Praise for
Becoming a Blessed C

BECOMING A BLESSED CHURCH

Forming a Church of Spiritual Purpose, Presence, and Power

Second Edition

N. Graham Standish
Foreword by E. Stanley Ott

An Alban Institute Book

ROWMAN & LITTLEFIELD
Lanham • Boulder • New York • London

Published by Rowman & Littlefield
A wholly owned subsidiary of The Rowman & Littlefield Publishing Group, Inc.
4501 Forbes Boulevard, Suite 200, Lanham, Maryland 20706
www.rowman.com

Unit A, Whitacre Mews, 26-34 Stannary Street, London SE11 4AB, United Kingdom

Copyright © 2016 by Rowman & Littlefield

Unless otherwise indicated, scripture quotations in this volume are from the New Revised Standard Version of the Bible, copyright © 1989, Division of Christian Education of the National Council of Churches of Christ in the United States of America, and are used by permission. All rights reserved.

The Vineyard Guild Prayer on page xx is reprinted by permission of the Vineyard Guild, Inc.

British Library Cataloguing in Publication Information Available

Library of Congress Cataloging-in-Publication Data

Names: Standish, N. Graham, 1959– author.
Title: Becoming a blessed church : forming a church of spiritual purpose, presence, and power / N. Graham Standish.
Other titles: Becoming the blessed church
Description: Second [edition]. | Lanham : Rowman & Littlefield, 2016. | Rev. ed. of: Becoming the blessed church : forming a church of spiritual purpose, presence, and power. c2005. | "An Alban Institute book." | Includes bibliographical references and index.
Identifiers: LCCN 2016005950 (print) | LCCN 2016007256 (ebook) | ISBN 9781566997911 (cloth : alk. paper) | ISBN 9781566997928 (pbk. : alk. paper) | ISBN 9781566997935 (electronic)
Subjects: LCSH: Church renewal. | Christian leadership.
Classification: LCC BV600.3 .S735 2016 (print) | LCC BV600.3 (ebook) | DDC 262.001/7—dc23
LC record available at http://lccn.loc.gov/2016005950

Printed in the United States of America

To the members of Calvin Presbyterian Church

You have been such a blessing to me.

CONTENTS

FOREWORD

I sat in the hospital waiting room with just one other person, a fellow waiting for a doctor to return with a prescription. Someone walking by said hello to the man, and he replied, "Have a blessed day." A short time later, I said to him, "Now that's a great phrase, 'Have a blessed day,' because it says you are trusting God to do the blessing." The man turned to me and beamed. "That's right!" he said and went on to describe the power of his experience of Christ, explaining, "Blessed means 'He will make you rise!'" After the doctor brought his prescription, this gracious man stepped into a nearby elevator, turned around, and said to me, "Have a blessed day." I waved and said, "He will make you rise!" and the man was gone. I thought, "Wow! What a marvelous way to think about being blessed. If God is going to make you rise, then God is going to bring life and love and power and presence into your life and into your church. That's blessedness!"

Years ago George Odiorne wrote about the "activity trap" in which we can get so enmeshed that we lose sight of why we are doing what we are doing. He observed that the activities become false gods or ends in themselves. In the church's own "activity trap" of people and programs, we can easily lose sight of our Lord. We lose touch with what it means to experience God's love, presence, and power. It is easy to be so consumed by what we are doing for God that we miss the experience of being with God, the experience of being blessed. Such is a common experience in mainline congregations.

With the concept of the blessed church, Graham Standish brings us back to an understanding of what it means to be the church that experiences God as well as serves God. A blessed church, Graham says, "is a glimpse of what a church can be. It is a vision, a glimpse of a healthy church uniquely grounded in a relationship with God that allows blessings to flow through it." Plainly put, the people of a blessed church experience *God* rather than merely experiencing church. They may talk about God and serve God, yet their overarching desire is actually to know and experience God in some personal and direct way.

We are experiencing a surge in thought, research, reflection, and publication about the health, dynamics, and effectiveness of the transformational congregation. Yet among the principles and patterns being offered to us, one overarching issue dominates all thinking about the transformational church. A church is alive *not* because its organization is busy. Churches are alive because God is alive. Blessed churches are in immediate touch with the living God.

We long for our congregations to pulse with life and energy, to hope that our most significant experiences of God's presence and work among us are yet to come. Most of us know intuitively that our congregations' present experience of God is not "all there is." Because it is so easy for us to be caught in the trap of "present demand," serving the program of the church while losing sight of our original purpose, we need a guide into the experience of the blessed church. Graham Standish clearly identifies the factors that have led many congregations into a lifeless functionalism and the God-given means by which our congregations may become "blessed" churches. As he says, "Becoming a blessed church means becoming awake, aware, and alive to the fact that Christ is in our midst, giving us guidance, life, and love." May God bless your journey as you become the blessed church. May God make you rise!

E. Stanley Ott, PhD
President and Founder
Vital Churches Institute
http://www.vitalchurchesinstitute.com

PREFACE TO THE SECOND EDITION

When I originally put in place my ideas about creating a more spiritually vibrant church upon coming to Calvin Presbyterian Church in 1996, and after I wrote about them in the original edition of *Becoming a Blessed Church*, I never anticipated the impact both would have on me and on hundreds of pastors and churches across the United States, Canada, and in such far-flung places as Taiwan, Australia, and New Zealand.

Personally, the impact has been a busier travel and speaking schedule, but it's also been a joyful experience of helping many, many pastors and churches become healthier. Since its publication in 2005, I have traveled across the United States and Canada at least 15–20 times a year. That may not be much for a professional speaker, but doing this while being an active church pastor is a lot. Although I've written six books and speak on a variety of topics related to spiritual formation, discernment, and prayer, the topic I am most asked to speak on is how to form a blessed church.

I've had the opportunity to speak to gatherings of Presbyterians, Methodists, Episcopalians, Lutherans, nondenominational evangelicals, members and pastors of the United Church of Christ, the United Church of Canada, the Christian Reformed Church, Mennonites, and so many more. I've had the opportunity to hear from people all over North America and beyond tell me how their churches have become transformed because of a greater commitment to prayerfully seeking and doing what they sense God is calling them to do. I've heard from small-church pastors in South Dakota and large-church leaders in coast-al Florida. Along the way I've had some really interesting experiences.

For example, at one conference I was challenged by a participant, asking me whether what I've suggested really works. Before I could answer, another participant stood up and responded that her small, rural church had been doing what I've suggested for a year, and it had transformed them—that they were growing for the first time in many, many years.

At a conference in Florida, I was told by a member of a large, suburban Methodist church that their board had studied *Becoming a Blessed Church* and had decided to implement many suggestions. They noticed a dramatic decrease in conflict and a significant increase in ministry and mission. When a new pastor was assigned to them by the bishop, they told the pastor that they would like him to read *Blessed Church* so that he would understand their approach. He said, "This must be the work of the Spirit. I've already been using that book in my present church, and I was so worried that I wouldn't be able to con-vince you to do so, too."

The executive presbyter (like a regional or conference minister in other denominations) of a presbytery (a diocese-like governing body) in my denomination once told me about an experience in her presbytery based on the book. An interim pastor had been called to a struggling church in the presbytery after the previous pastor left. This church once had been an influential, 2,000 member church but now struggled with fewer than 75 worshiping in a sanctuary that seated 800. She suggested that they do an eight-month study of the book in order to discern their future. At the end of the process, they sensed a clear call to close their church, sell the building to a growing Latino Pentecostal church, and give half of the proceeds to a new church plant across town, while giving the rest to a transformational church effort being spearheaded by the presbytery. The executive said to me, "They gave life to a new, growing church. They gave life to themselves by becoming part of that church. They gave life to a Pentecostal church. They gave life to our presbytery. It was amazing to witness."

The point is not that by following the guidance in this book churches have gone from being small churches to being vibrant, large churches. It is that prayerfully discerning and doing God's will leads to tremen-dous, Spirit-filled possibilities that opened up as the congregations became open to God's guidance. As they became more prayerful in their leadership and actions, they discovered God leading them in directions that they couldn't see before. They were mired in a functional way that meant treating the church as a mere business or organization. They became more open to a spiritual way like that described in the book of Acts—a deeply prayerful community, filled with God's Spirit, that's always available to do God's will.

So if the book has had this kind of impact, why the need for a revised edition? I have two answers. First, when I wrote *Becoming a Blessed Church*, I never expected to follow up with two other books that would take these beliefs about creating a Spirit-led church even further. I didn't expect to write a book on leadership, which became *Humble Leadership*. I didn't expect to write a book on transforming worship based on the central question "What kind of worship are we called to offer to reach the people God is calling us to reach?," which became *In God's Presence*. With the publication of *Humble Leadership*, I developed a growing sense of disappointment with what I had written on leadership in *Becoming a Blessed Church*. It didn't help people develop the spiritual kind of leadership I had hoped it would and that *Humble Leadership* had.

A second reason for the revised edition is that I wanted to write about insights I've gained over the course of the past 10 years. Many people have stretched me by asking me more detailed questions about what we've been doing at Calvin Presbyterian Church over the past 20 years. These have been questions about how to discern, how to teach a congregation to become more deeply spiritual, and how to overcome conflict when trying to transform the church.

For example, in many conferences where I've spoken I've been asked to talk more about the process of discernment. So few pastors are taught the principles of discernment in seminary, and so few church members are exposed to the 2,000-year history of prayerful discernment in the Christian tradition, that distinguishing between typical theological analysis and prayerful discernment is hard. Thus, most churches that would like to adopt a more prayerful approach are lacking in a basic understanding of the elemental processes of discernment that are part of this approach. Also, most churches don't know how to train members to become more discerning and more open to God's calling. Nor do they really know how to move their churches in a more discerning direction without causing greater conflict with those committed to a more functional approach.

So in this revised version we decided to take out the last three original chapters on leadership, believing that the guidance in *Humble Leadership* was better, and to introduce three new chapters based on the questions people have asked, and challenges they've offered me, over the past 10 years.

Thus, the new chapter 6 focuses on discernment. It explores the Christian tradition of discernment and how it can be done on a personal and communal level. It also guides those interested in making their churches more discerning in how to lead leaders to adopt a more discerning approach.

The new chapter 7 focuses on how to train members in a spiritual approach through the development of a small group and educational program devoted to teaching prayer and discernment. Something I realized over time is that at Calvin Church we didn't just expect leaders to be more discerning. We trained them as leaders while we simultaneously created a multifaceted program that introduced members to the 2,000-year Christian emphasis on spirituality and prayer.

Many modern Christians don't even realize that most of the great movements within Christianity began with prayer and discernment. Nor are they aware of the great spiritual writers throughout Christian history who were often the progenitors of later reform movements. These were people such as Athanasius, Benedict of Nursia, Dorotheus of Gaza, Guigo II, Patrick of Ireland, Francis of Assisi, Augustine of Hippo, Meister Eckhart, Thomas à Kempis, Brother Lawrence, Ignatius of Loyola, Catherine of Genoa, Teresa of Avila, Martin Luther, John Calvin, George Fox, and John Wesley, as well as more modern influencers such as Evelyn Underhill, Thomas Kelly, C. S. Lewis, Thomas Merton, Henri Nouwen, Richard Foster, and those from Eastern Christian traditions such as Father Arseny and Elder Thaddeus of Vitovnica. So many have been a part of this spiritual tradition and have written vibrantly with the Spirit's hand. Creating a small group and education program that taps into this tradition becomes the vehicle in which an ethos and culture of prayer and discernment is created.

Finally, the new chapter 8 offers a way of transforming a church by training leaders in discernment and then calling on *them* to lead the church through transformation. This is a bit different from the approach many pastors take, which is to take the lead themselves in personally guiding, prodding, and pushing a congregation to change, which often leaves pastors exposed to resistance and conflict. This chapter explores the nature of human resistance and offers a path to overcome that resistance through the use of transformational task forces.

Ultimately these are new chapters built on questions and experiences that have come up in the years since I first wrote *Becoming a Blessed Church*. I hope they will be a blessing to you.

ACKNOWLEDGMENTS

When my wife, Diane, and I were getting married, we hired a bagpiper for the ceremony. We've long since forgotten his full name, but in our minds he will always be fondly remembered as "Bagpiper Bob." We remember Bagpiper Bob not only for how well he played at our wedding but also for his vibrant faith. When meeting him, you knew immediately that God was alive in him. He continually weaved wonderful phrases about faith into his conversations, with each one offering a pearl of wisdom. During one conversation, he said something that I have never forgotten and that I keep at the center of my life and ministry, especially when I am down, frustrated, or confused. He said, "You know, God never sets you up to fail." I don't remember why he said it, but it was such a positive statement about God and faith that I decided then and there to hold onto that belief and never let it go.

Bagpiper Bob was right. I've discovered throughout my ministry that God never sets us up to fail, and that if we are faltering and have faith God sends all sorts of people into our lives to pick us up and make sure we don't fail. It doesn't mean that we won't go through difficult times. It doesn't mean that we won't suffer, struggle, falter, or fall. It simply means that if we have faith and trust in God, help will find its way to us. Our part is to have faith. This book is a testament to how God helps us personally and congregationally. I've discovered through experience that when we have faith, God blesses us. And I want to acknowledge these blessings and share my gratitude.

First, I thank God for allowing me the opportunity to study with Adrian van Kaam and the faculty at Duquesne University's Institute of Formative Spirituality. Even though the program no longer exists, it blessed many of us who studied there over its 30-year history. Van Kaam had a comprehensive, integrative perspective on life that started with the spiritual and integrated theology, philosophy, social sciences, physical sciences, art, literature, music, and so much more. He helped me to see that while everything may start with the spiritual, the spiritual's focus is bringing everything together in harmony. Through my studies with van Kaam, I learned to see life, faith, theology, and the church through more spiritual and mystical eyes. Much of what I write in this book has been influenced by insights I gained through my studies in spirituality. Studying with van Kaam opened me to the possibility that God can be experienced in the church if we focus on creating communities of communion—what a novel concept!

I truly appreciate the directors of the doctor of ministry and certificate in spirituality programs at Pittsburgh Theological Seminary, past and present, as well as those in the doctor of ministry faculty at Tyndale Seminary in Toronto—Charles Hambrick-Stowe, Jim Davison, Mary Lee Talbot, Susan Kendall, and Jim Davison at Pittsburgh Seminary, and Paul Bramer and David Sherbino at Tyndale Seminary—who have allowed me to teach classes on congregational spirituality and spiritual leadership. These classes have pushed me to work out and articulate the ideas that would eventually form the original version and the revised version of this book.

I am also grateful to the members of the Vineyard Guild, and especially the Vineyard Guild board of directors and my small-group cluster, who have been such a support for me over the past 15 years. The Vineyard Guild is an organization devoted to nurturing spiritual leadership, and its members have been wonderful to me in their willingness to let me blather on about my ideas that appear in both versions of this book. They have contributed much to this book just by offering their own ideas and experiences, some of which are reflected in the stories in these pages.

In addition, I thank the researchers of the Project on Congregations of Intentional Practice, Diana Butler Bass and Joseph Stewart-Sicking, who initially made the folk at Alban Institute aware of me and my interest in the subject of congregational spirituality.

I am greatly appreciative to Richard Bass and the Alban Institute for their willingness to publish this book. I am especially grateful to my project editor, Beth Gaede. She has been a true blessing. It is not often that a writer has a project editor who will go overboard to make a book better. Beth has done that. She has complimented me when my ego was fragile, challenged me when my theology and articulation were sloppy, and redirected me when I was stuck in the thickets. The editorial work on this book was a real joy. And in this I include the work I have done with my copyeditor, Jean Caffey Lyles. Again, she has been wonderful in helping me articulate my thoughts more clearly. Such a blessing.

I also truly appreciate Sarah Stanton at Rowman & Littlefield for being open to the possibility of creating a revised version of *Becoming a Blessed Church*, which has allowed me to include insights I've gained over the past 10 years since its original publication—as senior pastor of Calvin Presbyterian Church, from questions in response to hundreds of talks on the topic throughout the United States and Canada, and from my work in mentoring pastors and churches as a spiritual director and ministry coach. All three have given me deeper insights into this vision of recapturing the spiritual in congregations and have allowed me to dig deeper into my understanding of discernment, leading others to grow spiritually, and how to transform a church.

I appreciated the staff at the Starbucks coffee shop in Cranberry Township, Pennsylvania, where I spent almost every day of a month-long sabbatical writing this book in July 2003. I managed to write five chapters sitting at my little table, and the staff was wonderful in supplying me with endless cups of tea. I also appreciate deeply the session of Calvin Presbyterian Church who allowed me to take my original sabbatical and then again a semi-sabbatical in the summer of 2015 as I revised previous chapters and added three new chapters.

As I stated in my dedication, I am deeply indebted to the members of Calvin Presbyterian Church in Zelienople, Pennsylvania, where I have served as senior pastor since 1996. They have helped me live out the lesson a respected pastor I know taught me years ago: "Graham, only one in 10 pastors ever serves in a church he or she loves. If you are in one, don't ever leave unless God hits you with a thunderbolt and says in a booming voice, 'Go forth!'" I am fortunate to be in a place I love. I cannot tell you enough how much I appreciate the members, elders, and staff of this church because of their love, their faith, and their willingness to indulge me in all my quirks.

I want to thank my wife, Diane, and my twin daughters, Shea and Erin, for their support and love. Diane has served as the primary editor for most of my books since my doctoral dissertation, and I am thankful that she has always been willing to do so. Imagine not only having to hear your husband talk all the time and spout his strange ideas but then being willing to edit hundreds of pages of material and read these same ideas over and over again. This willingness says a lot about Diane's love and how fortunate I am to be married to her.

Finally, I want to thank you for letting me share my ideas and experiences with you. You also are a blessing, and I hope that you will hear God's voice and sense God's presence in these pages. To prepare you as you embark on this journey, I leave you with a prayer that has been my daily prayer, the Vineyard Guild Prayer:

> Holy God, Beloved Trinity, let me always be rooted in you so that I may live in you and you in me. Bless me so that your grace may flow through me, allowing me to bear your fruit to a hungry and helpless world. As I wander, prune me of all that inhibits your growth in me. Let me do nothing apart from you so that your joy may be complete in me. In Christ's name I pray. *Amen.*

Part I

Becoming a Blessed Church

For as long as I can remember, I have struggled with church. I think it has been one of God's holy jokes to call me to be the pastor of a church, to spend my life in the very place that I had struggled with for so long. Most of my earliest memories of church are not particularly wonderful. I remember sitting in church and being told constantly to "Quit fidgeting," "Don't sniffle," and "Be quiet." I remember being given a weekly assignment, as part of my confirmation class, to listen to the sermon and outline what it said, and then trying to cheat from my cousin's notes because I had no idea what the preacher was saying. I knew that the church was supposed to be a place of God, but I had a hard time sensing God there. Instead of being confirmed in the church, I walked away from the church after confirmation class because I had become disillusioned with the church. Looking back 35 years later, and especially on my 27-year career as a pastor, there have been times when I jokingly concluded that my being called into ministry was simply God's holy joke on me. You see, I am now the one who invokes fidgeting in young children and bewilderment in teens. Why would God call that fidgety, discontent child to become a pastor?

Regardless of how I now feel about the church, much about the Christian church turned me off as a teen. I was a turned-off teen in a tuned-out culture. The churches of my youth seemed devoid of God, and living in a culture that increasingly denigrated Christian religion helped me to tune out the church. As a youngster and a teenager, I had a tremendous spiritual hunger and a deep thirst for God that wasn't satisfied in the church of my youth. I sat through worship service after worship service, feeling little of God's presence. I don't want to give the impression that the church actually *was* devoid of God, only that I rarely sensed God's presence. There is a big difference between the two. I was a cynical teenager in a generation of baby boomers who consistently denigrated the church at every opportunity. How was I supposed to encounter God in church when the pop icons of the early and middle 1970s were so critical of the church? What's clear is the modern bias against religion and church is even more pronounced now, with the category of "nones"—those who have no religious affiliation— being the fastest-growing religious group today.

Second, I thought the church was a place of hypocrites. I couldn't get beyond the fact that I saw so many adults listening, singing, and praying on Sunday morning but doing and saying nasty things the rest of the week. Was there anyone who didn't look like a "saint" on Sunday and act like a "sinner" on the other days? Of course there were many, but I didn't notice them. I was too focused on the "sinners" to notice the "saints."

A new pastor came to the church when I was 15, one who offered a glimmer of God's presence, but by then I was too cynical and jaded to profit from his ministry. So I walked away from the church with the intention of never returning. I sought God elsewhere. Psychology became my religion. I went to college and studied to be a counselor. I developed a belief that if psychologists ran the world, the world would become a happy place. Working as a counselor in a psychiatric hospital for several years cured me of that naïve belief. The hospital was, in my experience, the most unhealthful place I had ever been, and not because of the patients. Those of us on staff didn't practice what we preached. We were unhealthy people trying to help other unhealthy people, and it didn't always work.

At this time I began to dabble in Eastern and New Age thought. I was practicing what I now call "ABC" spirituality—anything but Christianity. I read books about the psychic Edgar Cayce. I read books by a New Age guru who said he was a Tibetan lama. I read books by psychologists turned spiritual guides. And for a time all of them fed me, but it soon became apparent that they weren't offering truly nourishing food.

None of them led me to encounter God. That didn't happen until I had a mystifying experience that opened me to the possibility of Christ.

The experience came through a patient I was counseling who had a mystical experience that continues to influence me to this day. A young man of 16, he had been brought to the hospital after engaging in bizarre and dangerous behavior. He was diagnosed with a bipolar affective disorder (manic depression), and his bizarre behavior stemmed from an extreme manic state, in which psychotic episodes are not uncommon.

No improvement was evident during his first few weeks in the hospital. The treatment team decided that if he didn't improve soon, he would be sent to a long-term facility. I didn't expect him to improve much either, but he surprised me one evening when I walked into his room for one of our counseling sessions. For the first time since I had known him, he seemed clear in his thoughts. He began by saying that he wanted to tell me something, but that he was afraid I would laugh at him. I assured him I wouldn't and encouraged him to talk. So he told me his story.

A few evenings before, he had been lying on his bed when he noticed something in the window. It was Jesus. Now, being a person who didn't know what to do with the whole idea of Jesus, having walked away from the church years before, I didn't know what to say. So I said what all counselors are trained to say in such situations: "Ahhhhhh, tell me more." He told me that Jesus had been standing in the window, and behind him was a forked path. Along the left path were strewn, in his words, "bums and guys on skid row." Along the right path were strewn, in the patient's words, all sorts of successful people. I had no idea what to say. Spiritual experiences were not covered in my counseling training. In fact, I had been taught to ignore anything spiritual. But I had to deal with this one or I would lose my patient. After thinking for a long while, I asked him, "What do you think Jesus was telling you?" He thought for a moment and said, "I think Jesus is telling me that I have a choice to make right now. If I keep going the way I'm going, I'm going to end up on skid row with all the bums, but if I make the choice to join Jesus, I can be successful like all the men on the other path." Not knowing what else to say, I said, "I think you'd better listen to Jesus." He did and immediately began to improve.

At a counseling session a week later he told me that he had had another experience of Jesus. This time he and Jesus were standing on the 50-yard line of a football field. A chain-link fence separated them. Looking backward, he saw that the grass was dead from the end zone to the 25-yard line, while the rest was green. Again, I asked him, "What do you think Jesus is saying?" He said, "I think Jesus is telling me that I have gone from death to life, but I still have obstacles to overcome to join him." I said, "I think you'd better listen to Jesus." And he did. He was discharged to his home within a week. He was a different person. His encounter with Jesus had changed him.

Now I don't want to dismiss the impact of the medication he was receiving, but I also can't dismiss his experience of Jesus, because that experience totally changed his thinking about life. He accepted responsibility for himself and his behavior, and he became determined to get better. Jesus had used this young man's illness to show him a better way, and he took it. I saw his father a year later in a mall and asked him how his son was doing. He told me that his son was doing beautifully, he was looking at colleges, and that one would never know that he had been ill. The father then told me that we were miracle workers. I didn't know how to tell him that it wasn't me—it was Jesus.

This experience changed me because it altered my perceptions of how God works. This young man had encountered Christ, and the encounter had changed him. This is what I had been missing and what I had hungered for in my youth. I had not encountered Christ in church, but I had encountered him in a psychiatric hospital, even if it was vicariously through a patient. That experience left me questioning every assumption I had previously made about Christianity, the church, and God. It didn't immediately lead me back to church, although that process began soon afterward.

Over time the stresses of working long hours in the hospital for little pay took their toll. I burned out at age 24. I was so disillusioned with the whole field of psychology and counseling, even more than I had been with the church. I was in a crisis. I had lost my sense of purpose, and I felt isolated and alone. So I quit and moved home to live with my parents while I searched for another career.

I quit right in the middle of the recession of 1983, which left the area around Pittsburgh, Pennsylvania, where I lived, with a 12 percent unemployment rate. There were no jobs. I became more and more despondent as the months passed. Where was God? Why wasn't God helping me to find a new career? Why did it seem as though every door was closing before me? I felt as if I were drowning. A lifeline had been thrown to me a month before I quit my job as a counselor, but it took months of floundering before I could grab it. My father had told me about a program at Pittsburgh Theological Seminary. I could get a master of divinity degree there and a master of social work from the University of Pittsburgh. I laughed. "Dad, could you actually see me as a minister?" "Sure," he replied, "I've always seen you as a minister." How ridiculous—me as a pastor. The funny thing, though, is that deep down I had that same feeling about myself. Somewhere deep inside, in a place that I really didn't have the courage to look into, I knew that I was called to be a pastor, but I was in no state to accept that knowledge. I rejected and repressed it. It took a long period of unemployment and a state of desperation finally to give me the courage to recognize that I was being called to become a pastor—to become a leader in the very body that I had tried so hard to reject and ignore. But more about that in a bit.

In the midst of my struggles I decided to join the church in January 1984. In joining the church, I became aware of something that I had refused to see before. Of course the people in the church were hypocrites. Of course the church was flawed and full of faults. I was just as aware of their faults and flaws as before, but now I recognized something even more important. I was a hypocrite, too. I was just as flawed and faulty. What better place was there for me than a church?

The choice to join the church came one evening several weeks before Christmas as I cried to God in prayer about my life. I could no longer take my loneliness, my lack of purpose, and my growing despair. I decided to make a commitment to God—to Christ. I would join the church because I needed others to join me on my journey, just as I needed to join them on their journey. The funny thing is that after making this decision, I began to experience God more tangibly in my life. Coincidences opened doors that had previously been shut. People came into my life who gave me guidance. I began to experience God all over the place. My decision to join the church was leading me to experience God tangibly, even though the church itself hadn't really changed. What changed was that I was now extremely open to God for the first time.

After making the decision to join the church, deciding to enroll in seminary was fairly easy. My intention was to go to seminary so that I could return to my career as a counselor, but this time equipped to deal with the spiritual issues that typically arise in counseling, issues that I had been discouraged from addressing in my previous work as a counselor. I went to seminary while simultaneously working on a master of social work (a counseling degree) at a local university to train to become a better counselor. Through my studies I regained a sense of purpose and formed a plan to return eventually to working as a counselor, one prepared to address spiritual issues as they arose in my practice; but God thwarted my plans once again. (Through experience I've discovered that God seems never to be content to let our plans be *The Plan*. God always has deeper plans.) I thought God's plan was that I become a counselor again, but God put me back into the place that I had been trying to escape, the church. The discernment of my prayers and providential and coincidental events made it clear that God was calling me to become a pastor, to lead a church.

Still, I faced a problem. I had gone to seminary hoping to learn how to deal with the spiritual issues I had encountered in counseling others, issues that I hoped also to address as a pastor; but I never really learned to address them. I took courses in Greek and Hebrew. I took courses in pastoral care and the Bible. I took courses in ethics, Christology, theology, and the like, but I still didn't know how to deal with the spiritual issues people faced in their lives. I was no better trained to deal with the patient who saw Jesus in the window than I had been as a counselor six years before. I didn't necessarily know how to address the spiritual thirst of those in my care. I was still spiritually parched myself. How could I lead people to wells of living water when I had no map to find them myself or even a bucket with which to draw the water? I had found God, but I didn't necessarily know how to lead others to God. I didn't really know how to pray. I didn't know how to lead a Bible study. I didn't know how to do much more than tell people to be good. Knowing how unprepared I was, I hid my deficiencies and read everything I could in the area of spirituality. I was especially drawn to the works of mystics—those who had encountered God through deep experiences—who had written of their experiences. Eventually, I decided that I needed to study spirituality so that I could be trained to deal with the spiritual issues of those in my church as well as my own.

I began working on a doctorate in spiritual formation at Duquesne University in Pittsburgh. It was in studying spirituality that I finally found a map that enabled me to lead others to spiritual water and a bucket to draw it out for them. As opposed to theology, which is the study of God and life from a rational, analytical, and semiscientific perspective (using Scripture, tradition, and the insights of the Christian community throughout the ages as the material of study), the study of spirituality is the study of the lived relationship between God and us as well as the study of the practices and perspectives that lead to a deepening of the relationship with God. The theology I had learned in seminary was important, but the study of theology was an experience much like eating dry crackers. It could sustain me, but I couldn't completely swallow it. The study of theology seemed dry and fragmented. In contrast, studying spirituality was like being given water to drink, allowing me finally to digest and process all the theology I had learned years before. I not only became alive; I also began to wonder why the church hadn't given me water like this years before. Why hadn't the seminary given me this kind of water? Why hadn't I been taught that theology and spirituality were partners; that spirituality was the water that gave life to theological insight? Why did it take 14 years of struggling on my own to discover this water of life?

The problem was that my seminary studies emphasized studying and speculating about God. My studies in spirituality showed me how to encounter and experience God. Unless we encounter God, speculating about God becomes nothing more than abstract conjecture and theorizing that has little impact on daily life. When we have an actual encounter with God, though, this speculation deepens us by revealing the depths of God.

After I graduated with my doctorate, it became clear to me that I was being called by God to return to the church to form a model for how to create a more spiritually vibrant church. I was being called to take the insights and practices of the growing spiritual formation movement and to find a way to bring them into the life of the local church. The vision I had was not one of simply offering retreats, classes, and small groups on spirituality. The vision was to restore to the church a clear sense of God's purpose, a transforming sense of God's presence, and an expectant sense of God's power in our midst.

I was fortunate in 1996 to be given the chance to do just that. I was called to become the pastor of Calvin Presbyterian Church in Zelienople, Pennsylvania, a place of wonderful, spiritually thirsty, and charitable people. Over the past 20 years we have worked together to experiment with ways of forming a church of purpose, presence, and power. Through this book, I hope to share with you what we have discovered in our ministry together at Calvin Church: a way of doing ministry that leads to creating a church filled with God's blessings.

I have been frustrated over the years that a vast majority of the congregations in the mainstream denominations, and the denominations themselves, have adopted a functional style of church that cuts off their spiritual cores. What I mean is that too many churches focus only on function, on doing the activities of church, and not on the fact that at their heart churches are meant to be spiritual communities in which people form a relationship with and experience God (I'll explain more in chapter 2). In these churches there is little expectation that members will experience and encounter God or connect what they do to God's purpose, presence, and power. The problem in many of these churches isn't so much what they do but the spirit in which they do it. They worship, but not necessarily with an eye toward leading people to an encounter with God. They meet to do God's work, but not necessarily in ways that include prayerfully seeking God's will and way in their work. They offer prayers, but not with the expectation that the prayers will do much more than offer comfort and consolation.

Many denominations, churches, pastors, and members become mired in a series of worthless arguments in their attempt to diagnose why mainstream denominations and churches are in decline. Too many in the mainstream church think the problems have to do with theological positions, styles of worship, or availability of programs. So they say that the decline is the result of churches being too liberal or too conservative, or that the decline is due to our too-traditional worship. They say that we don't meet enough of people's needs and that we need to offer more programs.

When it comes to theological positions, I've noticed that there are many growing conservative *and* liberal churches, just as there are many declining conservative *and* liberal churches. When it comes to styles of worship, if growth is just a matter of becoming more contemporary, why do so many declining churches add a contemporary worship service but remain depleted? (Of course, many churches also remain traditional and slowly die.) Many churches continue to stagnate, even though they try to offer a multitude of programs that appeal to all. At the same time, many churches grow vigorously while offering little more than a caring community.

What I have consistently noticed in almost all thriving congregations, including Calvin Church, is that what makes the difference is the extent to which the community is open to God at its core. Many churches simply aren't open to God. They let the will, ego, and purpose of the dominant voices in their congregation, whether the pastor's or that of a few strong members, drive the agenda. Instead of seeking God's call and purpose, they argue over who is right or wrong. Declining churches tend not to be open to God's presence. They worship, meet, and engage in ministry and mission, but their sense is that God is in heaven, we are on earth, and all that matters is doing good deeds so that we can get into heaven. The congregants have no sense that Christ is in their midst and that this presence of Christ can bless them and make their churches places of love. So they continue to engage in the practices of the church, but they don't expect an encounter with Christ. Finally, these churches have no awareness that God's grace and power can work in their midst. They have no awareness of the Holy Spirit. They are unaware that when we become open to God, God's spirit flows through the church to make miracles happen.

This book is about how to open our hearts and minds to God in our communities in such a way that we become blessed in everything. It is not a book on how to turn a small church into a large church, although spiritual growth *can* lead to numerical growth. It is not about how to attract members, although that may happen because people are attracted to spiritually healthy places. It is not a book on how to become a successful pastor by the world's standards, although that may happen. Simply put, this is a guide on how to create a church that is open at its foundations to God's purpose, presence, and power. It is a book on how to create a spiritually deep congregation that becomes inwardly and outwardly healthy on every level: spiritually, psychologically, physically, and relationally (I'll say more about this topic in chapter 2). It is a book on how you can open your congregation to God's blessings so that these blessings flow through everything the church does, from meetings to ministry to mission.

My prayer is that as you read this book and begin to use what you discover in it, you will find your church growing in the way God is calling it to grow. Just as every pastor and layperson has a calling, so does every church. My prayer is that through this book, you will be able to discover the path God is calling your church to walk and that as you walk it, you will discover how to open up the congregation to discover God's blessings everywhere.

1

WHAT IS A BLESSED CHURCH?

What exactly is a blessed church? It is a glimpse of what a church can be. It is a vision, a glimpse of a healthy church uniquely grounded in a relationship with God that allows blessings to flow through it. Unfortunately, it is a vision too few churches have today, although many are glimpsing it. There are so many factors that keep churches from becoming blessed communities that it's hard to grasp the full ramification of this vision. To understand what becoming a blessed church means, it might be helpful first to look at the factors that need to be overcome to allow a blessed church to take root and grow.

Identifying what prevents churches from becoming blessed is a kind of chicken-and-egg thing. Is the problem that pastors and church leaders no longer have the vision, faith, and skills to lead churches to blessedness? Or is it that churches have become so dry, dysfunctional, and dead that they no longer have the ability to follow pastors and church leaders into blessedness? Both seem to be true. As I look back at my training to become a pastor, I have to admit that I wasn't very well trained to lead churches into blessedness. The seminary I attended tried to prepare me to become a pastor, but like many mainline denominational seminaries, it had an overwhelming focus on all things theological that didn't prepare me to become a pastor in a church where not everything is theological. I studied theology, Christology, eschatology, teleology, ecclesiology, bibliology, and a bunch of other "ologies." I studied church history, biblical languages, pastoral care, and ethics, but I learned very little about how to lead a church. The assumption, so well articulated by a Hebrew professor, was that "you can learn how to do all that church stuff when you get out of seminary." As he said, "Seminaries are academic institutions. You have to figure out the other stuff on your own." That's an amazing statement from someone charged with preparing pastors and church educators for ministry and church leadership.

The problem with so many mainline denominational seminaries is that their mission is often at odds with the mission of the early church, which was to bring people into a deep, spiritual, loving, saving, and healing relationship with God the Creator, Son, and Holy Spirit. Too often they see themselves primarily as academic institutions, like universities and colleges, where the focus is a rational investigation and study of theology, history, and the Bible. How does this emphasis fit with their calling to train pastors, educators, and leaders for ministry and mission? Is the main function of pastors, educators, and leaders merely to be theologians explaining the mysteries of life, or are they charged with leading others to this deep, loving relationship with the Trinity? If their calling is to train pastors, educators, or leaders, what model for ministry and the church do they use? Is it that churches should be little academic institutions where the pastors and educators act as resident theologians? Is it the corporate-culture model that assumes the church is an organization in which the pastor acts as CEO and the lay leaders act as members of the board of directors? Is it the pastoral care and counseling model that assumes the church is a counseling agency in which the pastor serves as the resident therapist? There's a lot of confusion about how to form a healthy congregation, and that confusion was imparted to me when I graduated from seminary. I wasn't sure what my role as a pastor should be or what model to follow.

My seminary professors reflected this same confusion. Few had served as parish pastors, and even fewer had served as pastors of dynamic, growing churches. The majority were trained mainly in academia, focusing on theological study, and so their teaching focus tended to be theological, not practical. This emphasis is in direct contrast with my graduate studies in counseling, where not only did every professor have training in the academic study of counseling, but all were still involved in private practice or as staff in a counseling agency. I noticed the difference in my sense of competence after graduating. As a counselor, I felt prepared for most situations, and when I didn't, I knew where to

get help. As a pastor, I felt unprepared. I'm not alone in feeling inadequately prepared for leadership. Many mainline pastors feel this sense
of inadequacy. As one pastor confided to me, "I came out of seminary
knowing how to exegete a passage, but I had no idea how to help a
person struggling to find a sense of purpose or to feel God's love."

Here's an odd little statistic to reflect upon—one that demonstrates
the problems with traditional seminary training. There is an inverse
correlation between denominational growth and educational expectations. The more education a denomination expects of its pastors and
educators, the more it shrinks. Christian Schwarz, who made a study of
the qualities of growing churches based upon a survey of 1,000
churches in 18 countries, found that seminary training has a negative
correlation to both church growth and the overall quality of churches.
His research found that only 42 percent of pastors in high-quality, high-
growth churches had seminary training, while in low-quality, low-
growth churches, 85 percent had graduated from seminary.[1] Traditional
mainline denominations all expect a fairly high level of education, and
pastors with a PhD or DMin are often the most respected in some
denominations. In contrast, the fastest-growing movements of all are
among the Pentecostals and nondenominationals, which require little
advanced education at all. They still may expect the pastor to be
trained, but the pastor often has on-the-job training, supplemented by
workshops, seminars, and in-house training programs focused specifically on church growth and discipleship. What inhibits the formation of
blessed *mainline* churches may be partly that pastors, educators, and lay
leaders have been inadequately trained not only in the practicalities of
church leadership but also in the knowledge of how to tap into the
power of God to guide and help them. Their training becomes so academic and intellectual that they lose the life-giving sense of God's call
that initially led them into ministry and that can sustain them in ministry.

It is unfair to place the blame squarely on seminaries. Congregations
present their own problems. They become so accustomed to a purely
programmatic and traditional mode of operation that they don't see the
possibility of creating a congregational approach that is more spiritually
open and that leads people to experience God more deeply and tangibly
in their midst. In fact, some churches become so accustomed to dysfunction that they don't realize they are dysfunctional. A seminary stu-

dent who served an internship in our church said something to me once that reflects how accustomed people can be to dysfunction. After participating in our church budgeting process (which entails bringing all committees together in a time of prayer to discern what God is calling us to do and putting aside squabbles and turf battles to seek what God wants), he said, "I didn't know it could be like this. I just thought that arguing and fighting over the budget was how it was done in all churches."

How does one lead churches like these out of the wilderness? Many pastors try. They eventually get chewed up and spit out when their congregations steadfastly resist all efforts to construct a more spiritually open approach. Some churches become so dysfunctional that their histories look like the story of a revolving door. One pastor after another comes to the church with much fanfare. Each lasts from one to three years and leaves, disillusioned by the hostility and inhospitable treatment she or he experiences while trying to lead the church out of dysfunction. In fact, many of these churches, steeped in dysfunctional patterns, seem to know how to call only dysfunctional pastors who end up damaging the churches further because of their addictions, affairs, or embezzlements.

A final problem lies with us pastors, educators, and leaders. Many of us come to ministry with broken lives that may leave us psychologically and spiritually wounded. On the one hand, our wounds can become detrimental when they interfere with our ministry because we have denied and repressed them, refusing to do what is necessary for healing (whether that means undergoing self-examination, therapy, or spiritual direction). On the other hand, our wounds can become a source of strength if, through our self-examination, therapy, or spiritual direction, we are able to use our wounds to deepen our compassion, understanding, and care of others. Whether these wounds become a detriment or a strength depends upon the pastor's, educator's, or leader's willingness to face her or his woundedness, be healed from it, and make it a source of strength.

God seems to call broken people to ministry. I don't know why, but it's true. Notice the people God called in the Bible. Joseph, a cocky little guy hated by his brothers, was sold by them into slavery. Moses was a murderer on the run. Ruth was a widowed foreigner whose descendants included King David. King Saul was afflicted by an oversized ego and paranoia. David was the runt of his litter and eventually became an adulterer. Solomon instituted a terrible death-squad campaign upon becoming the ruler of Israel. Jeremiah seems to have been mentally ill. Many of the disciples were ignorant and selfish. Mary Magdalene was possibly demon possessed. Paul was a persecutor of Christians and aided in the killing of them. Yet God called them all. God calls broken and flawed people.

That does not mean that people called by God should remain broken and unhealed. God also calls them to seek healing. They bear responsibility for doing the best they can to live a healthy life—one that is spiritually, psychologically, physically, and relationally balanced. Becoming whole may entail going to a counselor for psychological and relational health; seeking out a spiritual director for spiritual health; engaging in a diet and exercise program for physical health—all of which many of us pastors are loath to do. Too many pastors today don't bear enough responsibility for their own health and well-being. As a result, they become unhealthy leaders leading unhealthy congregations.

What is the path out of this wilderness? How do we lead our churches out of dysfunction and into blessing?

RATIONAL FUNCTIONALISM

To place the blame *solely* on academic seminaries, dysfunctional churches, and unhealthy pastors is not quite fair. They are all symptomatic of a far greater problem. The bigger problem is something I call "rational functionalism"—a disease that has afflicted all mainline denominations and as a result afflicts their seminaries, churches, and pastors.

Rational functionalism is the tendency of denominations, their congregations, and their leaders to subscribe to a view of faith and church rooted in a restrictive, logic-bound theology that ignores the possibility of spiritual experiences and miraculous events, while overemphasizing a functional practice disconnected from an emphasis on leading people to a transforming experience of God. On the one hand, rational functionalism turns faith into an intellectual endeavor rooted in an excessively rational, empirical, quasi-scientific approach. This approach to faith is a by-product of the Enlightenment, whose focus was on the rational and scientific pursuit of truth. Rational functionalism is rooted in the idea that we can uncover the mysteries of life and the universe mainly through rational thought and disciplined investigation. From this perspective, God is a puzzle to be solved through an approach that mirrors the scientific method as closely as possible. If that isn't feasible, then it restricts the inquiry to the laws of human logic and analysis.

The rational functional approach can reduce a congregation's practice to the attempt to lead people into a positivistic, logical exploration of religion and faith. The idea here is that a theological, historical, sociological, psychological, anthropological, economic, and philosophical understanding of the Christian faith will enable us to discern the laws of God and human life more clearly, and we can therefore learn to live better lives. In short, this approach reflects what a national leader in my denomination once said to me: "If we can just get people to think right theologically, then all of our problems will go away." The problem is that faith is more than just a logical, empirical inquiry into God and God's ways. It involves our minds, spirits, bodies, relationships, and beings. To address the human seeking for God from only a rational, logical, theological perspective is limiting.

One danger of rational functionalism is that it can cause pastors and leaders to become overintellectual in their approach to faith. God becomes an abstract notion, not a presence whom we can experience, form a relationship with, and love. Increasingly, these pastors and leaders endanger their faith. They don't know what to do with God. They especially don't know what to do with Jesus and the Holy Spirit. They can appreciate Jesus from a historical perspective, but what do they do with the resurrected Christ who, according to Scripture, is incarnated in the world, in relationships, and in the human heart? What do they do with the Holy Spirit, who inspires, heals, and miraculously touches life? Ultimately, they become so intellectual in their approach that they not only lose their own faith but struggle with leading others to faith.

I am not advocating that pastors and church leaders should remain theologically and historically ignorant or that we should blindly accept everything in the Bible as historical fact. Just because I'm advocating a more spiritual approach does not mean I'm suggesting that we get rid of theological understanding. I'm simply advocating that we ground our theological explorations in spiritual experiences. Understanding Scripture and Christian faith from a more critical and academic point of view is a good thing because it can help us to understand the context and intent of Scripture, thus helping us hear God's voice more clearly when we read Scripture. Unfortunately, when academic inquiry and scientific skepticism become stronger than an emphasis on forming faith and leading people to an encounter with God, the church declines because people are no longer led to form a living faith in God that can transform their lives. The church becomes little more than a social agency filled with well-meaning but spiritually dead people.

In churches caught in the grip of rational functionalism, sermons tend to become academic papers read to the people in the pews. They don't address more basic issues: How are we supposed to endure living with pain, loneliness, and turmoil? How are we supposed to find God amidst life's darkness? Bible studies focus on the historical, sociological, economic, and cultural issues of the time with the intent of uncovering what theological message the writer of a Bible passage is trying to impart. They don't address more basic issues: What is God saying to me through the Scripture about how to live my life? What is God saying to me about what God is doing in my life, especially in the face of my suffering? How is God calling me to love others and to reach out to those who are suffering, both near and throughout the world, and who are in need of God's love as well as mine?

The primary problem at the core of rational functionalism is that it fails to treat God as a tangible presence. God is treated mostly as an idea or thought, or as an entity we encounter when we die, rather than as a tangible presence in the here and now. There is no sense that God's kingdom is all around us and that this kingdom is a spiritual reality in which we can experience God directly.

A second problem with rational functionalism is that it functionalizes the life of the church, turning everything from worship to committee meetings into routinized events with little connection to a larger purpose. In the rationally functional church, the focus is on maintaining the institution, not on creating experiences through which God can be encountered and experienced in our midst. What matters most is preaching in *the* prescribed manner, adhering to particular rituals in *the* traditional way, and singing only *the* traditional hymns. Guiding people to a tangible encounter, experience, and relationship with Christ isn't much of a concern. Teaching people how to discover the power of the Holy Spirit in their midst is never emphasized because the object of the church has been reduced to doing what we've always done, to functioning the way the church has always functioned simply for the sake of functioning. Guiding people to discover the Creator's call in their lives, calling them and us to live deeper, richer, and greater lives of love and service, is ignored in favor of guiding people simply to function as Christians have always functioned. In short, the message is reduced to (as someone once told me) a formula: "We should be Christians because Christianity is good and ethical, and we should be good and ethical people. The church's role is to teach us to follow the Golden Rule."

According to church-growth researcher Bill Easum, a leading writer on mainline church health and vitality, this kind of functionality (what he calls the "machine metaphor") has "made it easy for church leaders to relate to the 'church' as an institution rather than a spiritual community. It also made it easy to honor educated leaders who often ridiculed emotion and feelings. Symbols easily became the reality instead of pointing to it, . . . logic replaced passion and experience. The materialistic world was real, whereas the inner world of the soul was little more than illusion."[2] The result, according to him, is that "institutional churches function like corporations. Pastors are CEOs. Policy manuals replace ministry. Pastors attend seminary and are referred to as 'professionals.' Denominational structures and financial needs grow faster than those of congregations. Job descriptions replace calling. Degrees are more important than proven competency. . . . In such a church, leadership is based on credentials, and faith is something to be learned. This metaphor is evident in churches that place a lot of emphasis on administration, credentials, denominationalism, meetings, and defending the faith."[3]

Ultimately, becoming a blessed church means overcoming rational functionalism. In blessed churches, people not only *expect* to experience God, they *do* experience God. Their expectations open the door to God, who stands knocking. They *expect* to hear the Creator's voice guiding the church to what it is called to be and do. They expect to encounter and be blessed by Christ. They expect the power of God the Holy Spirit to flow through their life and the church's, blessing them in so many ways.

THE PROBLEM OF CHURCH GROWTH

Becoming a blessed church does not necessarily mean becoming a growing church, at least not in numbers. Many of the large, fast-growing megachurches around the country are what I would call "blessed churches," but many are not. Numerical growth is not a defining characteristic of a blessed church, even though many think it is. In fact, the plethora of church-growth materials on the market nowadays can be a problem for many churches and their leaders who seek to grow blessed churches. Why? Because not all churches are in situations that allow them to replicate the growth of these megachurches.

The books written by megachurch pastors are filled with insights and tips on how to create a large, growing church. Many of these books have influenced my ministry and my life. The problem is that almost all these books fail to account for three primary factors that contribute to their growth—conditions that most churches can't replicate. First, most of these churches are new church developments, seeking to attract only members of younger generations, so they don't run as forcefully into the problems inherent in turning around an established church that includes members of multiple generations. Instead, they have had the advantage of being able to create their own customs, follow new ideas, and focus much more of their energy on ministry rather than on maintaining buildings. Established churches can be difficult to turn around because their members often resist change and transformation. They cherish their customs, their worship, and the ways they have always done things.

In addition, mainline churches are being challenged to respond to the demands of multiple generations, all seeking something different from worship and the church. Often the oldest generations seek to hold onto tradition. Baby boomers, born between 1943 and 1960, tend to want stimulation and excitement in worship, but in a new package, which may mean contemporary worship that eliminates traditional symbols and rituals. Generation Xers are often idiosyncratic, wanting churches to tailor their efforts to their age group's varied interests and tastes (which can be almost impossible for churches to do). Finally, millennials, those born between 1982 and 2000, tend to love traditional symbols and experiential rituals while still expecting them to reflect a mixture of traditional and contemporary effects. They also seek community based on acceptance and tolerance. At the same time, they have grown up in a culture that increasingly declares religion and church to be irrelevant, meaning that they have been raised to be church resistant. Holding the interests of all these generations can be extremely difficult, making revitalization of a mainline church a much more daunting task than simply starting a new church that targets only one or two of these generations. Many of these megachurches have succeeded by ignoring the older generations, even shifting their approaches in a way that encourages the older members to leave the church as it changes to target younger members, something the mainline churches cannot do.

Turning a firmly entrenched church around to make it grow numerically takes a set of skills that many pastors don't have, either because they lack the proper training, the right personal attributes, or both. It takes a special set of skills to help a struggling congregation make the transition from, as pastor and author Stan Ott says, a *traditional* church to a *transformational* church.[4]

A second factor that uniquely contributes to the growth of megachurches is that they are either planted or replanted in growing communities. There is a direct correlation between a growing community and a growing church. For instance, my own church, Calvin Presbyterian Church, has nearly tripled in size since I became its pastor. Certainly a big factor in this success is that Zelienople is a growing community near one of the faster-growing areas of the country. With the exception of Pentecostal churches, it is rare that churches grow in declining communities, and unique factors contribute to the growth of Pentecostal churches.

Third, the large, growing churches tend to target and attract people who are seeking a church that does things differently. They draw members who are adaptable to change and are willing to risk, and who *don't want to be in a traditional church*, no matter how alive it is. The people in mainline churches are often the people left behind by members who have left to seek a more contemporary church. They fear risk and don't want change. They sometimes love their traditions more than they love God.

The challenge for most mainline churches is how to get church leaders, especially lay leaders, to lead an anxious, resistant, and risk-averse church to grow when they are anxious and resistant themselves.

Many mainline churches lack a vision for change, the confidence to make changes, and the desire for change. They want stability. Their focus has slowly become fixed on themselves and their survival (and sometimes their death). Seeking what God wants is not high among their priorities. In many ways, they become stuck. They don't want to die, but they don't know how to live. They want God to speak to them, but not if it means making changes.

Many of the pastors who lead these churches are afraid themselves. They fear leading these churches to God and transformation because of the backlash they may experience from members. They feel like failures because their churches aren't growing, and they feel like cowards for not taking more risks. I don't want to make it sound as though great pastoral leadership means changing everything. As you will see in the following chapters, I believe that change should be rooted in God's calling. Change may also mean maintaining traditional rituals and programs but adapting them in ways that make them fresh to new generations.

As I stated above, becoming a blessed church may not lead to church growth because the focus of a blessed church is on opening to God in our midst, not on adding members. Growth in numbers becomes a by-product of growing in a relationship with God. The focus of a blessed church is on doing what God is calling us to do, having the confidence to know that God is in our midst, and relying upon God's power to get results. This focus may not lead to numerical growth, but it does lead to health. In other words, by focusing on leading people to spiritual encounters and experiences of God, the church and its members end up forming healthier and more vibrant relationships with each other, relationships that emerge out of the deep spiritual connection with the Trinity and with each other. The more the church focuses on grounding its ministry and mission in a dynamic relationship with the Trinity, the more its members and other participants engage confidently in ministry and mission that make a difference in the local community and in the world, if only in a small way. As the church grows in its relationship with God, the members become increasingly aware of God's power in their lives. In short, becoming a blessed church means becoming a place where God is present and God is experienced. Lives are thereby healed.

If becoming a blessed church means becoming more open to God and God's power in our midst, why doesn't that automatically translate into church growth? The answer is fairly simple. Becoming a blessed church means discerning and doing what God is calling us to do, and some churches simply aren't called to grow. In fact, sometimes churches are called to die. How many of the original churches founded by Paul and the other disciples still exist? Just as people have a term of life, so do churches. Sometimes, becoming a blessed church may mean finding a way to die with faith, hope, and love. This is a hard idea to grasp in our evangelical age when success in ministry is measured by the size of a church, but sometimes churches have to die to give new life to others.

A woman told me of her experience with the death of a church that brought new life to two other churches. She served on a presbytery (the regional judicatory body of the Presbyterian Church) committee to determine what to do with the church building of a Presbyterian congregation that had shut its doors and ceased operation. The decision had been made to sell the building. Two bids came in, one from an Episcopal parish, the other from a fundamentalist Southern Baptist congregation. The Southern Baptist bid was $30,000 higher than the Episcopal, creating a dilemma. The members of the committee wanted the extra $30,000, but they didn't want a fundamentalist congregation to occupy the church building. A fight erupted within the committee. Finally, the committee leader asked the members to be quiet and to go out and pray for an hour to see what God wanted them to do rather than argue about what each wanted.

When they resumed talking, someone offered an alternate suggestion, one heard in prayer. Why not sell the building to the Southern Baptists and give the extra $30,000 to the Episcopal parish? That way, new life would be given to two churches out of the death of one Presbyterian church. The committee spent time praying about it, and all agreed. But they had one problem. How would they get the presbytery to go along with their suggestion? Wouldn't their suggestion be seen as poor stewardship, since the building was presbytery property and the presbytery could use the $30,000? Indeed, at the next presbytery meeting, a bitterly divisive argument erupted among the 120 pastors and elders. Finally, an 85-year-old woman slowly walked up the aisle and stepped to the microphone. Stamping her cane on the floor for emphasis, she said, "Can't this presbytery ever do the right thing? They heard this answer in prayer!" In that moment, everyone knew that following the committee's suggestion was what God wanted. In that moment, the presbytery became blessed, and because it did, God became ever more present to two churches of widely different theological beliefs. This kind of thing happens in a blessed church. People seek what God wants, and when they do, they discover God's unexpected blessings.

THE MARKS OF A BLESSED CHURCH

I've spent most of this chapter discussing what a blessed church is not and what keeps churches from becoming blessed churches. Let me now offer a vision for a blessed church.

I believe that above all, mainline churches are called to become blessed churches, to become places where God's blessings are tangibly experienced. They are called to be healthy places where people devote their lives to God the Creator, Christ, and Holy Spirit, and where healing occurs. These are some of the marks of a blessed church.

The blessed church sees itself as the body of Christ. This is the first mark of a blessed church. To do so, the church and its members must quit considering itself to be something akin to a business, an organization, or even a family. The church has attributes that are similar to a business, an organization, and a family, but it is unique. Nothing else in the world is like a church. As Rick Warren, a leader in the church-growth movement, says, "The church is a body, not a business. It is an organism, not an organization. It is alive. . . . The task of a church leadership is to discover and remove growth-restricting diseases and barriers so that natural, normal growth can occur."[5] Blessed churches are the body of Christ, and they take that fact seriously. In 1 Corinthians 12 Paul outlines a vision of the church as a living, breathing, acting body with Christ as its head. Too few churches hold onto that vision. The blessed church is the body of Christ that follows Christ's guidance to feed, nourish, and care for itself in a way that allows it to grow and become a servant to the world.

The leaders of the body know that Christ is the head, and so they continually and prayerfully seek Christ's guidance. They are like the nervous system. They move the body to act and react in certain ways, but they remain very much aware that their source has to be Christ—God's presence—in their midst. The rational, functional church forgets that Christ is in its midst. Seeking Christ's wisdom and way becomes an overwhelming passion for the blessed church, and its leaders regularly seek in prayer Christ's wisdom and way. For pastors, this means becoming people who pray, especially when they are too busy to pray. Prayer is central to the life of the blessed church. It is like the nervous system of a body. It is through prayer that the body hears what the head desires, and it is through prayer that the body communicates with the head. This emphasis on prayer must begin with pastoral leadership. If the pastor does not lead out of prayer, then the body is unlikely to pray, and without prayer the body becomes disconnected from the head. It will end up either running functionally and frenetically like a chicken with its head cut off, or it will die.

On a practical level, the meetings and matters of the blessed church are grounded in prayer as its leaders seek what God wants over what they want. Dying churches are ego driven. Blessed churches are Christ guided. Blessed churches root their ministries and mission in prayer, act confidently on what they hear, and let God take care of the results. They don't achieve these practices perfectly by any means. Faith is always sprinkled with fear and doubt in even the most faithful leaders. Still, in the end, they do their best to act in faith rather than fear.

A blessed church has a vibrant sense of faith, hope, and love. When a church lacks the faith to trust God to work in its midst, the hope to believe that good things are possible, and a basic love of God and others, it begins a slow descent toward death. So much in a church depends upon leadership—not just pastoral leadership but lay leadership as well. A church always mirrors its leaders. If the leaders are self-focused and selfish, the church will be, too. If the leaders are tentative and fearful, the church will follow suit. If the leaders are ambivalent about God and growth, the church will also be ambivalent. In the same vein, if leaders have a strong sense of faith, hope, and love, then so will the church and its members. That faith, hope, and love will carry over into members' lives so that they become more faithful, hopeful, and loving with their families, in their workplaces, and in responding to the suffering of the world.

A blessed church has a deep faith in God and God's power. What does it mean to be a church of faith? Sadly, far too many Christians confuse faith and belief. Faith is much more than belief. It is a deep trust in God. It is an abandoning to God in which we surrender our control and power, trusting that God will act to accomplish something through, with, or among us—something wonderful and powerful that we cannot accomplish on our own. The leaders and members may be anxious about change, but in the end they always opt in faith to do what they prayerfully sense God calling them to do. They may not clearly know what the outcome of their act of faith will be, and their options may feel risky or dangerous, but when given a choice between acting fearfully to protect themselves and acting faithfully to serve God, they act in faith—though it may mean taking a path that seems uncertain and frightening.

Besides having a deep faith, the leadership has a strong sense of hope for the future. This hope prevails even during bad economic times, amid troubling world and national events, and despite congregational crises. Church leaders have a strong sense that God is with them and will make good things happen, especially if they remain faithful, even if it means going through terrible times of struggle and turmoil.

Finally, the leaders have a strong sense of love for one another and the church's members, a love that leads the members eventually to reach out and love others, even those who are different. They don't react to failure and problems with anger, frustration, or impatience. They understand what it is to be afraid and to make mistakes. So they act with love. With this kind of leadership, members become people of faith, hope, and love, and this love becomes almost tangible to those visiting the church. This quality of tangible love is apparent in large blessed churches but especially evident in small ones.

A blessed church is filled with God's purpose, presence, and power. I believe that we *experience* the Trinitarian God as purpose, presence, and power.[6] For example, one of the most tangible ways we encounter God as Creator happens as we become increasingly aware of what our *purpose* is as a church and as individuals. We encounter God in Christ when we sense Christ's *presence* in the life of the church—in worship, word, sacrament, music, drama, activities, meetings, and one another. We encounter God the Holy Spirit when we witness the *power* of God making coincidences (providences), miracles, and amazing events happen (although the Holy Spirit also works in ways that are often unseen and unencountered). Blessed churches have a relatively clear sense of what their purpose is and why God the Creator called them into existence, even if they are hundreds of years old. They tangibly sense Christ's presence. They expect the Spirit's power to work everywhere in the church, blessing the ministries, mission, and members of the church.

The blessed church embraces the sacred. The blessed church emphasizes symbols, sacraments, and rituals in a way that helps people encounter God in every dimension—spiritual, mental, emotional, subconscious, physical, and relational. Such churches emphasize rituals, sacraments, and symbols because they know that these have the power to connect people to the Trinity in sacred ways that the spoken word and music cannot.

For example, the sacraments of communion and baptism are central to their lives. Blessed churches recognize sacraments have the power to reveal and connect a person with the divine—a power that cannot be fully explained or duplicated in any other way. So the blessed church emphasizes the power of these sacraments and places them at the center of congregational life. For instance, at Calvin Church we celebrate communion once a week in our first worship service, once a month in our second. This frequency is not typical of Presbyterian churches (typically Presbyterians celebrate communion between five times a year and once a month), but we recognize the power of communion to connect people with God's love and presence. We recognize that the sacred can be revealed through nonsacramental rituals, too. For example, we offer regular healing services as part of our worship, and we have a healing prayer ministry that reaches out to those suffering with physical, mental, and emotional illnesses as well as other needs. Again, making healing rituals and prayers part of the worship and life of the church becomes a powerful way of connecting people to God's presence and power in their lives.

Blessed churches embrace the sacred also by placing banners, crosses, statues, and other artistic expressions of the divine throughout the sanctuary. Displaying religious and spiritual artistry runs counter to the emphasis of many contemporary churches, which often strip their worship spaces of all symbols and sacraments. The blessed church tries to create sacred spaces that reveal the Trinity through sacrament, art, architecture, and creative use of symbols and space to reveal the sacred and to connect people with the divine.

One key to embracing the sacred is ensuring that rituals, symbols, sacrament, art, architecture, and space are used in ways that lead people to encounter God. The focus cannot be only on offering symbols and sacraments the way the church did 200 years ago. The sacraments and symbols can and must be transformed so that they use the language and expressions of today in a way that invites newer and younger Christians to experience the power these elements have had for Christians for more than 2,000 years. When we resist transforming the language and expression of our sacraments in meaningful ways, holding on instead to the language and pacing of previous generations and eras, we make tradition and custom more important than an encounter with Christ.

Transforming sacraments and symbols creates a difficult choice because it forces the church and its leaders to maintain a tension between remaining true to a tradition and creating a new tradition. In other words, we have to maintain fidelity to the intent and purpose of the sacrament or symbol while transforming it and while resisting the temptation to create something new simply for the sake of newness. The best transformation of a sacrament, symbol, or ritual happens when we understand fully its purpose and power, while transforming it in a way that touches and affects new generations. The essential point is that the blessed church appreciates deeply the power of the sacred to be revealed and experienced through much more than the spoken word or music. The blessed church recognizes that the sacred can emerge through symbols, sacraments, architecture, and art, especially when we ask God to guide us in discerning how to reveal God.

The blessed church is not afraid to serve God in its own way. It is not concerned with fitting into a mold of what church should be nor of what its denomination expects it to be. Instead it is concerned with responding to God's call and God's call alone. Each church has its own calling, ministry, and mission. Calvin Presbyterian Church's calling is going to be very different from that of a northern urban church, a church in Orange County, California, a church in rural Alabama, or a church in the deserts of Arizona. Our mission is not as clearly on our doorstep as it is for some churches. We don't have homeless people sleeping on our steps, nor do we have an influx of migrant workers each summer. We don't necessarily come as clearly face-to-face with our mission field. While an urban church may be called to give direct service to the poor and the homeless, or a church in Orange County, California, may be faced with reaching out to thousands of unchurched people moving into the area, much of our mission beyond evangelism is in giving money to support mission rather than engaging in a more active, hands-on mission. Some people may criticize us for that, but it's our calling. In fact, we felt that calling so clearly a few years ago that we restructured the way we give to mission. Instead of being a church that gives a huge chunk of money to the denominational mission programs, we decided to devote our yearly mission giving (we generally give between 19 percent and 23 percent of our yearly budget to mission) to what we call the Special Mission Fund. This fund is set up to respond to the more immediate needs of those with whom we come in contact. The fund helps a paralyzed woman purchase a voice-command control box to operate her television, telephone, and other appliances. It helps a poor woman with six children find temporary housing. It supports a faith-based organization that needs seed money. It helps an abused woman rent an apartment to start a new life. It supplements the welfare income of a man with epilepsy and supports him in the process of receiving a house built by Habitat for Humanity volunteers. The point is that this mission fund is set up to respond to God as God is calling us to act in mission.

The ministry of a blessed church is always unique. It is a custom fit to its members and its community. I cannot stress sufficiently how important it is for blessed churches to serve in their own distinctive ways. Some Christians are always willing to tell others what they should be doing. Blessed churches resist the idea that they should do what others outside their situation demand, even if the hearts of the demanders are in the right place. The blessed church is harmonious with its own calling. It doesn't respond to people who say, "You should do this because it is what churches are supposed to do." Instead, it responds to only two questions: "God, what are you calling us to do?" and "How do we best respond to God in our own situation and context?" Bruce Smith, our music and youth director, likes to say that Calvin Church has an unofficial motto: "Calvin Church—we're not for everyone." What he is saying is that we tend to respond to God in the way we feel called to respond. If you don't want to be part of a church that responds to God in this way, there are other congregations. We want people who feel called to the same ministry and mission that we do. We want to respond to God in our own unique ways.

THE "BLESSED" BODY OF CHRIST

Describing the blessed church with precision is difficult because in many ways it is something experienced that cannot be outlined. There is no such thing as a perfectly blessed church because there is no perfection in the human realm. Instead, what people notice is that there is something special, something sacred and mysterious going on that leads people to encounter and experience God. Not everyone who enters a blessed church experiences this, especially if one is looking for something else. Some people who visit Calvin Presbyterian Church really are looking for a different experience. They may want a church with a particular political or social agenda, a church with less commitment or perhaps more rules, or a church that will expect less active participation. They are seeking a particular form of worship. They are looking for a church with mostly folk in their own age bracket The mark of a blessed church is not that everyone who enters the sanctuary is "slain in the Spirit" and walks away in the conviction that this is the *only* home of God. The ultimate mark of a blessed church is that the people called to become part of it sense God's presence and power working among them, even if they can't put their finger on exactly how this presence is manifested or how the power is working.

In a blessed church, rational functionalism has been chased away. People don't discuss theology so much as they discuss life, and in the process they experience the theological teachings of the church coming alive. In a blessed church, the pastor doesn't do everything. Instead, the love of the members and the leaders for one another does everything. I've experienced that activity at Calvin Church. I don't have to be the main love giver when people go through trauma. The members of the church do it without being trained or educated to do so.

As we will see in subsequent chapters, becoming a blessed church means becoming what a church already is: the body of Christ in a particular place. It is a place in which people form a vibrant sense of faith, hope, and love that comes naturally from being part of a community of faith, hope, and love. The blessed church is a place in which people tangibly experience God as purpose, presence, and power; and because they also embrace the sacred, they experience God through sacred symbols, sacraments, art, architecture, and more. Blessed churches are places where people serve God in ways that are unique to them and their context because they are trying to live in harmony with their calling. Ultimately, blessed churches are places that have discovered *the* great spiritual truth of congregational life: God wants to bless us, God wants our churches to thrive in their own way, and all we have to do is create the conditions for God to be welcome.

REFLECTION QUESTIONS

1. Read 1 Corinthians 12:12–21. Reflect on what specific changes would have to be made in your church to make Christ the head and to nurture health in the body.
2. Read 1 Corinthians 13. Reflect on concrete ways to make faith, hope, and especially love stronger in your church.
3. In what specific ways is your church caught in rational functionalism? How can you break its grip on your church?
4. In what ways does your church bear the marks of a blessed church

   - as an organic incarnation of the body of Christ, rather than an organization?
   - as a place of faith, hope, and love?
   - as a place filled with God's purpose, presence, and power?
   - as a place that embraces the sacred? and
   - as a place that serves God in its own unique ways?

2

SETTING A SPIRITUAL FOUNDATION

What was the defining moment of the Christian church, the moment that gave it birth? It wasn't Christ's birth. His birth gave us God's revelation *in* a person rather than *through* a person (as God was revealed *through* the prophets). Jesus revealed that God is among us, and he taught us how to live in God's kingdom and presence. Still, Jesus' birth was not the defining moment of the Christian church. Nor were Jesus' death and resurrection the defining moments. They revealed that God's love is the greatest force in the universe, and they define the Christian *faith* but not the church.

The defining moment of the Christian church, and its birthday, was the day of Pentecost, a day too many mainline Christians neglect. Acts 2:1–12 tells us that the disciples and followers of Jesus gathered to wait. They weren't sure what would happen, but Jesus had told them that they would receive the gift of the Holy Spirit after he had ascended. At their last supper together, he said, "If you love me, you will keep my commandments. And I will ask the Father, and he will give you another Advocate, to be with you forever. This is the Spirit of truth, whom the world cannot receive, because it neither sees him nor knows him. You know him because he abides with you, and he will be in you" (John 14:15–17). He also said as he ascended into heaven, "But you will receive power when the Holy Spirit has come upon you; and you will be my witnesses in Jerusalem, in all Judea and Samaria, and to the ends of the earth" (Acts 1:8).

Jesus' disciples and followers waited on the day of Pentecost, and "suddenly from heaven there came a sound like the rush of a violent wind, and it filled the entire house where they were sitting. Divided tongues, as of fire, appeared among them, and a tongue rested on each of them. All of them were filled with the Holy Spirit and began to speak in other languages, as the Spirit gave them ability" (Acts 2:1–4). Pentecost was the defining moment for the Christian church, the moment when the followers became the church—the community of Christ. They were no longer simply following the teachings of Christ, although Christ's teachings were their foundation. They were no longer simply trying to imitate Christ. The moment they became filled with the Holy Spirit was the moment the church became a living organism, just as Adam became a living being when God breathed the breath of life into him.

According to Genesis, what defined and gave life to all humans was God breathing God's breath, God's Spirit, into the first human being: "Then God formed [the human] from the dust of the ground, and breathed into his nostrils the breath [or Spirit] of life" (Genesis 2:7). From the Genesis account it is made clear that it is God's indwelling Spirit that gives us life and distinguishes us from all other life forms. The gift of the Holy Spirit makes us uniquely aware of God and of the fact that God has created us. The same can be said about the gift of the Holy Spirit filling Jesus' followers and disciples on Pentecost. In that moment the church was given life and became a living organism. The followers no longer saw God as residing only in heaven or in the temple of Jerusalem but now saw themselves as the body of Christ, as Christ's presence on earth: "For in the one Spirit we were all baptized into one body—Jews or Greeks, slaves or free—and we were all made to drink of one Spirit" (1 Cor. 12:13).

The day of Pentecost was a defining moment because from that day on, the Christian church became increasingly clear each day about what it was—the community of Christ filled with the Holy Spirit. Through the power of the Holy Spirit, Christ's followers now had the living and transforming Christ alive within them, allowing them to become the living, breathing body of Christ in the world. Together and individually, they could incarnate Christ. Christ had not only ascended into heaven. Christ was still alive in the world through the community of Christians acting in the world as they shared God's healing and saving grace with the rest of the world. Without the day of Pentecost, without this "being filled" by the Holy Spirit, the Christian movement would have died. Like many fleeting movements, Christianity would have rested on a series of teachings and commandments, not on a living experience and incarnation of God.

RESPIRATORY FAILURE

Despite how crucial the events of Pentecost were to the formation of the church, Pentecost isn't emphasized in many of today's mainline churches because we mainline Christians don't know what to do with the Holy Spirit. We're very comfortable with God the Father. We're relatively comfortable with Jesus, even if we can't always decide whether Jesus was God or just a great man. But the Holy Spirit seems nebulous, enigmatic, and unpredictable. We have no clear sense of who the Holy Spirit is, what the Holy Spirit does, and what will happen to us if we become open to the Spirit. We mainline Christians are an orderly bunch. We want our religion, our worship, and our experience of God to be organized, predictable, and calm—at least those of us do who have remained behind after the great exodus of members from our churches over the past 40 years.

Many of today's mainline members fear the Holy Spirit because of what they see in the Pentecostal movement, which tends to focus mostly on the Holy Spirit. Mainliners see people speaking in tongues and cover their mouths. They hear people prophesying and shut their ears. They see dancing, swaying, and shouting and cover their eyes. If being open to the Holy Spirit means becoming like that, they want nothing to do with it. The Holy Spirit can just fill someone else, thank you very much.

Unfortunately, too many of our churches, by ignoring and remaining closed to the Holy Spirit, have developed respiratory failure. Since we no longer breathe with the breath of the Holy Spirit, we neither *aspire* to become open to the Spirit nor allow ourselves to be *inspired* by the Holy Spirit. As a result, our churches eventually *expire*. We suffer such chronic respiratory failure—the failure to breathe in the Spirit and life—that our churches eventually take their last breath and die.

Essentially, too many mainline Christian churches—urban, suburban, and rural— are losing or have lost their spiritual core, their vibrant center. They are missing something deeply spiritual, but because they don't know what they've lost, they wheeze along, desperately trying to grasp anything that promises to sustain them. They try this or that program but fail because the programs are missing the very thing that people are searching for: the breath of God in their midst, the work of the Holy Spirit that reveals Christ and leads them to live in harmony with God's plan.

Here's an example: Do you know what has often been one of the most popular evangelizing programs over the past 25 years? It is the "bring-a-friend-to-church" program. Years ago, church researchers noticed that up to 85 percent of the newcomers who eventually joined growing churches had originally visited the church at the invitation of a friend who was a church member. So the creators of "bring a friend" tried to recreate this statistic in a functional, programmatic way by developing materials to encourage churches to designate a particular Sunday when all members would bring at least one friend.

The essential problem with this program was succinctly identified by one of my cousins. She told me that her church had a "bring-a-friend-to-church" Sunday, and she didn't know what to do. She had joined the church because she wanted to expose her children to religion, but she didn't necessarily like the church. As she said, "I'm kind of embarrassed about my church. I'm not sure I want to bring a friend, because then I have to explain why my church is so dead." What good does it do to bring a friend to church if the friend can't encounter God in that church—if it is spiritually vacant?

These programs mimic the functional aspect of what takes place in growing churches, but they lose sight of what is going on spiritually— the spiritual vitality at these churches' cores. They fail to understand that growing congregations don't need to institute bring-a-friend-to-church programs because their members already want to bring their friends. The members sense that God's Spirit is alive in their church, and they want to share their experiences. They are excited about their church because they know it is a place of aspiration and inspiration. Not everyone who visits a church feels as completely inspired as its members, but many do. Their church is a place that breathes life into them.

volved. God becomes a theological principle we speculate about rather than a spiritual presence we encounter and experience. When we become aware of how lacking we are in spiritual animation, we then question what we are doing in the church. We look at our worship and ask, "Has our worship become routine, or does it have a sense of spiritual vibrancy at its core? Has our education program become functional, teaching kids *about* God instead of leading them to form a relationship *with* God?" We ask, "What in our church has become merely functional, and what can we do to recapture a sense of liveliness?"

Not all churches are willing to ask these questions. Churches that remain unaware of this slide into functionality eventually slip from functionalism into *dysfunctionalism*. "Dysfunctional" is a psychological term used in family and marital therapy. People make the mistake of thinking it means "not functioning." It doesn't. It means "functioning in pain." When we are dysfunctional, we still function, but everything we do causes pain. Dysfunctional families still have dinner together, go to the zoo together, and take the kids to dance classes and soccer games. The difference is that all of their interactions are painful. Family members, and especially parents, argue and snipe about everything. The dinner table becomes a battleground. Rides to events become torturous. Family functions become laborious, leading all to depression and despair.

Churches that slip into dysfunctionalism do function, but they function in pain. They hold worship services, participate in committee and board meetings, make decisions, do mission work, and more, but they do so in dysfunctional ways. Sermons become berating diatribes as the pastor criticizes the congregation for failing to give enough money, to show up often enough for worship, or to volunteer enough. Church members snipe behind the pastors' backs or send them nasty letters, criticizing them for not visiting members often enough, preaching well enough, or inspiring them enough. Fights within the church erupt over budgets, plans, and more. Energy is drained from the church over every little detail. The question becomes, "What's holding this place together?"

By the time a church slips into serious dysfunctionalism, it is difficult for it to decide to move back toward spiritual vibrancy. When it does, often it does so because some catalyst sparks the movement, such as a scandal that forces the church to look at itself honestly, the intervention of denominational authorities who impose strict sanctions on the church, or the realization that the church will soon die if something isn't done. In other words, what motivates the church to recapture a sense of spiritual zest is the church's hitting rock bottom and deciding to change at its foundations. Sadly, most dysfunctional churches don't make this choice. Instead, they slip from dysfunctionalism to what I will call simple *disfunction*.

Disfunction simply means that the church stops functioning. This doesn't happen all at once. In fact, it generally happens very slowly. Oddly, when a church slips into *disfunction*, it can enter a period of relative peace as the church slowly dies. The people who argued and fought have either left, died, or accepted the inevitability of death. They don't have problems with the pastor anymore because they can't afford a pastor. Instead, they have a series of part-time interim pastors, each of whom stays for only a short time, or they find a lay pastor who will hold their hands until death comes. The ministry of the church is pretty much relegated to offering a basic worship service on Sundays and to finding someone "pastoral" to serve as a chaplain to the dying congregation. In many ways, it is like being with a family that has a loved one in long-term hospice care. Everyone knows that death is coming, and people become more caring and respectful of each other as they prepare for the inevitable. Churches that slide into *disfunction* and begin the dying process aren't going to improve no matter what happens. They don't have the capability. There's no critical mass to build upon. What remains in these kinds of churches is simply a profound sadness. They know they are dying and that death is inevitable.

WHERE HAS ALL THE VIBRANCY GONE?

The person who made me most aware of the cause of the mainline church's loss of spiritual vibrancy was a man I studied with for more than five years while working on my doctorate in spiritual formation, Adrian van Kaam, a Roman Catholic priest and psychologist who created Duquesne University's Institute of Formative Spirituality. During his lifetime he wrote numerous books on spiritual formation, and he had an understanding of spirituality that goes beyond anything that I have seen in my own work or that of anyone else writing in the field of spirituality.

Van Kaam understood that the true health of an organization or person comes from being fully integrated. For him, the integration of the four primary dimensions of our lives, which he calls the transcendent, functional, vital, and sociohistoric, is what keeps us healthy and energized.[1] For clarity's sake, I have altered his language slightly. In essence, he is saying that to be healthy, we need to integrate and balance the *spiritual, mental, physical,* and *relational* dimensions of life. Unfortunately, we find this kind of integration all too rarely in individuals, organizations, or churches. Without this integration there is no vitality.

Integration begins with the spiritual dimension of life, which is concerned with living in harmony with God and God's will. When we are open to the spiritual dimension, we increasingly seek God's will and begin to sense what God wants for us and from us. When our spiritual dimension is strong, we aspire to what God wants and become inspired by God. The stronger the spiritual dimension is in our lives and churches, the more God's will and ways seem to flow through our thoughts, plans, and relationships.

Whether we are talking about an individual or a church, being integrated means to live life in such a way that the spiritual, mental, physical, and relational dimensions of life all work together with a sense of consonance that brings wholeness and holiness to life. Unfortunately, we live in a culture in which these dimensions are split from one another and in fact are often at war. They are split because at the foundations of our culture, we have cut off the *spiritual dimension,* which, among other things, is also the *integrating dimension.* It is concerned with balancing life as God intended. At the foundations of our culture, we have accepted a mechanistic, rationalistic, scientific view of life that either denies the existence of God or relegates God and spiritual concerns to the margins of life. This view of life denies or ignores the spiritual dimension. The result is that we live in a fragmented world in which people think that having a perfect body, being rich, being powerful, or best, all three, will lead to happiness. Our modern view of life is very different from the ancient view of life. In the ancient world, God and the divine were considered to be part of the very fabric of life. Ancient people considered every part of life to be infused with the

spiritual, and they had a sense that they were part of some divine drama. Having lost much of this ancient, integrated understanding of life,
we have difficulty attending to the deeper interests of life. We are no
longer concerned with our ultimate purpose or how to live a deeper,
richer, more loving life. What we seem to care about is the surface of
life.

Each dimension, when it is open to the spiritual dimension, has the
potential to reveal deeper spiritual truths. For example, theological
thinking has the power, via the mental dimension's openness to the
spiritual, to reveal the wonders of God and the universe. Art and music,
through the physical dimension's openness to the spiritual, reveal God's
beauty and grace. Relationships, when open to the spiritual, can embody God's love. Unfortunately, when any of the dimensions are cut off
from the spiritual, they lead us to become consumed with their more
shallow aspects.

For example, some people become dominated by the mental dimension, becoming obsessed with gaining and wielding power, wealth, and
control. Others become dominated by concerns of the physical dimension, becoming obsessed with physical appearance, exercise, diet, sex,
drugs, alcohol, pleasure seeking, and the satisfaction of urges. Those
who are dominated by the relational dimension become obsessed with
fitting in or standing out. They become slaves to fashion, custom, and
conformity. We can see the separation of the spiritual from the other
dimensions in the domination of our culture by the lifestyle industry's
obsession with physical beauty, sexual gratification, and the need for
constant stimulation and attention. We can see it in the political and
corporate realms, where politicians care only about who has power,
wealth, influence, and control. We can see it in the dominance of the
fashion and entertainment industries that bombard us with messages
about what clothes to wear, what cars to drive, and what gadgets to
acquire while simultaneously stoking our desires for food, sex, and ad-
dictive substances and activities.

Van Kaam stresses the importance of the spiritual dimension to the
life of an individual, an organization, *and* the church. He says that the
spiritual dimension is the integrating dimension of life. It holds all the
other dimensions in consonance. It is the dimension most concerned
with living according to God's purposes. When the spiritual dimension
is strong, it does not dominate the other dimensions by denying or

controlling them. Instead, it guides and integrates the other dimensions so that we can live according to God's purposes in every dimension. The spiritual dimension guides us so that we can aspire to be healthier mentally, physically, and relationally, even if we live amid conflicts and struggles. Living an integrated life does not keep us from experiencing life's turmoil and pain, but it does open us to God's guidance, which enables us to live through these times in God's ways and, in the end, to transcend them in a way that leads to wholeness and holiness. Churches especially need the spiritual dimension to be a strong, guiding force in members' life together. The stronger the spiritual dimension is in our churches, the more we try to live with one another according to God's purposes.

What makes the spiritual dimension the integrating force is its role as the dimension most concerned with openness to God's Spirit. When our spiritual dimension is strong, we aspire to live according to God's calling and seek the inspirations of the Spirit that teach us how to live holy, whole lives. When we aspire to live as the Creator calls us to live and are inspired by the Spirit, the spiritual dimension guides the mental, physical, and relational aspects of our lives so that they come together in relative consonance. In short, when the spiritual dimension is strong in our lives and churches, it leads us to live healthier, holier, and more whole lives—lives grounded in God and God's love.

RESPIRATORY FAILURE IN THE CHURCH

Like individuals, church communities are meant to be healthy bodies whose dimensions are integrated in healthy ways. Unfortunately, because we have cut off the spiritual in many churches, they have become unhealthy places. They become dominated by the mental and relational dimensions while simultaneously suppressing the physical dimension. You may know churches in which the mental dimension dominates. You may be a member of one. Such churches have slipped into functionalism, or worse, dysfunctionalism. Board and committee meetings often break down into ego-driven fights over who is right and who is wrong. Members of the church divide into theological and political camps as the need to be right and to wield power becomes more important than following the call of Christ to humbly love, support, and nurture each other. These churches become ruled by members and pastors who care most about achieving their ambitions, controlling the decision-making processes, and dominating the community with their positions or beliefs.

Here's an example: Early in my ministry, I served in a growing church that needed more space for its programs. The pastor had asked a member of the church, a man whose business was real estate development and construction, to draw up tentative plans to build an addition onto the church. The plans addressed the needs of the church in a well-thought-out way. The first floor would house a new classroom and an expanded choir room. The second floor would house a multi-use room with a small kitchen and fireplace. Soundproof dividers could be used to create a more intimate space around the fireplace, but the room could also be expanded to host lectures and small congregational dinners. The plans also called for adding an elevator and renovating existing rooms for new purposes. The plan was to build the expansion on the side of the church facing a large parking lot and 16 acres of wooded property.

The plans were presented at a board meeting. Questions were asked, and everyone pretty much agreed with the plans. Then one man said, "I agree with the need to build this, but I don't agree with where it is to be built. I think it should be built on the other side of the church," facing a large field. An argument ensued as the board divided into two camps: those wanting the addition built on the parking lot side, and those wanting it built on the field side. For the next few meetings, the discussions continued with no resolution. Both sides were adamant. To end the arguments, it was decided that a task force should be formed to refine the proposal and settle the dispute. The commission worked for eight months and ended up being somewhat divided itself. Eventually, the senior pastor left the church, partly because of the ego-driven stalemate. Thirteen years later the addition remained unbuilt. In fact, the church has since had more conflict and has shrunk to little more than one-third its former size.

I don't write this to be critical of these people. I think all the people involved in the dispute were good, honest people. The problem was that the spiritual dimension was just too weak in that church and its board. No one ever considered stopping the discussion and saying, "What do you think God wants?" I became aware of how God averse they were when I led that board in an exercise designed to make board members more aware of the need to follow what God wanted. One board member said to me after the exercise, "I don't like this at all. It is much easier to make a decision when you don't have to figure out what God wants. I would rather decide what I want." Making "deciding what I want" the key concern is the hallmark of a church that has cut off the spiritual dimension and is now caught in the dominating grip of the mental dimension as egos and a desire for power and influence.

Overcoming enslavement to the mental dimension is difficult. It requires training and guiding the leaders and members to put aside their own egos, ambitions, and need for control and to seek and follow the Spirit. If the leaders remain resistant to the spiritual, then other leaders who are more open to the Spirit may have to be found. Seeking Spirit-led leaders, however, requires depending on the guidance and grace of the Holy Spirit and may require the patience of Job to wait for God to reveal these more spiritually open leaders. The patience of Job is a particular asset in leading small churches with little growth, where the same leaders serve on the board year after year. In their case it may be a wise step to shrink the size of the governing board, even if that means shrinking it to the bare minimum of three members. It is better to have a tiny board of faith-filled, Spirit-led leaders than a large one of functional leaders who care little about what God wants. In fact, cutting the size of boards is a good idea in churches big and small because the smaller a board is, the more it is forced to delegate and to trust in the Holy Spirit while also building a greater sense of trust among members.

In some churches, where the spiritual dimension is cut off, the relational dimension dominates. You know these churches. They are the ones that become slaves to the phrase, "But we've never done it that way." They are afraid of change because of a need to conform to the church's past, to rules and customs created by people long gone who were responding to a different age. They are afraid to change because so much has changed around them. They want the church to be the one place of stability in their lives. They become mired in functionalism, doing things only because that is what we do, have done, and always have done. In seeking functional stability they slowly kill the church by sapping its spiritual vibrancy. To keep the church stable, they have to make sure that no one ever joins, no new ideas are ever implemented, and no inspirations of the Holy Spirit are ever followed. Overcoming this tendency to conform to the past can be hard. It means opening the people to the guidance of the Holy Spirit in ways that lead frightened members to feel safe. It may require that the pastor and other leaders maintain a strong and patient faith coupled with a gentle approach that enables them to listen to God while simultaneously making steady, God-inspired, incremental changes. Too many pastors and leaders try to change things too fast. Even God-inspired changes take time.

The modern Christian church generally ignores the physical dimension when it comes to physical health. At the same time, the church obsesses about the physical dimension when it comes to dress, race, sexual orientation, and sex. The people of these churches become obsessed with how people are dressed, what color their skin is, what their sexual orientation is, and who is sleeping with whom. The church was more concerned with other aspects of the physical dimension in years past, especially during the Middle Ages, when the focus was on asceticism, fasting, and celibacy. Still, fixation on the physical dimension remains strong in some circles, especially in matters of sex. I'm not advocating a permissive attitude toward sex. What I am saying is that in churches where the spiritual dimension is diminished or cut off, people become obsessed with sex to the point that the church becomes divided over sexual issues and God seems absent.

Meanwhile the Christian church generally ignores other connections between the physical and the spiritual, such as the connection between prayer, healing, and health. Adherents of the New Age movement have filled the void created by the modern church's neglect of the physical by emphasizing the connection between the spiritual and the physical. With their emphasis on yoga, aromatherapy, massage, Reiki, therapeutic touch, crystals, healing, and the like, they have tried to reconnect the spiritual and the physical. Only recently have Christian churches begun to try to reconnect the two. Many churches have discovered or rediscovered the power of candles, labyrinths, incense, yoga, massage, contemplation (what many call "meditation"), prayer-based dieting, and more. In fact, the reconnection of the spiritual and the physical has led many churches, including nondenominational churches that have traditionally stripped their worship of Christian symbols and of sacraments other than baptism, to recognize the importance of sacraments in opening people to God's mystical presence. As a result, many are now creating new worship services that emphasize Christian sacraments and symbols. Still, most of our churches remain resistant.

THE POWER OF THE SPIRITUAL

When the spiritual dimension is strong in a church, members are able to experience God. They discover that God isn't "out there," that God is "above all and through all and in all" (Eph. 4:6). As members become more open spiritually, they become more open to an intimate relationship with each person of God: Creator, Christ, and Holy Spirit. They have an intimate encounter with the Trinity, even if they don't necessarily describe this encounter in Trinitarian terms. They come to know God more than they speculate about God. As a result, they also grow in their ability to encounter and experience God in Scripture, others, their own hearts, and the events of life.

Certain signs can reveal fairly quickly whether your church community is open to the spiritual—to the Holy Spirit—and therefore to becoming integrated. The first sign of openness to the spiritual is the extent to which *Robert's Rules of Order* dominates the proceedings of the church. Standardized parliamentary procedures are good for helping a church and its committees maintain order, but they aren't designed to help us discern God's will. The more determined the church's leaders are to follow these rules to the letter, the more the spiritual is cut off. The more they are able to supplement these rules with a determined effort to discern God's guidance and voice in prayer, the more open they are to the Spirit.

Robert's Rules has been a blessing to churches by helping churches become more orderly and less disorganized (at least when comparing church life before the creation of such procedures, when meetings were often chaotic and confusing). At the same time, strict observance of them can stifle the life of the church because over time a church can become a slave to the functionality inherent in *Robert's Rules*. As functionality grows what increasingly matters is following the rules, not Christ; following the will of the majority, not the will of God. What matters most is doing things in an orderly way, not in a Spirit-led way. Order and procedure become more important than seeking and serving God.

A second sign of being a spiritually integrated church is found when we ask a simple question about worship: What kind of worship is God calling us to employ so that we can reach the people God wants us to reach?[2] Answering this question involves answering other questions: Whom are we trying to reach? What do we have the talent to accomplish? What is the calling of our church? Is it to grow in size? *Can* we grow in size? What is God's purpose in our midst? These questions cannot be answered all at once but must be constantly asked and the answers patiently discerned.

Churches that have cut off the spiritual aren't really as concerned about what worship God is calling them to offer nor the question of whom we are trying to reach. Instead, "cut-off" churches tend to fight over worship styles, music, hymns, and the like. They get caught up in trying to conform to the music of the past or in trying to force upon others the music of the present. They don't ask the fundamental question, "What worship styles, music, and hymns is God calling us to use?" I've witnessed this fight in our church. At Calvin Church, we in the leadership of the church are pretty determined to form worship styles and use music that we feel called by God to use. I suppose you could call our style "blended," but in reality we just go in the direction we feel called to go. The term we use is "integrated worship," since our approach is to integrate different approaches to worship, including traditional, contemporary, jazz, blues, and folk music as well as elements we've adopted from Reformed, Episcopalian, Catholic, contemporary, emergent, Lutheran, Taizé, Baptist, and other traditions. We've kept some traditional things (wearing robes and singing some older hymns), we've adopted some contemporary things (using contemporary songs, lighting, and instruments), and we've even reintroduced Christian traditions long forgotten by Presbyterians such as using real wine (along with the customary grape juice) for communion, chanting, hanging symbolic banners, and emphasizing the liturgical seasons. We try to create worship that is God-inspired.

As in all churches that embrace change, especially change for God's sake, we have received complaints. For one particular six-month period I consistently heard complaints from two members about our worship. Both members are good people, yet both came to worship with their own beliefs about what kind of worship we should offer—their kind of worship. On most Sundays, one man in his 80s would sarcastically say on his way out, "What's the matter with the organ? Is it broken?" He was referring to the fact that we played most hymns and contemporary songs on piano, electronic keyboards, guitars, string bass, and drums. Meanwhile, a woman would complain to me that the hymns we sang were too traditional: "Contemporary worship is the wave of the future. We should be going all contemporary." It was hard for either of these worshipers to accept that we were trying to follow what God was calling us to do in our church, not what churches did 40 years ago or what "seeker" churches are doing today.

A third sign of spiritually open churches is that the preaching emphasizes teaching people how to become open to the spiritual, to the divine, to God. In far too many of our mainline churches, preaching tends to be excessively theological or speculative rather than inspirational and applicable. Such sermons may be theologically deep, exploring the mysteries of God and the universe, but they don't necessarily help people live or give them guidance on how to encounter God. A sign of spiritual openness is that while sermons remain theologically sound, their main focus is addressing the questions people are silently asking instead of the questions theologians ask. We address such questions as these: How will this help me discover and hear God? How will this help me serve God in my church, home, workplace, and all other arenas of life? How will this help me discover God's presence and guidance in the grief and darkness of divorce, disease, downsizing, and death? Spiritually grounded sermons try to answer these questions in relevant, honest, and inspiring ways.

The final sign of a spiritually open church is that it integrates all the dimensions in healthy ways. For example, a healthy church is organized and has ambitions, but the leaders care most about humbly seeking God's guidance in prayer rather than pridefully attempting to achieve what they want. For a leader, being spiritually integrated may mean helping the church achieve or accomplish something that I, the pastor, don't think is right but that other leaders have discerned in prayer. The spiritually integrated church also cares about relationships and traditions. What matters most is steeping the church in loving God with everything it has, loving others as ourselves, and not reflexively conforming to or rebelling against certain traditions and customs because of fear, anxiety, and confusion about what to do to survive. Finally, the spiritually integrated church cares about and addresses physical issues.

It cares about teaching members how to develop healthy eating, drinking, sexual, and other physical habits.

BEING REFILLED WITH THE HOLY SPIRIT

How do we form a church that is spiritually vibrant and integrated? It begins with both pastoral and lay leadership. The pastor first must make a foundational decision to become spiritually open at her core. If the pastors (especially the lead or senior pastor) are closed to the Spirit, the church will be, too, no matter how many members are open to the Spirit. The pastor must become a person of prayer and discernment who seeks God's guidance in everything. The pastor must pray for the church and for the members. The pastor must pray over her sermons, asking that the sermon ring with God's voice, not her own. The pastor must pray for the board, committees, task forces, and teams of the church. The pastor must pray sincerely over his own ministry, asking whether he is God-inspired and led or ego driven and prideful. The pastor must also pray for God to reveal and bring forth other leaders who are faithfully and prayerfully open to God's Spirit. Finally, the pastor must lead the leaders to become more open to the Spirit as individuals and as a group.

Everything said about the pastor also is true of lay leaders. The lay leaders must take God seriously. They must want God to guide them in their leadership and personal lives. If lay leaders refuse to become open to God, they will end up leading the church on a path of disease. The church will slowly sicken and perhaps even die.

Church leaders can take specific steps to encourage openness to the Holy Spirit. First, they need to make a thorough assessment of the whole church body to determine the extent to which the members are foundationally open to God. (See appendix A, "Assessing the Church's Spiritual Openness.") The point of this assessment is not for the leaders to beat up on the church but to assess honestly the extent to which the church is open to God. The other point is for leaders to begin making concrete, prayerfully discerned, Spirit-inspired plans to open the church more fully to God.

Second, the leaders can ask questions of themselves to gain a sense of whether their leadership is open to God. For instance, do they plan their meeting agendas in ways that actually seek God's presence and guidance? Most churches that follow the traditional agendas of *Robert's Rules of Order* do not. I do not suggest jettisoning these rules and guidelines. I suggest augmenting them. For instance, in our church we made a decision to reformat our agenda to create space for God. (See appendix B, "Session Agenda.") We restructured our meeting more in the shape of a worship service, with the agenda resembling a worship bulletin. We also decorated our meeting room with religious art and symbols so that it becomes a more worshipful space.

We begin meetings by lighting a candle in a time of centering prayer, after which we sing a hymn, pray together, and then have a time to share what is going on in our lives. We then engage in a time of study, which can mean studying Scripture, books intended to open the church to new possibilities, or short studies using the writings of great spiritual writers throughout history. In recent years we extended this practice so that now all of our committees and task forces begin their meetings with a 20–30 minute period of spiritual study (for samples of these materials, please go to http://www.ngrahamstandish.org to find a three-year cycle of committee and board studies).

We then move to the typical work of a board, but with a difference. We don't start with motions and debate them. We start with recom-mendations and allow the discussions and dialogue to shape the motion (more on this is discussed in chapter 6), which is then voted on. In other words, we encourage dialogue that leads to discernment rather than debate that leads to division. Before voting on the agreed-upon motion, we spend time in prayer (30–60 seconds, depending on the difficulty of the issue), discerning whether this action is one that God is calling us to take. The question asked for each vote is, "All who sense this is God's will, say 'yes'; all who don't, say 'no.'" The point is to emphasize that we are prayerfully seeking together what God wants, not what we want. It is amazing how simply changing the question for the vote changes the emphasis. When we ask, "All in favor, say 'yes'; all opposed, say 'no,'" we are asking leaders to ignore what God wants in favor of what they want. We are saying that we aren't willing to intensively seek what God wants and assuming that God's will always rests with the majority. By pointed-ly asking people to discern whether something is God's will, we are saying that we care most about seeking what God wants.

At the end of the meeting, we take time for each member of the board to pray, and then we close by saying the Lord's Prayer together. Many good resources are available for helping leaders decide how to restructure meetings in a more spiritually vital, integrated way. Among the best are Danny Morris and Charles Olsen's *Discerning God's Will Together* or Roy Oswald and Robert Friedrich's *Discerning Your Congregation's Future*.[3] One note of caution, though. While these books can open us to becoming more spiritually available in the work of the church, even these programs can be too orderly. Remember that the original church did not have *Robert's Rules*. Instead, people simply tried to root themselves in discerning the will of Christ. It is more important to create a culture or ethos of spiritual openness than to follow a program of spiritual openness. I tend to believe that the simplest approach is best. (I discuss this topic in more detail in chapter 3.)

Other practices can help the church leadership become spiritually centered. For instance, retreats and training sessions can be held to train leaders in prayer, discernment, and spiritual openness. In denominational traditions where the pastor does not moderate the church board, it can be difficult to institute these kinds of changes when the lay moderators are trained more in a functional, corporate, or organizational approach to meetings. Yet the pastor still maintains a spiritual authority and can insist on training leaders in spiritual practices of prayer, study, and contemplation.

It is also helpful for church leaders to share the leadership if they seek to create a culture of spiritual openness. Leadership boards should be willing to delegate and decentralize so that decisions can be made by committees, task forces, and teams without micromanagement by the leaders. This willingness is a huge part of being spiritually centered. In a healthy, growing, spiritually vital church, the leaders don't always know everything that is going on. I know that in my church I don't have a handle on everything. I can't. It's become too large for that. I ask the leaders to let me know the things they think I need to know, but for the most part I have to be willing to trust them. More than that, I have to be willing to trust the Spirit to take care of things I don't see or don't know about. This doesn't mean that I abdicate my responsibilities. All it means is that if I try to be in control, I push out the Spirit. My role is to share control with the other leaders and the Spirit so that the Spirit has room to work as it will, not as I will.

The amazing thing that I've experienced is that whenever I trust in God, great things happen. I've never been disappointed. If I prayerfully sense that a new program or approach should be instituted but we have no one to run it, I will pray about it and try to wait patiently. It is amazing how often something does happen after I have given the matter to God in prayer. A new member joins the church who can run the program, or someone else comes forward to do it. It may take a while for this to happen, but it always does if I pray and have patience.

For example, years ago when we needed to create our first website and had no clue how to do it, we struggled to find someone who could do it. We approached teenagers, thinking they would know what to do, but teens often don't follow through. Frustrated that we couldn't find anyone, I finally suggested in a committee meeting that we needed to pray and wait for God to call someone forward. So we prayed, and I continued to pray on my own. About a week later a new member came forward and said, "I noticed you don't have a church website. I've always wanted to create a website. I'm not working for the first time in 20 years, and this will give me a something fun and creative to do." She created the site from scratch and did an excellent job.

When we needed a new treasurer, one came forward to take the position and revolutionized our bookkeeping process. In 1998, when we needed to buy property to expand our program, a house next door to the church came up for sale as if on mystical cue. Also, because we were in the middle of a capital campaign at the time, we had the money on hand to buy it outright without going into debt. Over the ensuing three years, two other houses came up for sale, and because of a series of interesting providences, we were able to buy both. The three properties became instrumental in a $1.6 million expansion and renovation completed in 2007. What I've noticed is that every time the leaders of the church pray together, seek God's will, and trust in God, miraculous coincidences happen *all the time*.

Ultimately, becoming a spiritually vibrant, blessed church means becoming a church that cares deeply about being centered in God's will in everything so that God's blessings flow through meetings, worship, program, mission, and every other part of the church's life. It means becoming a church that is prepared to be blessed by God to do what God is blessing.

REFLECTION QUESTIONS

1. How have your denomination and congregation suffered from respiratory failure by being resistant to the Holy Spirit's work?
2. How has your church lost its spiritual vibrancy? Is it immersed in functionalism or dysfunctionalism?
3. In what ways is your church unintegrated? In other words, how has the spiritual dimension been unintentionally cut off, and what dimensions are now vying for control of the soul of your church?
4. What steps can your church, and especially your leaders, take to become more open to and guided by the spiritual dimension and so recapture a sense of spiritual vibrancy?

Part II

Forming a Church of Purpose, Presence, and Power

If I were to pinpoint the biggest problem in the mainline church today, it would be that the modern church has succumbed to treating God as a theological ideal, as an abstract concept rather than as an experience, an encounter, an embrace of one with whom we can have a deep and transforming relationship. Too many churches never emphasize the encounter with God that leads to an experience of God but instead emphasize a knowledge of God that leads to—well, where does it lead? Because we too seldom ground our understanding *of* God in a relationship *with* God, we don't truly understand the teachings of the Christian faith. The odd thing about Christian beliefs and doctrines is that they don't really make sense until we experience their truth through an encounter with God.

Most of the essential beliefs of Christianity—the incarnation of God in Christ, the virgin birth, Jesus' death and resurrection, the coming of the Holy Spirit, and many more—become real only when we tangibly experience their truth through an encounter with God. For example, while we can cognitively understand the doctrine of the Trinity with our minds by studying the theology of the Trinity, it is not until we spiritually encounter and experience God as Trinity that we are able to begin to understand God as triune. The simple fact is that most modern mainline Christians don't know what to do with the Trinity because it has been treated predominantly as a doctrine throughout the centuries rather than as an experience. These Christians believe in God. They believe in the Creator. They believe in Jesus. They believe in the Holy Spirit. But they don't know how God can be one and three at the same time.

To witness how much mainline Christians struggle with the concept of the Trinity, all it takes is engaging them in a discussion about the Trinity and what they think of it. You will find that they hold a vast variety of opinions and beliefs. Many mainline Christians, in their more candid moments, confide that they don't understand the Trinity. "Why not just call God 'Father' and get on with it?" they think privately. When they pray they tend to pray to "Father," "Mother," "Father-God," "Creator," or "Creator-God." While they may say they are Trinitarian, in practice they focus mainly on God as Father, Creator, or even Mother. They have experienced God as being one God, similar to the Jewish or Muslim concept of God as the Source, the Creator, the Master of the universe, who completely transcends this world. The problem is that because they experience God as one God, they don't know what to do with Jesus or the Holy Spirit. They haven't experienced God as Christ or Spirit, and so they may consider themselves to be Christian, but their faith is mostly Father, Creator, or Mother focused. As one person who joined our church said, "I consider myself to be Christian. I pray every day; in fact I pray all the time. You wouldn't believe how much I pray. And I experience God all the time, but I don't know what to do with Jesus."

In contrast to this focus on God the Father, evangelical Christians talk mostly about Jesus. They talk about the importance of being "Christ centered" and being saved only by a "personal relationship with Christ." They suggest that those who don't focus mainly on Jesus aren't really Christian. They believe in God, but to them Christ is the most important person of the Trinity. Their experiences are centered on Christ Jesus.

Charismatics and Pentecostals emphasize the Holy Spirit. They emphasize praying in the Spirit, being baptized in the Spirit, being filled with the Spirit. They believe in Jesus and pray to the Father, but it is the Holy Spirit who consumes their thoughts because the Holy Spirit is the person of God they truly encounter and experience tangibly.

For the many Christians who don't really experience God as three persons, the Trinity remains a theological and doctrinal idea they say they ascribe to but they don't fully believe. They recite the creeds but don't understand them. For example, what does the Apostles' Creed mean when it says that we believe in "God the Father Almighty" and "in Jesus Christ his only Son our Lord"? Does this mean that the Father is the only person of the Trinity who is really God, while Jesus, being the Son, is something like the vice president in charge of salvation? What does it mean that Jesus is Lord? Does that make him merely a man imbued with divine powers? Does that make him a prophet with mystical powers? Does that make him something like God but not really God? Is Jesus God? If Jesus is the Savior, then what do the Father and the Holy Spirit do? Do they save, too?

And what is the Holy Spirit's role in our life? Is the Holy Spirit just the spirit of God, kind of like an emanation from God, or is the Holy Spirit God?

All these are questions that people in our pews ask privately but are much too polite, timid, or embarrassed to ask publicly. Few would ever consider asking the pastor, "Can you explain the Trinity to me?—because I have absolutely no idea what it's all about." A lot of pastors, if asked, would squirm in response, reluctant and embarrassed to admit they, too, are baffled. Most people just say what a friend of mine once said: "What difference does the Trinity make? It's just a concept, a thought. As long as you believe in God, it doesn't matter." It's hard to argue the point, because to disagree is to come close to making our relationship with God come down to getting God's name right. From a practical standpoint, my friend may be right. Does God get upset when we don't call God "Father"? Does God get upset when we don't call God "Jesus"? I've met Christians who seem to think the latter. An evangelical pastor once criticized me because I kept talking about God rather than Jesus. Isn't Jesus God? If Jesus is God, why does it matter if we call God "God" and not "Jesus"? Will God deny us our salvation if we don't call God "Jesus"?

Ultimately, most mainline Christians simply don't know what to do with the Trinity. Is this a problem? From a purely practical perspective, it may not matter much. I've noticed that God seems to be willing to bless churches whether they are truly Trinitarian or not. God has blessed many mainline churches that are almost solely Father, Mother, or Creator focused; evangelical churches that are almost solely Jesus focused; and charismatic churches that are mainly Spirit focused. God seems to want a relationship with us regardless of what we call God.

While it may not matter much whether we are Trinitarian from a functional perspective, it does seem to matter from a "blessing" perspective. What I mean is that if we are in a church that feels called to become a blessed church, the more intentionally Trinitarian we become, the more we open avenues to God's blessings in our midst. My belief is that the way to forming a deeply blessed church lies precisely in leading our congregations as a whole, and our members as individuals, into a deeper encounter and experience with God as all three persons: Creator, Christ, and Holy Spirit.

How do we go about creating a more intentionally Trinitarian community? I think it begins with recognizing that above all, the concept of the Trinity is a paradox. The Trinity makes no rational sense. How can God be one and three at the same time? If we really believe we are monotheistic, then how can we say God is three? From a purely logical perspective, God can't be. Almost all the major beliefs of Christianity are paradoxes.[1] Does it make sense that God would become human in Jesus Christ? Does it make sense that God, as a human, died? Does it make sense that God, who is dead, would be able to resurrect God? We don't believe these things because they follow human rules of logic. We believe them because we have spiritually grappled with them, and over time our experiences of God have led us to believe in our hearts, whether or not we understand in our heads. In other words, we believe in the Trinity because we've experienced it, not merely because someone taught us that it is true.

The Trinity is a paradox we come to experience as true when we form a relationship with God as Creator, Christ, and Holy Spirit. When we engage our congregations in these same paradoxical experiences, they come alive.

I believe that our churches need to be mindful of being Trinitarian if they are to become truly blessed churches. We need to be people who are (1) grounded in the purpose that God the Creator created us for; (2) alive to the presence of God in Christ in our midst; and (3) open to the miraculous power of God the Holy Spirit flowing through everything we do. We need to create communities that are grounded in God's purpose, alive to God's presence, and open to God's power.

To become truly blessed, our churches need to become Trinitarian both in faith and practice, not only in doctrine and belief. We need to form churches that prepare people to encounter and experience God as Creator, Christ, and Holy Spirit throughout their lives. I ask readers in the next three chapters to focus on the Trinity as an *experience of and an encounter with God as Purpose, Presence, and Power*. I offer an approach to forming a church that is grounded in God's purpose, presence, and power. I believe that if you use this approach in your congregation, it will allow God's blessings to flow more strongly in your midst. [2] In chapter 3, I will focus on ways to form churches that are steeped in the work of the first person of God, God the Creator—God the *Eternal Purpose*. In chapter 4 we will discuss how to form churches that are alive to Christ, God as *Incarnational Presence*. Finally, in chapter 5 we will examine ways to become open to the Holy Spirit, God as *Inspiring Power*.

3

GROUNDED IN GOD'S PURPOSE

Many of today's mainline churches are wandering aimlessly in the desert, wondering what to do to inject new life into their churches. I've talked to many pastors and leaders of these churches in my work in retreats, at conferences, and as a spiritual director. They struggle painfully as they try to find the right approach, the right program, the right system to get their church moving and growing. They go to conferences and workshops that promise them a fast-growing, healthy church if only they do this or that. They return from the conference or workshop armed with new ideas and renewed energy, only to find three months later that they are back where they were before—demoralized and drained of energy.

Why? Why are so many pastors, church leaders, and churches wandering in the wilderness? They're wandering for the same reason the Israelites wandered in the wilderness for 40 years: they weren't grounded in God's purpose. The Israelites were called by God to serve God. Unfortunately, during their years in Egypt they forgot their calling. They became a timid and oppressed people, crying in their misery but unwilling or unable truly to follow God's call. They believed in and worshiped God, but they weren't truly grounded in God's call and purpose, and so they became disconnected from their purpose—to be a people of God who lived according to God's law and grace.

Moses was the first Israelite to discover God in the wilderness and to rediscover God's purpose for the Israelites. In the wilderness, God called Moses to lead the Israelites out of captivity and into the Promised

Land. By means of that leadership, Moses rerooted them in their purpose: to be God's chosen people and to live by faith in God. Being God's chosen people had been the Israelites' purpose from the moment God said to Abraham, "Go from your country and your kindred and your father's house to the land I will show you. I will make of you a great nation, and I will bless you, and make your name great, so that you will be a blessing" (Gen. 12:1–2). Abraham's purpose was to be the father of God's chosen people, a people who would reveal God to the world. As both Abraham and Moses became grounded in God's purpose, they were filled with the life and grace of God. In other words, both became *alive* to God's presence and *open* to God's power, which inspired and empowered their service to God.

Focusing specifically on the Israelites and how they rediscovered a sense of purpose through Moses' leadership, we can examine their struggles to embrace their purpose as they embarked on their journey, on what was initially to be a fairly short journey. At first, their journey was amazing. As long as they were grounded in God's purpose, wonderful miracles led and sustained them. They followed God, who appeared as a pillar of cloud by day and a pillar of fire by night. When they hungered, God provided manna and quail from heaven. When they thirsted, God provided water. As long as they remained true to God's purpose, blessings flowed, but when Moses left the Israelites to meet God on Mount Sinai and to discern even more clearly God's purpose, the people became afraid. Lacking a leader grounded in God's purpose, they desperately sought anyone who could offer them a purpose, even a false purpose. They built a golden calf, hoping that this false idol would give them a new sense of purpose. It didn't. Their subsequent 40 years of wandering were a time of becoming grounded more solidly in their purpose: to be a people prepared for the Promised Land.

As the Israelites demonstrated in the desert, fear grows when purpose is lacking, and this same fear afflicts churches. Too many of our modern churches don't know their purpose. They don't know what they were created for. Having lost a sense of connection with God as Purpose, they wander aimlessly. In reaction to this loss, they run about trying this or that program, this or that worship style, this or that approach to ministry and mission. Sometimes such efforts lead to temporary growth and rejuvenation, but more often they simply lead to confusion, conflict, chaos, and decline.

For churches to become blessed churches, the first thing they must do is to become grounded in God's purpose by reconnecting with God the Creator, God the Eternal Purpose. They must become more aware of who they are and why they exist. The more firmly grounded in its purpose a church is, the more it opens conduits of grace that allow God's blessings to flow. For a church truly to become a blessed church, it must become grounded in a deep experience of and relationship with God as Purpose.

PLANTING A GARDEN FOR GOD

Churches are like gardens in that they grow best when planted and cultivated according to a clear plan and purpose. In fact, certain types of gardens resemble specific kinds of churches.

For instance, the formal English garden is a carefully planned plot of flowers, shrubs, walkways, fountains, and walls. Typically, a whole slew of professional gardeners meticulously maintain it. Its purpose is to provide a beautiful and inspiring landscape to awe and inspire visitors. As a result, it is most impressive when seen from afar. It is highly ordered and organized, so one must be careful not to handle anything too much. Its purpose is to induce awe and inspiration, not interaction. Traditional, cathedral-inspired churches are somewhat like these gardens. They are beautiful, magnificent, well-organized places. They have awe-inspiring stained-glass windows and expensive pipe organs. They are meticulously maintained by a large staff. Their purpose is to provide a space where people are inspired to worship the transcendent God in holy space. Like the formal English garden, the structure and architecture of this majestic church dwarf us as we worship God from afar, a God who seems so distant, transcendent, and otherworldly. Among members there isn't much sense of a relationship. People of these churches come to worship to be awed, inspired, and transported into a mystical, sacred world.

The cottage garden is built around a home or cottage using a variety of plants. It provides beauty, shade, screening from nosy neighbors, inspiration, and comfort. It takes only a few people to maintain it. This is a garden to be enjoyed at close proximity, not witnessed from afar. When we sit on the patio of the cottage garden, our senses come alive with textures, smells, sights, sounds—and sometimes tastes, even if they are faint. Some churches are like cottage gardens. I believe that my own Calvin Presbyterian Church is more like a cottage garden. Its purpose is to provide shade for those scorched by life's heat, small-scale beauty for those needing respite from life's ugliness, inspiration for those seeking God's Spirit, and comfort for those suffering pain. In these churches much more interaction connects the members. These are not awe-inspiring churches in architecture and program but churches that cause people to feel at home, comfortable, and part of a beautiful nook in an otherwise busy world.

Then there is the vegetable garden. Its purpose is to feed others. Many churches are like vegetable gardens. They are mission-focused churches, often in the inner city, whose purpose is to feed others physically, mentally, and spiritually. Sometimes they ship their food (their mission and missionaries) off to other places to feed people they don't know. More often they simply offer food to those in their midst. Like those working in a vegetable garden to grow food, they focus on feeding those who hunger for love and God.

The herb garden's purpose is to provide spice and healing. Many of the herbs are medicinal, while others add flavor to food. Some churches are places of healing for those who are broken and hurting, salving their wounds and helping them discover God's love. They also provide flavor to the lives of people whose existence has become bland and flavorless. Healing services, as well as inspirational songs and messages, figure prominently in these churches.

Another garden to consider is the wilderness garden. Planted on a large tract of land, it has some organization, but the gardeners also have a propensity to let plants and flowers grow wild. These gardens offer delightful experiences but have dead patches as well. They can be places of inspiration but also mazes where people get lost and confused. The closest parallel to this garden in the religious world may be the New Age movement. Much in the New Age movement is inspiring and nourishing, but other aspects are deadly and misleading. Discerning which is which can be difficult.

Finally, there is the conservatory. A conservatory is a large structure containing many kinds of gardens. Upon entering, you are immediately immersed in a leafy jungle. Turning to the left you find a manicured flower garden. Soon you come to a room with a small pond and fountains. To the right is a small English-style garden, appropriate for weddings. The conservatory also has Japanese, butterfly, desert, tropical, and country gardens. Each room of the conservatory offers a contrast. Visitors are invited to spend as much time as they want in each garden or to walk through all. Some churches are like conservatories, especially the large nondenominational churches that present a range of experiences. They offer a wide variety of Bible studies and small groups as well as all sorts of worship, mission, ministry, Christian education, and spiritual experiences. They try to offer a bit of everything.

Why this comparison of churches to gardens? Because just as there are many kinds of gardens in the world, there are many kinds of churches. Unfortunately, we live in a cookie-cutter world and would prefer to find the *one* model that fits all churches. But like gardens, churches are meant to be unique. The point is that when planting a garden, gardeners have to be true to their purpose. It makes no sense to treat a vegetable garden like a formal English garden because heavily pruned vegetable plants will produce nothing. It makes no sense to treat an herb garden like a wilderness garden because weeds will grow and choke the herbs. To plant and cultivate a healthy garden, we have to be as clear as possible that we are being true to the garden's purpose. Otherwise, the garden becomes chaotic. Weeds proliferate and choke the life out of some plants, while other plants die from too little or too much water and fertilizer. A particular church should be treated like a different church only when it becomes clear that it has a new purpose, that it is called to become a new kind of church. When a congregation intentionally follows a new purpose, a time of crisis and difficulty will follow, but because God is calling the church to transformation, the transformation will succeed in the end.

Rick Warren has said that the church is alive, that it is an organism rather than an organization, and that the focus of leadership is to nurture the church so that it can grow in a healthy way.[1] He says that the task of church leadership is to discover diseases and barriers to growth, but there is more to leadership than that. Just as gardeners have to be sure what kind of garden they are growing, church leaders have to be clear about what kind of church they are growing.

A model for the kind of organic church growth that we have been discussing comes from John 15, where Jesus says that he is the vine, we are the branches, and the first person of the Trinity, "the Father," is the vinegrower. The vinegrower, God the Creator and Purpose, plants the vineyard for a purpose: to bear fruit that feeds and nourishes others. When we fail to live according to God's purpose, our fruit withers on the vine and eventually is pruned. For the church to become truly blessed with God's grace and bear fruit, it must live and grow according to the purpose it was created for. Church leaders need to be clear about God's purpose for the church rather than trying to graft on an unsuitable purpose. Nothing is more frustrating for pastors and members than wandering aimlessly with no guiding purpose, or worse, aggressively following a purpose for which the church is unsuited. Unfortunately, this is happening all over as denominations and their local churches try to follow models created for nondenominational contemporary churches. Some will thrive by doing so, but many more will simply experience frustration and conflict.

When churches are unclear about their purpose—what God created them to be—they begin to look like my garden. I am only an average gardener. I have been guilty again and again of choosing plants that I thought would look good around my house but that weren't right for our soil, the amount of sun they received, or the lack of attention I would give them (my garden could be called an absentee-landlord garden: I plant and neglect). I've killed more than my share of trees and shrubs by planting the wrong plants in the wrong places.

Many churches are guilty of similar gardening sins. They try to plant just anything—a program designed for large churches in their small church; an evangelism program designed for transient suburban communities in their shrinking rural town—and then wonder why the garden keeps dying. They create a contemporary service but fail because they don't have the talent or charisma to pull it off. They try to get an older, suburban congregation excited about inner-city mission and wonder why no one will sign up to help. They never ask, "God, what is your calling for us?"

WHAT IS OUR PURPOSE?

All churches are started for a purpose. All churches are started in response to God's call, whether it is the calling of a pastor planting a new church or of a group of immigrants coming together to worship God according to their traditional languages, beliefs, and practices. Looking at the history of any church reveals that it originally had a strong sense of purpose. Perhaps it was to reach out to farmers. Perhaps it was to reach out to people in the inner city. Perhaps it was to reach out to people in a new suburb. Perhaps it was to be a place to raise families. Perhaps it was to reach out to boomers or generation Xers. Whatever the purpose, these churches were once clear about their calling. But over time, churches forget. They forget that God created them for a specific reason. When churches forget, they lose their sense of connection with God.

Whenever we lose a sense of connection with our purpose as a church body, we lose our connection with God as Purpose. We can try all we want to be a place of Christ and the Holy Spirit, but if we have lost our purpose, we drift and suffer. Many churches are adrift because they have no real sense of what God is calling them to do or be. This is not just a contemporary phenomenon. Even the first Christian churches lost their purpose. In the book of Revelation, we find a clear example of churches that have lost their sense of purpose.

In Revelation 1:17–3:22, God's angels deliver messages to seven churches. Five of them are sharply criticized; two are praised. The five are criticized for one simple reason: they abandoned their purpose, their calling. The church at Ephesus was criticized for abandoning its original call to love (Rev. 2:2–4). The church at Pergamum was criticized for promiscuity and for mixing other faiths with their Christian faith (2:14). The church at Thyatira was criticized for letting a false prophetess lead the people to promiscuity and false practices (2:18–20). The church at Sardis was criticized for being dead (3:1). The church at Laodicea was criticized for being lukewarm (3:15). Two churches were praised, the ones in Smyrna and Philadelphia. They were praised because they remained faithful to their calling, even though they suffered all sorts of afflictions, especially the slanderous accusations of some of the Jewish residents who saw this Christian movement as a threat.

To begin the process of becoming a blessed church, we must communally ask a basic question that lies at the heart of the life, ministry, and mission of a church: "God, what is your call for us?" Rick Warren underlines this idea: "If you want to build a healthy, strong, and growing church you *must* spend time laying a solid foundation. This is done by clarifying in the minds of everyone involved exactly why the church exists and what it is supposed to do." He goes on to say, "A clear purpose not only defines what we do, it defines what we do not do."[2] Bill Easum, in his book *Leadership on the Other Side*, echoes this emphasis by saying that every church has DNA, a kind of genetic code created by God, at its core. Every church is a living, breathing organism that lives according to its DNA: "When churches know their DNA and individuals use their genes to enhance the DNA, growth *just happens*. Just like grass grows and fish swim, organic churches grow."[3] He goes on to say that the church's DNA "defines who we are without making us all exactly the same. It allows each part of the Body of Christ to be different while focusing on the same God-given mission." To come alive, a church must live according to its DNA, its purpose, its call. It is in actively seeking God's call for us that we form a deep and guiding relationship with God, who created our cosmos, universe, galaxy, solar system, world, nation, community, and church with a specific purpose in mind—a purpose in harmony with God's eternal plan for everything.

The more we ask, "God, what is your call for us?" and patiently listen for the answer, the more we become a blessed church. The less we ask this question, the more God's blessings are dammed up. Prayerfully seeking God's will is like divining and drilling for living water. We have to make sure that we are drilling where the water is—not where we want it to be. Here's an example. A friend of mine discovered how powerful living according to God's purpose can be when he was the executive presbyter of a presbytery (a regional Presbyterian governing body) in northeastern Ohio. He was asked by a small congregation to help it prayerfully discern its future. This struggling church was slowly dying, so he spent a weekend with the leaders, helping them discern what God was calling them to do. The purpose of the discernment was specific: Do we close our doors or stay open? Surprisingly, at the end of the weekend they never really answered that question. Instead, they clearly sensed that God was calling them to start a new church. You could hear the objections that would eventually be, and were, shouted by other members of the presbytery at the next presbytery council meeting: "How could they possibly start a new church? They don't even know how to grow their own church. This is crazy! You need to go back and get the answer to the original question!" In essence, my friend's response was, "Are you saying that in all their prayer they couldn't possibly have heard God, but that all of you who haven't spent any time in discerning prayer have?"

The church decided to follow God's calling, and an amazing thing happened. The members started a new church, it grew, and miraculously, so did their own congregation. Ironically, they had reconnected with God's original purpose for them. Part of their mission, starting in the early 1800s, had been to plant other churches in the area—having started almost 20 of the region's 80 Presbyterian churches. In their discernment they had rediscovered God's purpose for them, and in the process they became blessed by God. They had reconnected with God as Purpose and in the process had become a blessed church.

PRAYERFUL DISCERNMENT OF OUR PURPOSE

Many churches desperately seek ways to ground their ministry and mission in God's purpose and call but aren't sure how to do it. Too often the models they use come from the secular world—not necessarily a bad thing. The secular world, especially the corporate business world, has developed some remarkable processes for determining an organization's purpose. These processes are designed to define a purpose succinctly for the creation of vision and mission statements as well as strategic and tactical plans.

Many churches follow these secular models for good reason: they are effective. Still, the processes they use aren't rooted in *discerning God's purpose for the church*. They are rooted in *determining what the members want the purpose of the church to be*. There is a huge discrepancy between the two. One is grounded in God and the guidance of Proverbs 3:5–6: "Trust in the Lord with all your heart, and do not rely on your own insight. In all your ways acknowledge God, and he will make straight your paths." The other is grounded in us—our goals, desires, and egos. I'm not suggesting that we avoid secular models and programs but that whatever process or model we use, we make sure that its objective is seeking God's purpose, not our own purpose masquerading as God's.

I once took part in a process, as a consultant, to help a church discern the purpose of a new ministry—a process adapted from the corporate world. The church had been given a large grant to create a spirituality center focused on deepening the faith and spirituality of members, friends, and visitors of this large, urban church.

Almost 50 people gathered one weekend to identify the purpose of the program. Much energy was devoted to the process as people talked about their hopes for the program, brainstormed possibilities, and targeted areas of focus. In the end, the result was somewhat confusing because there was too much: too many ideas, too many different focuses. The problem inherent in the process was that it used all of the most modern techniques but never asked the crucial question, "What is God calling us to do?"

Over the years I have kept an eye on this center from a distance. I have noticed that it struggled for a time to gain an identity. The center has done wonderful work, but it was difficult for those involved to discern what to do and what not to do. At times they tried to do too much, and at others not enough. In the end, I'm not sure that the program fully discerned its purpose. Too many people were involved, including me. I'm not sure I should have been invited, nor should the rest of the consultants. Probably it would have been much more effective had those feeling a call to this ministry sat together in simple discernment and listened for God's voice in their midst (we will talk about these kinds of processes below and also in the context of personal and communal discernment in chapter 6). They might have gathered interested people and invited them to meet over several months, together reading Scripture and relevant contemporary writings (writings that help people grow spiritually). They then might have spent time in prayerful discussion, trying to gather a sense of what God was calling them to do and how to implement these ideas concretely. I'm convinced that it could have had a much more powerful start had it been clearer about trying to discern God's purpose.

I believe that the simpler the approach, the better. The key to discerning and articulating God's purpose lies in seeking a simple process for discernment. So how do we go about choosing or creating a simple process for discerning God's purpose? I offer a process in appendix C, "Discerning God's Purpose for the Church," but other processes are available. I also encourage you to develop your own process, one that is compatible with the needs of your own church. The key is choosing or creating one that is rooted in prayerful discernment and the leadership group's temperament (for example, if the group is mostly filled with extroverts, spending 20 minutes in silent discernment will probably not work). Still, several elements are important in forming a prayerful discernment process:

- Choose or create a discernment process that emphasizes prayerfully seeking God's will and call;
- Invite into the discernment only those leaders who are deeply interested in God's will rather than their own;
- Allow time for prayerful discernment, with an emphasis on listening for God's voice;
- Formulate a succinct statement that captures the essence of the discerned call.

The first element of discerning God's purpose entails *choosing or creating a discernment process that emphasizes prayerfully seeking God's will and call.* Many processes created by organizational experts can help organizations and companies figure out their vision and mission. These processes are great for secular groups, but they are not right for churches. The main focus of any church is prayerfully seeking what Christ, the head of the church, wants for the church. To discern the purpose of the church requires a process that emphasizes prayerful listening. It requires spending time with relevant Scripture that sheds light on how to hear God. For example, the following Scripture passages open people to ways of hearing God: Proverbs 3:5–8, 1 Corinthians 12:4–31, Ephesians 3:14–21, John 15:1–17, Ephesians 4:1–16, John 13:1–20, 2 Timothy 2:14–19, and James 4:1–10.

Any good discernment process also invites people to discuss the present situation of the church as well as possibilities for the church. It allows for brainstorming, but always with an emphasis on what God may be calling us to do. Finally, it invites people into the hard but fruitful work of prayerfully sifting through all possibilities to center on those that most strongly seem to come from God.

For help in better understanding group discernment, several resources are available—for example, *Listening Hearts,* by Suzanne Farnham, Joseph Gill, Taylor McLean, and Susan Ward; and *Discerning Your Congregation's Future* by Roy M. Oswald and Robert E. Friedrich.[4] Over the past 10 years many wonderful resources have been written that delve into personal discernment and can be adapted to communal discernment.

Whatever process is chosen or developed, expect people to resist it initially. Unfortunately most members of modern mainline churches aren't particularly mature spiritually. The reason is that our churches haven't emphasized spiritual growth. We don't necessarily expect our members to be biblically literate. Our Christian education tends to emphasize imparting religious and theological information rather then nurturing spiritual formation. Most of the spiritual nurturing that people get comes through worship. Unfortunately, the typical worship service does not require the kind of self-examination, study, and practice that leads a person to grow spiritually. Combine all of these factors, and they suggest that our members are not very mature spiritually.

In fact, too many of our church leaders aren't spiritually mature, so it is important to train them in spiritual discernment. Unfortunately, too many church leaders are chosen for their functional abilities to organize and get projects done, not for their spiritual maturity. They may be good problem solvers in their work and in other facets of their lives, but this doesn't necessarily mean they will be people of faith committed to discerning God's will instead of problem solving. People who are used to problem-solving analysis don't like doing discernment. Earlier I quoted a leader in the first church I served who said, after participating in an exercise designed to help the leaders listen for God's will, "I don't like this 'trying to hear what God wants' business. It's too hard. It's much easier for me just to decide to do what I want." He recognized the importance of listening to God but also his own resistance. Resistance to discernment cannot be overcome through coercion. It is overcome by gently helping people to identify the source of their resistance and then patiently encouraging them to try something new and God-centered. We need to help people recognize that although discernment is scary—after all, we are stepping boldly into what God wants, not what we want—we can trust God to continue caring for us throughout our seeking.

Discernment is also not a one-time process. It requires that we constantly refine our discernment. Even when we have discerned what God is calling us to do, we have to return to discernment again and again to discover what new and wonderful things God may be calling us to do. Discernment is a lifelong commitment for the blessed church and its members.

The next step is *inviting into the discernment process only those leaders who are deeply interested in God's will and are willing to put aside their own will*. There is no way to overemphasize this point. Too often the people we ask to determine and articulate a church's vision are more interested in what they want than in what God wants. Whenever that is the case, the resulting purpose statement ends up reflecting the members' will rather than God's. Seeking what members want rather than what God wants is a major problem in the modern church. For that reason I am not a big fan of church surveys that care mostly about what the people in the pews want. This does not mean that church surveys aren't valid and should never be used. I just think that we need to be aware that when we base our decisions on surveys about what people want, we may be missing what God wants. Most declining and dying churches are declining and dying precisely because they have focused too much on what their own members want rather than on what God wants.

Spiritual leaders point and motivate people to go where God is going, not where the people want to go. The best leaders encourage people to want what God wants. What God wants and what members want are not necessarily the same, and we need to recognize that church members are not mere consumers. I became very clear on that point when I was an associate pastor serving in my first church. The personnel committee used an evaluation process taken from the committee chair's employer, a large corporation. The group didn't change the evaluation form much other than to replace the title of the evaluation from the company name to the name of our church as well as to change the name of the corporate position from "customer service associate" to "associate pastor." The questions asked in the evaluation weren't particularly suited to evaluating a pastor. For example, the form asked: "How well does the associate pastor respond to *the consumer*?" The implication was clear. As associate pastor my responsibility was to please the consumers—the members of the church—not God. I wasn't evaluated on whether or not I prayed, helped people connect with God, or did what God was calling me to do. Secular models focus too much on what members (consumers) want and not on what God wants.

What do members usually want? Most members want stability. They want the church to respond to *their* needs and desires. If new members join, old members want new members to bring their wallets and energy but not necessarily their ideas, needs, and desires. They don't want too much change. Unfortunately, surveys never ask the question "OK, enough about what you want. What do you sense *God* wants?" What if God wants the church to change? What if God wants the church to grow? What if God wants the church to engage in a new mission or ministry? What if God wants the church to reach out to the new people moving into the area? What if God wants the church to move or die? (I do believe that sometimes God calls churches to die.)

I am not suggesting that leaders ignore what members want. Certainly God can speak to us through the voices of our members, and often God does. Still, good leaders also have to have the wisdom to distinguish God's voice coming through the members from the members' voices drowning out God. Perhaps a way around this tendency to seek what the people want rather than what God wants is to design surveys that invite people to engage in a time of prayer and to write down what they sense God wants for the church.

The third step in discerning God's purpose is *allowing time for prayerful discernment, with an emphasis on listening for God's voice.* The process of discernment is very different from the way most of us have learned to determine a course of action. Most of us have been trained in analysis rather than discernment. Analysis is the process of dissecting a problem to figure out its root. It literally means to "loosen throughout" or "tear apart" something to figure it out, and then we offer solutions based on human logic. In scientific and technological fields we analyze something by tearing apart a machine, a substance, or a molecule to find the problem, and then we apply human logic to determine how to fix it. When we analyze a problem in business or politics, we break everything down and determine the weakness of an approach or argument, and then we use rational projections to apply a solution. Too often we apply these same methods of analysis in the operation of our churches. When addressing a situation or a problem, we analyze rather than discern, and in the process we can end up with an elegant human solution that moves in a completely different direction from what God wants. At times what God wants doesn't make human sense, yet it is what God wants that God blesses. If all we do is analysis, we can end up missing what God is ready to do in our midst. Discernment discovers what God is doing.

Discernment is more like sifting or panning for gold. We slowly sort through all the junk and false answers to discover God's answer at the center—the nugget of gold in the midst of worthless pebbles. Discernment requires faith, prayer, and patience. It calls individuals and groups to sit and wait for God's answer, even if it takes months to discern. Discernment is not a quick process, and its slowness can frustrate those for whom haste is a constant imperative. God can take a while to provide an answer. It can take us a long time to sift through all the noise of the world and finally hear God's whisper. It requires letting go of not only the voices of convention, security, and stability but also the voices of pride and fear that can scream out from within all of us. For help in discerning a particular issue, see appendix D, "Discerning Direction for a Particular Issue."

The final step of discernment is *formulating a short, succinct statement that captures the essence of the call*. Too often churches create elaborate vision and mission statements that no one follows because they are too long and involved. It is difficult to distill our discernments into a short, succinct statement of purpose, but when we do, the statement can guide everything we do in a church. For instance, Calvin Presbyterian Church's purpose statement describes the congregation as "a spiritual family sharing the gospel of Jesus Christ and discerning God's purpose and will through sincere commitment, prayer, fellowship, teaching, and mission." Within it lie two phrases that articulate our purpose and guide me in my role as a spiritual leader. These two phrases are *a spiritual family sharing the gospel of Christ* and *sincerely committed to discerning God's purpose and will*. I can't think of anything more expressive of our purpose.

The phrase "spiritual family" was coined by a member during our discernment process. We were trying to express what our foundation is, and she expressed it perfectly: "I'm not sure what else we are, but this is my spiritual family. It's my home. No matter what is happening in my life, no matter how bad things get, I always know I can come here and people will care about me." Over the years, we have worked hard to nurture this identity as a spiritual family that shares the gospel of Christ. We are spiritual in that we know that it is not our biology but our faith in Christ's love and presence that binds us. We are also family in that we are trying to create a place that accepts all people to the best of our abilities while also nurturing them to mature spiritually. Our church is a place where all people, regardless of how hurt or broken they are, will find love from others. And sometimes we are like the family of the prodigal son. We are willing to let frustrated people go and to celebrate when they return. We are not very good in our church at stressing purity or righteousness. Some churches in our area call us the "church of sinners"—a description that we take as a good thing, even though it isn't meant that way. People who come here know that they aren't going to be judged. As one woman said, "I like Calvin Church because it is the one church where I am allowed to be divorced. People don't hold it against me, and they care about me." In the process of being a spiritual family, we try to be a healthy family. Certainly some dysfunctional people are in our church. We try to be compassionate with them without becoming ineffectual. In other words, we care about people, but we do not let their personal issues cause us to form detrimental patterns of relating with one another. It is our hope that by taking this approach we can nurture them to health.

The downside of being a spiritual family is that we are not as strong in some aspects of church life as we could be. We are not as strong in certain kinds of mission or evangelism as some churches are—perhaps because our commitment to prayerfulness prompts us to give God responsibility for leading us in mission and evangelism. In other words, we allow God to bring us mission opportunities to which we respond, and we let God be our evangelism program, calling people to become part of our community. The result is that our mission program is diverse, including mission trips, funds to help people in immediate need, a recent mission to partner with a church in crisis to grow again, and supporting my mission to help churches renew and grow. Also, despite *not* having a structured evangelism program, we have managed to triple our membership and more than double our weekly attendance over the course of 20 years. I believe that all these elements are part of becoming a blessed church. When we are centered in trying to do what God is calling us to do, God gives us opportunities to bless others through mission, and God brings people to the church who will bless us and whom we can bless. I believe that because we are trying to be centered in God's purpose, God blesses us by allowing amazing things to happen in our midst—miraculous and inspiring blessings—and they don't happen by our own hands or efforts. They come as gifts from God.

In addition to focusing on our call to be a spiritual family, we also stress "discerning God's purpose and will." We emphasize this aim in meetings of our governing board, committees, and congregation by grounding our work in one central question: God, what are you calling us to do? In personal counseling sessions I stress that people should seek God's will. Ultimately, becoming a church or a person of purpose originates in spending time in prayer, discerning God's will for us.

Even after having crafted that vision statement, we've still yearned to capture our purpose in more succinct statements. A few years ago we spent time working on a shorter statement that captured what we sensed was our most essential purpose: *Calvin Presbyterian Church: where faith, compassion, and authenticity meet.* We created this in a committee meeting where four members tried to prayerfully capture what seemed to be the most essential words reflecting who we were and are.

CREATING A CULTURE OF DISCERNMENT

It is not enough simply to discern a purpose for the church. We also need to create an ethos or a culture of discernment that permeates everything we do. We need to make discernment part of the overall life of the church. For example, in our board and committee meetings, do we operate in a way that is open to God's call and voice? Are we open to God as Purpose in our midst? If we are guided by *Robert's Rules of Order*, can we modify the procedures in a way that allows for discernment?

At Calvin Presbyterian Church we include several elements in our session meetings to encourage discernment. First, we create a spiritual atmosphere by modestly decorating the room where we meet with spiritual symbols and by placing a candle in the middle of the table. We light the candle at the beginning of the meeting and extinguish it at the end, just as we do in our worship service. As I mentioned earlier, we design the agenda for our session meetings so that it follows a worship agenda and looks like a worship bulletin, including time for music, prayer, study, discernment, and reflection. When we are making a decision, I ask people to spend time in silent prayer, putting aside their own desires to listen for God's call and voice. When I ask them to vote, I say, "All who sense this may be God's will, say 'aye.' All who don't, say 'no.'" If we fail to reach a consensus, I take this outcome as a sign that we have not listened carefully enough to God, so I generally ask the members to postpone the decision so that they can pray over it for a month and, we hope, discern more clearly God's will. I call this action "postponing in prayer." Then we take up the matter in the next meeting. If the elders still cannot reach a decision, I will continue to postpone in prayer. We usually move forward only when we have reached either *unanimity* (we agree unanimously) or *unity* (some still disagree, but they believe it is best to move forward together and support the decision because they aren't sure or convicted of God's will). We will explore this kind of discernment more deeply in chapter 6.

It isn't only in meetings that we are called to seek God's purpose. In every operation of the church we have to look for ways to seek God's will. For instance, at Calvin Church we try to bring listening to God into our budgeting and stewardship programs. For the budgeting process, we ask each committee in September to spend time in prayer asking what God is calling it to do in the next year (see an agenda for these meetings in appendix E, "A Prayerful Process for Discerning Committee Budgets"). Then in October, we bring all the committees together to discern the overall budget (see an agenda for this meeting in appendix F, "All-Committee Budgeting Process"). We ask all the committee members to put aside their commitment to their own committee budgets and to become part of the body as a whole, seeking what God wants for the whole church. Each committee presents its budget while others pray for that group's work and mission. Then we discuss and provisionally decide what the overall budget total should be. Afterward, all pray for God's continued guidance and blessings. Then we communicate to the members our plans for the following year, and in our stewardship program we ask them to pray about what God is calling them to give (see appendix G, "Guiding Members to Give," for information on how to create a prayer-based stewardship program, and appendix H, "Sample Stewardship Letters and Campaign Circulars," for these pieces used to communicate with the congregation). Since we instituted this process, we have consistently and significantly increased our budget each year, yet we have continued to end each year with a surplus. I am convinced it has to do with our grounding ourselves in God's purpose, which connects us with God's blessings.

Another area where God's purpose has to be emphasized is in preaching and teaching. To be a church grounded in God as Purpose, we need to preach consistently to people in a way that teaches them how to discern God's will in their personal lives. The more a church discerns as a body of individuals, the more a church can discern as a community. Classes, retreats, and programs for childhood through adulthood must be offered that teach discernment (of course, without becoming obsessive about it).

Finally, our outreach, both local and global, must be grounded in God's purpose. One reason so many churches struggle in outreach is that they try to do what they think they ought to do rather than what God is calling them to do. Every church has its own unique missional call that reflects its situation. We cannot follow the call of another church. We have to be true to God's call to us. A sure-fire way to ensure that a mission program will fail is to try either to do too much without ever asking, "Is all of this true to our purpose?" or to engage in mission that is not our discerned purpose at all. We are called to reach out to others for Christ, and we are called to stretch ourselves, but we still need to be mindful that what we are doing is according to God's will.

LEADING WITH PURPOSE

It is not easy to get a church to be centered in purpose. As stated earlier, people will resist the process because it is new and uncomfortable and because we are naturally, sinfully more interested in our own desires than God's. Still, good leadership finds a way to ground people in purpose despite their discomfort. Blessed leaders, leaders who are relatively clear about what God's calling is for them and the church, understand that members will be anxious and uncertain because they are not used to seeking God's purpose for themselves or the church. So blessed leaders must work hard to forge a strong faith in God as Purpose so that those with a weaker faith can lean on them. These leaders must be firm but gentle in their determination to follow God's purpose. They must lovingly and prayerfully encourage people to be grounded in purpose. They cannot coerce and force people. They must be patient, understanding that being grounded in God's purpose is something new and takes time.

Blessed leaders also must make sure that the church continues to seek God's purpose, because over time the functional tendencies of people will always pull the church back to a more functional style. They must make discerning God's purpose one of the bedrock norms of the church. How do leaders know when the congregation has become blessed? They know it when an issue comes up and the members remind the leaders to discern God's purpose. I've had this happen to me many times when I've been anxious about something and an elder or other church member has simply said to me, "Don't worry, Graham. Just try to listen to what God wants and it will all work out." That says to me that we are a church grounded in God's purpose and that I have done a good job of being a spiritual leader.

It is important to realize that though becoming grounded in God's purpose will breathe new life into the church, this does not necessarily mean that the church will experience explosive growth as a result. Churches are always bound by their available talent, context, and situation.[5] Not all pastors are dynamic preachers and organizers. Not all churches are located in growing areas. Not all churches have the resources to provide exceptional and groundbreaking programs. All that matters is that we do what we are called to do, how we are called to do it, and where we are called to do it.

Finally, in some situations you, the reader, will not be able to get the whole church to become more grounded in God because the senior or solo pastor and other key leaders are resistant. If you can't change the whole church, you can make sure that you and your committee, task force, team, or ministry are grounded in God's purpose. Do what you can and leave the rest up to God.

Ultimately, the foundational focus of a church in communion with the Trinity is to be grounded in God's purpose by forming a deep relationship with God as Purpose. By doing this, the church community begins to encounter the Creator as they experience God's blessings in their midst. It all begins with grounding ourselves in God the Eternal Purpose.

REFLECTION QUESTIONS

1. To what extent do you sense that your church has a clear purpose?

2. To what extent do you sense that your church's purpose is grounded in God's purpose?

3. How would you describe, succinctly, God's purpose for your church, even if you have never formally discerned your church's purpose?

4. What concrete things can you do to ground yourself and your church in God's purpose and steep the church in a relationship with God as Purpose, with God the Creator?

5. What particular steps can your church, and especially your leadership, take to become more open to and guided by the spiritual dimension of life?

4

ALIVE TO GOD'S PRESENCE

It is amazing what can happen in churches that are grounded in God's purpose. They form a strong sense of identity and are filled with a sense of direction. Their leaders and members exhibit humble conviction and resoluteness, even when trying to do something new and different. A church grounded in purpose is connected to the source of living water. It has the potential to become a conduit that allows living springs of water to flow in and through people's lives. When a church is grounded in purpose, it connects to the source of living water, but that does not mean living water—grace—will automatically flow through people's lives. More needs to take place. Being a church of purpose connects the church to living water, but it is by becoming a church of presence that the conduit between living water and the people of God is opened. To be a church of presence means to be a church that intentionally tries to awaken people to God's presence and grace in their midst so that they can connect with Christ more powerfully in their daily lives.

Churches that become alive to God's presence may not be perfect (no church is), but even in their imperfection they are alive because Christ—God as Presence—is in their midst. In these churches, the presence of God becomes tangible and evident to those who are ready to discover it. These churches have life and give life; they deepen and revive people in amazing ways.

Becoming alive to God as Presence, to Christ, is not synonymous with creating a large, fast-growing megachurch. In fact, becoming a church of presence can actually inhibit growth, at least at first. The focus of a church that's alive is spiritual growth—the deepening and transformation of people's lives—not necessarily physical growth (although the two are not incompatible). Some seekers will turn away from a church of presence because they do not want depth and transformation. Many want simple rules to follow and quick, easy, and clear answers to their deepest questions. A church of presence offers neither.

A church of presence offers a pathway for people to experience Christ. It calls them to commitment, prayer, sacrifice, love, and transformation. It teaches people that Christ is among us and in us but that we cannot encounter Christ with the depth that Christ desires unless we adopt practices and lifestyles that allow the life of Christ to grow in us. The example of what happens when we become alive to Christ comes through Paul's instruction to the Colossian church:

> As God's chosen ones, holy and beloved, clothe yourselves with compassion, kindness, humility, meekness, and patience. Bear with one another and, if anyone has a complaint against another, forgive each other; just as the Lord has forgiven you, so you must also forgive. Above all, clothe yourselves with love, which binds everything together in perfect harmony. And let the peace of Christ rule in your hearts, to which indeed you were called in the one body. And be thankful. Let the word of Christ dwell in you richly; teach and admonish one another in all wisdom; and with gratitude in your hearts sing psalms, hymns, and spiritual songs to God. And whatever you do, in word or deed, do everything in the name of Lord Jesus, giving thanks to God the Father through him. (Colossians 3:12–17)

Ultimately, Paul reminds us that as we practice faith together and share a Christlike lifestyle, we become alive to Christ in our midst. Becoming alive to Christ's presence is central to becoming a blessed church.

Too many of today's Christian leaders believe that bigger is better—an attitude that is a product of our culture—but some of the most deeply blessed churches are smaller congregations. Of course, many blessed churches are large, but in many cases the larger and faster a church grows, the less blessed it becomes because the focus is on breadth, not depth, on quantity, not quality. The appearance of blessing on the surface may obscure the fact that these churches are frenetic, showy places with lots of bells and whistles, filled with people who are not all that committed to Christ but who have become addicted to stimulation and entertainment in their spiritual walk. They want to experience Christ's presence but only if it comes wrapped in an enticing package.

Many Christians tend to think that contemporary is better and that offering a contemporary worship service is the answer to all our churches' ills. If only we become more contemporary, people will flock back to us. The flaw in this belief is that the youngest generation, the millennials (those born since 1982), are showing less interest in contemporary worship than they are in ancient rituals that connect them with something deeper that draws them into a more tangible experience of God. According to Neil Howe and William Strauss, generational researchers, millennials are "drawn to such complex ancient rituals as the Jewish Kabbalah, the walk of the labyrinth, the meditations of St. Ignatius, or the mantralike recitations of Taizé, in which kids sit in a candle-lit room and sing the same songs, over and over."[1] For millennials, ancient rituals are new, and contemporary is old. In fact, some "seeker" churches (those that emphasize reaching out to unchurched people, or "seekers") are beginning to offer more traditional worship services to attract those millennials who want stained glass, crosses, candles, art, sacraments, rituals, and the like. This desire for the mystical and symbolic explains why more and more younger people are attracted to the liturgies of the Orthodox, Roman Catholic, and Episcopal churches. They want an experience of Christ that touches all their senses. They want more than music and a message. They want a tangible sense that Christ is in their midst.

What people really want in worship and a church is an encounter and experience of God. The extent to which people sense Christ's presence and life through worship matters more than the style of worship. Of course, given the choice between a shallow but entertaining contemporary worship and a stodgy traditional service, neither of which really enlivens them to God's presence, people (including me) will choose the contemporary because at least it is stimulating.

Forming a church that enlivens people to Christ's presence means offering a church experience that invites and incarnates God as Presence, God as Christ. And make no mistake, many churches do not invite or incarnate Christ. They are more focused on maintaining denominational and congregational traditions than they are with letting Christ in—and Christ will not enter our churches uninvited. In Revelation he says, "Listen! I am standing at the door knocking; if you hear my voice and open the door, I will come in to you and eat with you, and you with me" (Rev. 3:20). In churches that ignore the knock or bar the door with a pattern of chronic conflict or indifference, Christ generally seems content to stand on the outside waiting. Only rarely will Christ surprisingly enter uninvited to transform the church. When Christ is left on the outside, churches become empty of presence. Sermons are preached, hymns are sung, and rituals are followed, but Christ is rarely encountered because he has been prevented from being present. Blessed churches open their doors to Christ and let Christ become a deep and life-giving presence in their midst, bringing life to the church and all who inhabit it.

AWAKE, AWARE, AND ALIVE!

I have heard many people in many places complain that their churches are dead, the sermons are boring and irrelevant, the music is laborious and archaic, the pacing is slow and tedious, and the people are lifeless. I've not only heard this criticism from others. I've made such complaints myself. I left the church at age 15 because of such experiences and returned to the church at age 24 despite them.

Churches feel dead when they are dead to Christ's presence. Sadly, spiritually dead churches can remain physically alive for many years, but eventually their spiritual death leads to physical death. Of course, members don't make the connection between a congregation's spiritual and physical deaths. They say that the church died because the congregants got old, the neighborhood changed, or the church was afflicted by a scandal years before. But these problems, while difficult to overcome, are not what caused the church to die. If the parishioners had been alive to Christ, they would have found a way to enable the church to survive and thrive, even in the face of the direst challenges. Ultimately churches have died because leaders and members were not willing to seek God's presence, which would lead and guide the congregation not only to survive but to thrive through the changes. God is present at the core of all our churches like a slumbering child, wanting to be awakened, wanting to play, wanting to bless us with his presence. When we realize that God is in our midst and ready to be awakened and then open ourselves to Christ and Christ's guidance, amazing things begin to happen in our midst. If we are to tap into this core, we have to take God's presence in Christ seriously enough to prayerfully seek and follow Christ's guidance, which is available to all who seek to follow.

Becoming a blessed church means becoming awake, aware, and alive to Christ's presence in our midst, giving us guidance, life, and love. I became aware of this truth after reading Thomas Kelly's *A Testament of Devotion* in 1989. Kelly was a college theology and philosophy professor at several Quaker colleges during the 1920s through the 1940s. His life was mostly unremarkable except that during the last three years of his life he delivered a series of talks to Quaker meeting houses in the Philadelphia, Pennsylvania, area that awed all who heard him. After he died, people realized that they had heard something authentic and true in his talks, and so the talks were collected in a book. Kelly's vision of church was so different from anything I had ever heard that it changed my whole way of seeing church.

Kelly had an understanding of Christ's presence in the church that was truly radical. He said that at the core of every true church lies a "blessed community"—a community of people at the center of the church who are so deeply grounded in Christ that the life of Christ flows through them into the rest of church. As he says, "Yet ever within that Society, and ever within the Christian church, has existed the Holy Fellowship, the Blessed Community, an *ekklesiola in ekklesia*, a little church within the church."[2] Perhaps you've met these people in your own church. They are deeply spiritual individuals whose connection with God causes them to radiate God's love and presence. They may not be leaders who sit on church boards and committees, but if they were missing, the church would crumble because they are the ones who embody the life of Christ. The more a church nurtures and cultivates this blessed community, this little church within a church, the more it becomes a blessed church that leads people to an encounter with Christ. Whenever the blessed community grows within a church, the whole community becomes transformed as more and more people encounter and experience Christ in their midst.

As the blessed community grows within a church, it becomes a transformed place, even if it looks the same. As Kelly says:

On all the wooing love of God falls urgently, persuadingly. But he who, having will, yields to the loving urgency of that Life which knocks at his heart, is entered and possessed and transformed and transfigured. The scales fall from his eyes when he is given to eat of the tree of knowledge, the fruit of which is indeed for the healing of nations, and he knows himself and his fellows and comrades in Eden, where God walks with them in the cool of the day. . . . And these are in the Holy Fellowship, the Blessed Community, of whom God is the head.[3]

In a blessed church the focus moves from maintaining right practices or beliefs to leading people to a communion with God. What matters most is allowing the life of Christ to flow through the church. People no longer become divided by theology, but as Kelly says:

Holy Fellowship reaches behind these intellectual frames to the immediacy of experience in God, and seeks contact in this fountainhead of real, dynamic connectedness. Theological quarrels arise out of differences in assumptions. But Holy Fellowship, freely tolerant of these important yet more superficial clarifications, lives in the Center and rejoices in the unity of His love.[4]

What is the nature of a blessed church—a church that is awake, aware, and alive? It is *awake* to Christ in that it responds to Paul's admonition to wake up: "Besides this, you know what time it is, how it is now the moment for you to wake from sleep. For salvation is nearer to us now than when we became believers" (Rom. 13:11). A blessed church is not content to do merely what has always been done. It truly wants to do what Christ has equipped it to do. The people of the church, and especially the leaders, deeply believe that Christ is in their midst, guiding, directing, and blessing them. They expect that something wonderful and mystical will happen in worship, meetings, classes, and small groups. They don't necessarily know what will happen, but they know it will lead to an encounter with Christ.

Blessed churches aren't just awake. They are also *aware*. They have what I would call a "mystical awareness" that God is present. This mystical awareness may not be a conscious awareness, but it is present nonetheless. These congregations look around and see evidence of God. They sense Christ's presence in the music, prayers, sermons, meetings, groups, fellowship, ministry, and mission of the church. They have

"Aha!" moments during the sermon and are aware that God has just spoken to them. They connect with someone in church, and they know that they have just experienced communion with God. They help another member in need, and at some level they know that they have just borne Christ to that person. This mystical awareness again emanates from the pastors and leaders of the church because they are constantly pointing out where God is present. When coincidences or small miracles occur, the leaders point them out and say, "There's Christ in our midst." In blessed churches, the people become increasingly aware that not only is Christ present in every person, but also that they have become the body of Christ (1 Cor. 12:12–31) and that Christ is working through everyone, even the least involved.

When a church becomes aware, a majority of members recognize that they are on a journey for, to, and with God, and that to sail across the waters they must keep Jesus as their North Star. No matter where they are, they keep their eyes on Christ, even if they don't know to call this presence "Christ." To them all that matters is that God is present among them and that they must follow where Christ leads.

Finally, blessed churches are *alive* to Christ, and because they are, Christ is alive in them. John 15 offers a powerful metaphor for this kind of aliveness. Jesus says that he is the vine and we are the branches, that those who live in Christ and allow Christ to live in them will bear fruit that feeds the world. This is a superb metaphor for being alive to Christ, telling us that if we become awake and aware of God's presence in our midst, the life of Christ will flow in and through us as we become alive in Christ. Our lives take on a new character and quality. When we become alive to Christ as a church, we are infused with an energy, a dynamism, that becomes apparent. Thus, becoming a blessed church is more than an approach or style of ministry and worship. It is a way of living as a church.

When the leaders of the church, both pastoral and lay, become awake, aware, and alive to God's presence in their midst, they create the conditions for astonishing things to occur. People begin to experience blessings in every part of their lives, and especially in the church. They continue to struggle. They still may become ill. They still may find themselves unemployed or divorced or suffer some other form of loss. But something else also happens. They become aware that God is with them, blessing them despite the pain and suffering of their lives. In the midst of suffering they experience faith, hope, and love. When a church is alive to Christ, its members notice God's grace and blessings working in their midst.

A story illustrates what it means to be an alive church: years ago a small monastery was nestled in the mountains of France. Once it had been the center of inspiration for pilgrims and seekers yearning for God. People came from all over Europe to discover God in the monastery. But then the monastery changed. It became proud. The brothers took themselves too seriously. Instead of being truly humble, they became proud of their humility. So began their decline. Fewer and fewer pilgrims sought their wisdom, and few monks joined their ranks. The brothers became rigid. They worshiped their past. They were spiritually dead and physically dying. In another generation all the monks would be dead, and the monastery would die with them.

One day a scraggly stranger came to the door. He smiled a toothless smile and asked for a place to rest for the night. He was invited in. The monks thoroughly enjoyed his presence at dinner and sensed a spiritual depth in him, though he was outwardly rough and smelly.

The next morning, as he was leaving, the stranger thanked the abbot profusely. Taking the abbot's hand, he leaned forward, and said in a soft whisper, "I need to tell you a secret, one that God has given me permission to tell you. Christ is here in your midst. The Messiah is masquerading as one of your brothers." The abbot was shocked: "The Messiah? Here? In this place? No, it isn't possible!"

He told the other brothers what the stranger had said. They also couldn't believe it. Then they began to think: Could it be Brother Joseph? No, he's too selfish. Could it be Brother John? No, he's much too strange. Is it Brother Bernard? No, he's too clumsy. No matter which monk they thought of, they couldn't imagine that brother being the Messiah. Still, what if the stranger was right? What if Brother Joseph is really Christ and just pretending to be selfish? What if Christ is Brother John, and he is just pretending to be strange? What if Christ is Brother Bernard and just pretending to be clumsy? So they started to treat one another as though each was possibly Christ, lest Christ be revealed as one of them. As they did, the monastery changed. The monks began to focus more passionately on God during worship, lest Christ catch them slumbering. They read Scripture with renewed fervor, lest Christ catch them daydreaming. As they did, they grew spiritually. Their prayers took on a new life. So did their teaching and service. And people noticed. Soon pilgrims and seekers came to their door to learn from their wisdom. New monks joined their ranks to learn the spiritual secrets. They became alive once again, and once again the monastery became a center of spiritual life for all of Europe. They became alive to Christ.

There is something essential in this story that we do not necessarily appreciate immediately, which is that the Christian belief in Jesus isn't just that he was the incarnation of God 2,000 years ago. It is that he was the presence of God in creation at the beginning of time, and he is the presence of God in us, in our churches, and in the world right now. We diminish Christ when we think of him as just a man 2,000 years ago. John's gospel begins with words that point to Christ's ongoing presence in creation: "In the beginning was the Word, and the Word was with God, and the Word was God. He was in the beginning with God. All things came into being through him, and without him not one thing came into being" (John 1:1–3). Paul echoes this belief: "For in him all things in heaven and on earth were created, things visible and invisible, whether thrones or dominions or rulers or powers—all things have been created through him and for him. He himself is before all things, and in him all things hold together" (Col. 1:16–17). Both passages say that Christ is more than the man. He is God's presence in creation, in the world, and in us. Christ is the presence of God that makes us alive and that our prayerful openness makes us alive to.

In churches that are alive to Christ, people encounter Christ because they seek Christ. Obviously, we can encounter Christ elsewhere because Christ is everywhere, not only in churches. If we are alive to Christ as God's presence, we can encounter Christ at home, in the workplace, on a mountaintop, in a park, on a golf course, in the supermarket—and anywhere else. Nonetheless, certain places are designed for holy experiences. Their architecture and atmosphere are designed for holy encounters. What gives the architecture and atmosphere the power to reveal the sacred is the intention of worshipers. When people become part of these holy places with hearts alive to Christ, they can encounter Christ there with a power that surpasses the presence they find in most other places.

When there is no expectation of encountering Christ, the church atrophies and dies. In many churches, despite their architecture and atmosphere, the members have little expectation of encountering

Christ. As Ben Campbell Johnson, a writer and teacher on spirituality and evangelism, says, "When there is no sense of the Divine, people go home empty. Soon they forget the main reason for church and worship. As the awareness of God withers, joy evaporates and persons find it increasingly difficult to speak of God to one another."[5]

TO PREACH, TEACH, AND HEAL LIFE

How do we specifically help people in a church become alive to Christ's presence? We do it by engaging in the same ministry Christ did, but in a way that is appropriate to our own situation and context. Essentially, we do it by forming communities that preach, teach, and heal *in* Christ's presence, as opposed to what many modern Christians do, which is to preach, teach, and heal according to our own abilities and insights. To preach, teach, and heal in Christ's presence means to embody Christ in what we do. As the following section will make more clear, when we become open to Christ's presence in our lives, we allow Christ's voice and power to be incarnated in us and our ministry, and we join Christ in his preaching, teaching, and healing ministry.

1. Preaching Christ's Presence

I have a confession to make. Most of the preaching in the mainline church bores me. This potentially embarrassing confession also implicates me. I'm sure I am guilty of boring quite a few members when I preach. Still, what bores me about most mainline preaching is that we pastors have turned an event that is supposed to reveal Christ into a dry, academic, intellectual activity focusing on abstract theological topics that have little relevance to real life. That doesn't mean that these topics are unimportant or that solid theological thinking and articulation aren't important. In fact, people in the pews need to be taught to think theologically as well as to become open to God spiritually. Good theology should lead to spiritual openness, and spiritual openness should lead to good theological thinking. The problem in so many churches is that the practitioners of much mainline Protestant preaching have forgotten to balance the theological with the spiritual, or even more important, to ground theological thinking and teaching in spiritual practice and experience.

It is not hard to see how theological thinking that is ungrounded spiritually can create uninspired preaching. For example, too many mainline Protestant pastors are guilty of "preaching their papers in public." They were taught in seminary to structure their sermons like academic papers that posit and prove a theological point, which they then read to the congregation while standing stiffly behind the pulpit and staring mainly at the manuscript. Even though many mainline Protestant preachers have utter disdain for televangelists and their preaching style, at least those preachers understand what sermons are. Televangelists understand their role in helping people encounter Christ. I'm not suggesting that we mainline preachers have to jump, shout, and prance like many of the televangelists, nor am I saying that I support their teachings, especially the teachings of the more fundamentalist ones. I, too, find many of the messages they preach offensive and simplistic. Still, we have to pay attention to something they understand: sermons are *oral* (and in some cases, when using multimedia resources, *visual*), not written, messages that lead to an encounter with the living Christ. They are meant to offer imaginative experiences in which people sense Christ and the Holy Spirit not only through words themselves but also through dramatic stories, gestures, inflections, and cadence.

What made Jesus' preaching so captivating and engaging is that he spoke through people's everyday experiences. Look at every film about Jesus' life. He walked among the crowds and told parables about planting, harvesting, shepherding, and the like, which reflected people's experiences. He spoke in their language literally and metaphorically. Too often today we don't preach to people's lived situations. Meanwhile, a number of popular religious books and websites reach millions of people every day because they use stories about people just like them who have encountered God's presence in their lives.

The problem for many of us mainline preachers is that we think it is beneath us to talk about ordinary people who experience God's presence in miraculous and dramatic ways. We think *these popular websites and collections of stories* seem sappy and too happy. But if we choose not to use these kinds of stories nor to speak to people's everyday experiences, then we need to recognize that people aren't flocking to hear us precisely because we are so abstract.

Despite the strength of the evangelical style, which is often more dynamic than the style of most mainline preaching, it overemphasizes the entry into the Christian life by being so "seeker-focused" that it ignores the call to spiritual depth. Mainline preaching generally has the opposite problem. As an evangelical friend once said to me, "The problem with us evangelicals is that we never let people grow to spiritual maturity. As soon as they become spiritual adolescents, we tell them to turn around and bring in the spiritual babes [the new Christians]. As a result, no one ever really grows to spiritual adulthood. On the other hand, you mainliners assume that everyone is in spiritual adulthood, and so you never really help people grow from spiritual infancy into adulthood. We need to find a way to lead people from infancy into maturity."

How do we preach Christ's presence? We do so by constantly and consistently saying to people, "Look, there's Christ in your midst, and there, and there, and there!" We do it by showing people that even if they are in darkness, they can find Christ's light shining through the love of a family member, the kindness of a friend, a phrase in a book, or the inspiration from a song. We can also preach Christ's presence by reminding people that Christ is in Scripture, in the sacraments, and in all of worship. We preach Christ's presence by pointing to the incarnation of Christ in everything: our sufferings, our joys, our relationships, and our hearts.

Whenever we preach Christ's presence, we also need to introduce the church members to practices they can embrace, attitudes they can adopt, and habits they can form that will lead them to experience Christ. We can use our sermons to introduce laity to practices of prayer, fasting, confessing, centering, simplifying, and other spiritual disciplines. Teaching people how to grow spiritually, especially through the use of spiritual practices and disciplines, may require that we share our own struggles to grow spiritually (a practice that may have been taboo in seminary preaching classes). When we *humbly* share our own personal struggles to encounter Christ, we tell people that they can trust us as guides and follow our guidance—because we share their struggle to grow spiritually and to encounter Christ.

Finally, it is important that we preachers become people of spiritual depth. We need to be people of prayer who preach out of prayer. For me, this meant drastically changing the way I traditionally prepared my sermons. Years ago I used to spend much of the week poring over biblical commentaries, trying to uncover the essential biblical message by researching the history, context, situation, intent, and focus of a biblical passage. I spent hours in preparation. Over time I realized that I was focusing so much on historical and biblical scholarship that I was not attending to God's message. Today my approach is different. I focus on praying through the Scripture, allowing myself to be led by Christ and the Holy Spirit to preach God's message. Sometimes this method leads me to do research, but at other times it means spending time in solitude reflecting on my experiences and using them as a template to guide others. Prayerful reflection can be research. The practical effect is that my sermons have become much more dynamic and piercing because Christ is much more present in my preaching.

In preparing a sermon, a preacher can ask several simple questions to help compose blessed sermons that lead others to encounter Christ:

- Have I prepared this sermon in prayer, asking God to speak through me?
- Have I taught something that will tangibly help people live healthier, more balanced, and more loving lives?
- Have I taught people how to follow Christ in practical ways that make a discernable difference?
- Have I preached out of my own spirituality, leading people to encounter Christ as I have?
- Have I preached in a way that makes people aware of God's purpose for them and Christ's presence in and with them?

2. Teaching

Much of what I just said about preaching can be applied to teaching in a church. There is a similarity between the styles of preaching and teaching in most churches, especially when it comes to adult education. My focus here will be mainly on educating adults, but I think the message can also be applied to children's Christian education.

The problem inherent in most mainline church education programs is that they emphasize *information* over *formation*. Informative education is interesting, helpful, and important, but for the most part it doesn't change lives. For example, the daily newspaper is informative. I read it every day, but it rarely changes my life (except, sadly, to make me more cynical). Formative education emphasizes teaching and learning that open people to discover how God wants them to live. It teaches people how to "form" their lives in God-directed ways that embody faith, hope, and love. It opens people to God so that they can be transformed to incarnate Christ's presence and love.

Informative teaching rarely has an eye toward how the taught information will form learners' lives. Classes on what the books of the Bible say, how to read the Bible in its historical context, Christian theology, and history often neglect what the Bible says to us about how to live life in meaningful and loving ways that serve God. When we teach informatively about outreach and social justice, we might help people better understand the impoverished and oppressed, but we often don't teach them how God is calling them to reach out to those in need. Such teaching also doesn't teach us how our own lives need to be transformed if we are to have compassion for the poor, the oppressed, and the outcast.

Informative teaching emphasizes concepts and constructs for their own sake. Formative teaching introduces concepts and constructs in the service of transforming lives, both ours and those of others, according to God's purposes. Formative classes have a direct impact on how people live, and specifically on how they live in a way that allows Christ to live in them. They deal with topics such as the formation of healthy marital, parental, friendship, and work relationships; prayer; forgiveness; recovery from addiction; discernment; practical servanthood; personal and communal evangelism; and community outreach. Even children's education can move from informatively teaching "just the facts" to formatively teaching how to live life in greater openness to God. Formative teaching does not preclude teaching about doctrines and mission. In fact, it strengthens them by giving them a spiritual foundation.

Stressing formation over information also applies to forming small groups. Resources need to be chosen that emphasize spiritual growth in practical ways. Material such as the Bible, devotional books, and the writings of the mystics, when approached formatively, change lives because God uses them to form and transform us. When we offer classes, groups, workshops, and retreats that emphasize formation over information, we change lives by opening people to Christ's transforming power.

3. Healing

While most mainline churches truly understand that Jesus came to preach and teach and that they are to be places of preaching and teaching, they've forgotten that Jesus spent as much time healing as he did preaching and teaching.

Our churches have abdicated their role as places of healing, which was part of the original church's calling. You can see this calling expressed in Jesus' teaching the disciples and followers to heal. The early church, as recounted in Acts, took seriously the calling to heal the sick. The apostle James even gives instructions to the church about healing prayer: "Are any among you sick? They should call for the elders of the church and have them pray over them, anointing them with oil in the name of the Lord" (James 5:14). Unfortunately, modern Christianity has given to the field of medicine the whole responsibility for healing while failing to recognize that we Christians have a role in healing, too. We are called to complement the healing that Christ does through medicine with the healing that Christ brings through prayers and relationships.

What does it mean to be a healing church? Using Calvin Presbyterian Church as an example, I can offer several answers. First, it means that we take healing prayer seriously. Most churches are afraid actually to pray for God's healing power. Their members are skeptical about prayer's effectiveness. Their faith in healing prayer has been poisoned by false Christians who have used healing prayer to bilk gullible people out of their money. The true church, though, is called to make healing prayer part of its ministry. Increasingly, mainline churches are offering healing prayer as part of healing worship services and in their regular worship services, and they are experiencing the healing of people.

For example, one person who opened me up to the power of healing prayer, especially as part of a church's ministry, was a friend in New York who had a healing experience as a result of a mainline church's healing service. My friend had years ago gone to a doctor who diagnosed her as having an illness that would probably be chronic. She was devastated. A few days later she was out walking in Manhattan, and while thinking about her illness and the ramifications for her life, she passed Fifth Avenue Presbyterian Church just as it was having its "Healing of Iona" prayer service. She entered the church and sat in the back, watching the people go to the front for prayer. Eventually she decided also to go forward, though she was skeptical. She received healing prayers from a minister and sat back down, thinking that nothing would happen. Suddenly, she felt something like electricity go through her, filling her with a kind of peace and joy. The feeling remained for a few days. When she went to the doctor the next week for a follow-up exam, he found no trace of the illness. She had been healed, and it happened because a church had the courage to offer the healing ministry of Christ as part of its ministry.

At Calvin Church we have two kinds of healing ministries. First, we offer a healing prayer ministry. We have called forth particular members of the congregation whom we have discerned are called to this ministry to offer prayers for those suffering with illness or other difficulties. We then train them in the tradition and practice of healing prayer. Requests for healing prayers come from sick and suffering members and nonmembers alike. Our healing prayer ministers go to those requesting prayer once a week for a 15-minute visit. As part of the visit, the healing prayer minister prays for the person, anointing him or her with oil, and also trains the person to pray for his or her own healing. For a sample of a resource for teaching people how to pray for healing, please see appendix I, "A Guide to Healing Prayer," or go to http://www.ngrahamstandish.org for a downloadable copy.

Second, we offer healing services on the first Sunday of each month as part of our celebration of the sacrament of communion. As people come forward for communion down our two aisles, a healing prayer minister and I stand in the center ready to offer healing prayer. Anyone who would like healing prayer before receiving the elements of the Lord's Supper steps into the center and can receive prayer from either of us. We ask what the concern is and try to make the prayer succinct but powerful. Afterward, we anoint the person's forehead with oil, making the sign of the cross in the name of God the Father, Son, and Holy Spirit. Then, the one prayed for reenters the line and receives communion, allowing the sacrament to complete the healing prayer. The initial decision to offer healing prayer as part of the sacrament of communion was not easy because we were like most other churches. Healing prayer was not part of our ministry. Still, we decided to offer it because we realized that healing is an essential part of our calling.

I also am involved in offering healing prayers as part of my own ministry. The amazing and wonderful thing is that we have had many healings in our church as a result of our various prayer ministries. I'm not talking about the "throw-your-crutches-away-and-dance-on-the-floor" kind of healing seen on television. Sometimes the healing is physical, but just as often it is mental, relational, or spiritual. The point is that as we've emphasized healing, people have been healed in many ways, and so has our church. For more information on healing prayer, two good resources are Agnes Sanford's classic, *The Healing Light*, and John Wilkinson's study of the biblical basis of healing, *The Bible and Healing*[6] (Wilkinson is a medical missionary and consultant on public health in Scotland). Also, most mainline denominations offer resources for integrating healing rituals into worship services. For more practical help on this topic, you might explore the Order of St. Luke, an ecumenical organization devoted to fostering healing ministries (https://orderofstluke.org).

Becoming a healing church also means emphasizing health and holiness in all that we are doing. For instance, staff and leaders in congregations need to emphasize healthy relationships along with an intolerance of dysfunction. We need to be clear that we expect staff and leaders to treat each other with Christ's love and care—the foundation of a healthy, holy church. Rabbi Edwin Friedman, a family systems therapist and congregational health expert, has published some wonderful resources on how to overcome congregational dysfunction, including his book *Generation to Generation: Family Process in Church and Synagogue* and the video *Family Process and Process Theology: Basic New Concepts*.[7] Ultimately, we need to remember that since churches are always about relationships—relationships with God, all of God's people and creation, and one another—the leadership and staff must exemplify good relationships. Sometimes modeling healthy relationships can mean letting go of leaders and staff who cannot relate with others in healthy ways—often a painful process. Still, when we hire people, we want to assess potential staff members' ability to relate healthily to others.

A final way that churches are called to be places of healing has to do with our understanding of the ministry of the laity. We need to reclaim their call to healing ministry. The past 100 years have seen a growing emphasis on the pastor as the agent of healing and health in a congregation. The pastor does all the visiting. The pastor is the one who cares for those in need. Unfortunately, this emphasis on the pastor as the main agent of healing and health keeps many churches from growing. All that time the pastor spends caring for individuals not only prevents her from attending to other aspects of ministry, such as preaching, teaching, and leading the church to be a place of healing, but it also keeps the church as a whole from taking responsibility for healing. The ministry of care and compassion in a church, what we today call pastoral care, is a ministry all the members need to be engaged in.

What I am proudest of is that Calvin Church is a community that loves and therefore heals. The people here understand that they are called to love, and so they do. I'm not going to say it is perfect, because I know that some people haven't felt loved by the church, but they are generally the exception. Many times I visit someone in need, only to discover that a member of the church has already been there. I have been told on quite a few occasions, "Graham, you can't do everything. We can care for people, too. If you can't visit someone, we understand. We're all responsible." Those are the words of a healing community. Ultimately, an alive, blessed church is a place where Christ can heal, teach, and preach, a place where everything we do somehow connects people to Christ's presence.

CALLING ALIVE LEADERS

If we are to become a church that is alive to God as Presence, where do we begin? Everything begins with leadership. If the leaders, lay or pastoral, are not alive to Christ, the church won't be either. As I said previously, too many churches cut off the spiritual dimension, and no-where is this lack clearer than in the process of nominating and calling forth leaders. Typically, the questions nominating committees ask about candidates run along the lines of "How organized is he? Does she have management skills? Is he good with his hands? Will she be able to coordinate the church dinner?" In some cases we don't even ask those questions. We just ask, "Will she or he say yes?" We don't ask, "Is she a person of deep faith and commitment to Christ? Will he prayerfully seek God's voice and lead us to follow God's will?"

We changed the way we call leaders at Calvin Church several years ago, and it has led to a dynamic change in our leadership. Since I came to Calvin, we have always had good people on the church board, but for many of them it was a whole new idea that we should prayerfully seek God's voice to lead us to follow God's will. They hadn't thought of church leadership in that way before. One of the foundational changes we made when I came to Calvin was to ask leaders to put aside their own egos as well as what they thought their pastor wanted and instead to emphasize prayerfully seeking and doing God's will. I stressed that they were called to listen for and to do God's will. They were not to be political representatives of the congregation or groups within the congregation, seeking mainly to do their will, but to be spiritual leaders. It was when we began seeking leaders who already had a willingness to seek God's will first that this church really became transformed. Our leadership was not bad before we changed our nominating focus. In fact, our leaders were exceptional. But now our leadership has a depth that is tangible, especially in times of crisis.

A guide to forming a more spiritually grounded nominating committee is included in appendix J, "Nominating Committees." We begin by inviting the nominating committee members to spend time in prayer, asking God to reveal whom God is calling to become an elder (in the Presbyterian Church [USA], elders are laity ordained to lead the church by serving on the session, the church's governing board; only elders can sit on the session, the church board). At Calvin Church we use the same process for calling forth any committee member whose position, because of requirements by our denominational constitution or the church's bylaws, requires a nomination and vote by the congregation. In our congregation this includes the nominating committee.

Returning to the work of the nominating committee, we ask it to assess the faith of the candidates first, their functional abilities second. The priority is on calling people of faith who will focus on doing God's will, not necessarily on getting people with organizational skills. After inviting the members of the nominating committee into a time of discernment, we ask them to come together and share their discernments and to form a list of potential candidates. The members of the nominating committee prayerfully come to a consensus about whom they sense God may be calling to be candidates. One of the most important qualities we ask the committee to look for is their sense that a candidate has a desire to seek God's will over their own, regardless of their experience with the process. We can teach discernment, but we can't teach a desire to discern. The committee then sits down with the candidate, explains the leadership position, and encourages the potential elder to spend time in prayer to discern whether she or he similarly feels called by God to become an elder. Appendix K, "Becoming an Elder at Calvin Presbyterian Church," is a sample of the guide we give potential nominees to help them in their discernment. We encourage candidates to say no if they do not similarly feel called to serve as elders. We also make sure they know that serving as elder is difficult and requires a commitment to the church and to the ministry and mission they oversee. We want only people who are committed to seeking and serving God's call.

The impact of the change in our process has been amazing. It is obvious that our leaders are people deeply committed to prayerfully discerning God's will. We have different perspectives and disagreements, but in the end the elders are committed to working in prayerful unity. We have gone through some difficult times and a few crises. It is important to remember that blessed churches aren't immune to crises. But because of the leadership's faith, commitment, and trust in God's leading, we have always found God's answers—answers that are deeper and more creative than anything we could come up with on our own.

Not only is it important to ask prayerfully whom God is calling to serve as leaders. We need to be just as discerning about who serves on a committee, team, or task force. Although the process of calling these people is less formal, the candidates still can be sought in prayer. The leaders need prayerfully to consider whom God is calling to serve with them and then recruit members based on their own prayerful discernment.

MEETINGS THAT COME ALIVE

Leaders in a blessed church need to be people of faith, but they must also guide others in a way that helps them form a prayerful faith. How meetings are run is crucial in teaching people how to be open to and trust God. Most churches are overfunctional in the way they run their meetings, from the church board on down. In the blessed church, the focus is not solely on following guidelines like *Robert's Rules of Order* but on heeding God's guidance. For guidance on how to create a more spiritually open and alive meeting where people seek God's guidance and voice, see appendix L, "A Guide to Holding Spiritually Grounded Meetings," as well as appendix D, "Discerning Direction for a Particular Issue."

In short, the way we try to hold meetings at Calvin Church (although we are not strict about it) is to invite people to discuss the issues but, in the end, to focus on seeking what God wants. As mentioned previously, this means starting with recommendations that we discern through dialogue rather than motions that are determined through debate. Sometimes this process involves prayer, although often the answer becomes apparent without prayer. We try to avoid what happens in many churches. In a typical church meeting, boards and committees figuratively and literally begin a meeting by inviting God into the room as they open in prayer and an opening devotion. Then, by what they do and how they discuss proposals and make decisions, they basically tell God to wait outside in the hall until they have made a decision. Finally, through their closing prayers they invite God back into the room to bless their decisions. In contrast, spiritual leaders ask God to be a part of the whole meeting. They ask God to become thoroughly part of the process so that they may seek and do what God is blessing rather than asking God to bless what they are doing. This process rightfully restores Christ to being head of the church.

ALIVE TO PRESENCE IN WORSHIP

While it is crucial for the leaders to become alive to presence, the foundation of the blessed church's life is worship that is alive to presence and that embodies Christ. Unfortunately, too many churches try to take a shortcut by focusing mainly on the *style* rather than the *soul* of worship. The question at the heart of a blessed church is not "What style of worship should we offer?" It is "What kind of worship are we called to offer that will lead people to encounter God as Purpose, Presence, and Power?" The latter question is the one that addresses the soul of worship by emphasizing that the focus of worship is God, not us.

At Calvin Church, our order of worship is grounded in our Presbyterian, Reformed tradition, but it also integrates elements from other traditions. We begin worship with a Taizé chant and lead people into silent prayer. Our worship service and space integrate the ancient and the contemporary. When we renovated our sanctuary, we asked: What is God calling us to do? Prayerfully looking at our demographics and community, we felt called to design a sanctuary that combined traditional symbols, ambience, and architecture with contemporary lighting, sound, and music systems. This blend fits our community, although it might fail in more traditional or transient communities.

We have also continually asked this question in regard to our selection of hymns, anthems, and other music, choosing music that we sense will best help the community as a *whole* to experience Christ. The focus in many churches is on choosing music that appeals to one segment of the congregation over the others. We try to avoid idolizing one style or era of music—classical, contemporary, or something in between—but to use whatever we sense will best help people encounter Christ. What matters to us is God's call, not the desire to idolize past traditions or to imitate current trends.

Another area in which Christ's presence is truly sensed and encountered is in the sacraments. It's unfortunate that in the zeal to move toward contemporary worship, sacraments such as communion have been de-emphasized in some congregations, especially in nondenominational ones. The irony is that even as many congregations have moved toward an emphasis on "seeker-friendly" worship, elsewhere in the church we see an emerging movement back toward ancient practices. More and more evangelical, nondenominational authors are calling churches to recover ancient practices to reach younger generations that seem to have an appreciation for experiential practices such as communion.

The spirit in which we offer communion and other sacraments is important. Sacraments can be offered in a ritualistic and dry manner that fails to create the conditions in which people can experience Christ's presence. There are ways of offering sacraments that make Christ's mystical presence in and through the sacraments more apparent, especially to newer or newly recommitted Christians. For example, at Calvin Church sometimes we serve communion in the traditional Presbyterian way, distributing the elements through the pews, but sometimes we call people forward, especially during our monthly healing services. The question for us is how to go about leading people to encounter Christ through these sacraments and to offer an experience of worship that helps people encounter Christ.

ALIVE TO PRESENCE IN MINISTRY AND MISSION

The final element in becoming a church that is alive to God's presence is maintaining a focus on what Christ is calling the church to do in ministry and mission. Ministry is generally considered to be how we serve God in the church—our pastoral care and programs targeted at the members—while mission is how we serve God outside the church by reaching out to those who are unchurched, hungry, poor, or otherwise in need. I have heard both laity and pastors complain that their church isn't sufficiently committed to ministry and mission. They grumble that their people are too self-focused. The problem may be not with the people but with the particular ministry and mission. The leaders may be pushing other members to engage in ministries and missions that are not God's call for them. Part of becoming a blessed church means actively listening to Christ's call to mission, whatever it is. As noted in the previous chapter, God has a purpose for everything, and the key to effective ministry and mission is discerning and responding to God's call for this congregation in this place.

Mission and ministry first need to be grounded in prayer. A large problem in the mainline church is that in sermon after sermon people have been told to feed the poor, change the political system, and reach out to the unchurched; to offer generationally sensitive programs for the divorced, single, grieving, and addicted; and to build this, transform that, solve this crisis, and eradicate that problem. People become overwhelmed by all the needs of the world. We should realize that we are only *part* of the body of Christ, not the whole body. God gives us specific ministries and missions to do while giving others different ministry and mission opportunities.

As I mentioned in the discussion on formative education, we need to reclaim the ability to discern how God is calling us to reach out to the world around us. The ministry and mission of Calvin Church are certainly not the same as that of a rural or an urban church. We are in another context and situation. We are called to different ministries and missions. If we are truly Christ's church, we need to focus on what we can do and are called to do rather than on the work we do not have the calling or talent to do. We ought to be aware that a lack of talent often reveals a lack of calling. We should ground what we do in prayer, seeking Christ's active guidance. The key is discernment that leads to activity for Christ's sake, not for activity's sake. When we direct our efforts to the ministries and missions to which Christ calls us, the work becomes God's work, not ours.

It is important to define our service to God first in spiritual rather than purely functional ways. The functional is an important component, but it must emerge from a spiritual yearning and aspiration to do God's will. Too often we functionally characterize ministry and mission as planned programs. When a church becomes truly blessed, ministry and mission just happen, whether planned or not. Our service to God is not restricted to activities that have been cleared by a committee or board (although what boards and committees do certainly is service to God). In a blessed church, ministry and mission have the opportunity to emerge more organically, meaning that the members are given permission and encouragement to respond to needs as they feel called, and the role of the church is to support them. For example, while the church may feel called to start small groups by creating a comprehensive small-group program, in the blessed church you will also find some people taking it upon themselves to gather once a week for prayer or Bible study. These spontaneous groups can serve as the seeds for a more extensive small-group program, or they can simply be the church's small-group program. Ministry becomes more flexible and spontaneous as people seek to encounter Christ in their own ways.

In mission, people look for opportunities in all areas of their lives to reach out to those in need. For example, one woman I know, who teaches children in a depressed area, took it upon herself to raise funds to buy shoes for poor children. Another family, seeing the struggles of a family with an unemployed father, gave a sizable and anonymous financial gift to help them through their tough times. Mission becomes organic, growing, and flowing in unexpected places and ways. It's not that Christ isn't present in churches where meticulous planning takes place through a centralized board; but by opening up the process and encouraging people to discern and respond on their own, we create the context in which Christ's presence grows stronger and moves in its own direction.

A problem facing many churches today, my own included, is that we tend to look at mission through "Christendom" eyes that recognize only overseas mission to the economically impoverished and hungry as valid outreach. We fail to recognize that we are in a post-Christendom era in which the people of our own culture have become increasingly impoverished and hungry spiritually. Because we do not always pay attention to God's call, we fail to respond when God calls on us to reach out to the spiritually starving on our doorsteps. We get caught in 1950s philosophies of mission and outreach rather than responding to God's present call.

The best example of someone who discerned God's call and responded in a unique way is Mother Teresa. Most people don't know much about her life. They think that she must have been born to be a nun and to reach out to the poor in Calcutta. The fact is that before she began her mission to the poor, she was the headmistress of an elite girls' school in Calcutta. Each day she looked out her window and saw the poor, and her heart broke. God used her breaking heart to transform her gradually and to call her to minister to the poor. Eventually she responded to God's call. She didn't do it by creating an elaborate organization. She did it the only way she knew how. She left the school each day armed with a bag of rice. She stopped at a corner and, using a stick, began writing in the dust to teach the children to read, making a promise that each child who learns the lesson is given a handful of rice. Over time, her mission grew. She was able to carry out this mission because she had a formative outlook on life that allowed her to be transformed by God because she first sought Christ's will in prayer.

Ultimately, being guided by the presence of Christ in ministry and mission requires members to be willing to discern how God is calling them to respond to the world's needs, whether as part of a committee or in their personal lives. (For help in understanding how to discern, see appendix M, "Four Principles of Discernment.") In a blessed church the members increasingly and creatively look at the world around them to see how God may be calling them to respond in their own ways. They respond to opportunities that seem in tune with God's calling.

Of course, when we look for opportunities, it is easy to become overwhelmed by the problems around us. We cannot take care of the whole world, but we can take care of that part of the world for which

God has given us a passion, a calling, and ability. When we are alive to Christ, God makes our mission and ministry clear. It is important, then, for pastors and leaders to nurture spiritual readiness on the part of the other leaders and members, stressing that God is constantly calling us to serve, whether as part of the church or in our own unique ways through our acts of love. True ministry and mission are a response to Christ, who is embodied in us and who seeks to reach out to others through us.

ARE WE ALIVE?

The hardest part of forming a Trinitarian church, a church of purpose, presence, and power, is forming one that is alive to God as Presence. It is hard because so many in the mainline church do not believe that God can be tangibly sensed in their midst. They focus on God in heaven or on Christ in history. Becoming a blessed church means being a church that reveals God's presence in everything so that people can encounter and experience Christ in every facet of their lives.

When a church becomes truly alive to Christ, it becomes a dynamic, creative place. It may not necessarily become a place of explosive growth because the factors that foster that kind of growth are not present everywhere. What does happen is that in worship people sense Christ's presence in their work for the church. They form deep relationships with others in the church, and they sense God's love in the relationships. They struggle and suffer the pains of life and discover God touching and caring for them through the people of the church. And as they do, they discover that they are not only in a place of God's presence, but they are living more and more according to God's purpose and are experiencing God's power flowing in and through them.

REFLECTION QUESTIONS

1. To what extent do you sense Christ's presence in your church?
2. To what extent do you sense that your church is purposeful about being alive to Christ's presence in preaching, teaching, and healing?

3. In what ways does your church close the door to Christ as Presence?

4. What concrete things can you do to help your church become more alive to Christ in its leadership, worship, ministry, and mission?

5

OPEN TO GOD AS POWER

In 1990, I first read about an amazing man who gave me a whole new vision for what is possible in a church. His name was George Müller, and he served God throughout the 19th century in Plymouth, England.[1] I mention him here because of how his life demonstrated what is possible when we become open to God as Power, to God the Holy Spirit. By the end of his life at the turn of the 20th century, Müller was one of the most famous Christians alive, giving talks to thousands of people worldwide. Few who knew him as a young man would have predicted that.

Müller was born in Prussia in 1805. When he was a young adult, his experience of God's presence through a group of Christians he had met revolutionized his life. Prior to that he had been a brilliant but hedonistic young man focused on drinking, gambling, and chasing women. He became a Christian, eventually moved to England, and became a pastor in Bristol. It was there that God's purpose, presence, and especially power transformed him. From that moment on, he decided to center his life in Scripture and to pattern his life on Matthew 7:7, where Jesus says, "Ask, and it will be given you; search and you will find; knock, and the door will be opened for you." Müller realized that if this passage was true, then God's power must be available to all, even if most Christians ignored it. If Scripture was true, then God must want to provide miracles. God must want to bless our work.

Müller decided to test his theory by relying on God's purpose, presence, and power for his life and ministry. His first experiment was to refuse a salary for his ministry. He decided instead to rely on God for his welfare as he continued to serve God. Over time, he discovered the extent to which God can bless what we do. He discovered the power of the Holy Spirit, which I'm going to refer to as "God as Power" because the work of the Spirit is God's power working in the world. Although Müller received no salary, the Spirit took care of him. Whenever he needed something, whether money, food, clothes, medical care, or anything else, the Spirit responded. For example, a man he barely knew might come up to him on the street and say, "I'm not sure why, but I feel that something is telling me to give you this," and then give him several shillings or a pound—exactly what he was praying for. Müller didn't engage in this experiment because he was lazy. In fact, he was anything but. He never prayed for anything beyond his most essential needs. Through prayer he discovered God's Spirit blessing him in everything.

A few years later, strengthened by his experience of God's power, Müller embarked on a new venture in faith—one that eventually made him known worldwide. He felt called by God to start an orphanage that would be rooted in prayer and providence and that would be a model of faith and love. According to his plan, discerned in prayer, the children would receive three meals a day, have their own beds and cubicles, own several pairs of shoes and changes of clothes, learn to read and write, and receive loving and respectful treatment. He would be severely criticized for this radical idea because, according to the conventional wisdom of the time, orphans were little more than street urchins to be ignored at best, abused at worst. Caring about them and educating them was considered a waste of time. Even more radical was his vision of grounding the orphanage in prayer. The orphanage solicited no donations, practiced financial accountability, focused always on the welfare of the children, and centered all decisions and actions in prayer. So instead of aggressively raising funds, the orphanage board and staff would instead go to God in prayer whenever they were in need.

Over the course of Müller's life, the orphanage grew substantially from the initial four orphans to more than 2,050 residents living on a campus of 25 acres. The leaders never asked for money, no matter how dire the need, but would always respond to their need by praying and trusting God in faith. Relying solely on prayer and faith, they raised the equivalent in today's dollars of $50 million to $80 million. Müller was a man of amazing faith who relied on God's power to flow through all he did.

Müller provided me with an alternative vision of what could happen in a church when we are truly open to God's power, the power of the Holy Spirit. For many mainline Christians who have been led to believe that God is distant and uninvolved in life, Müller's story is unbelievable because it says that God is actively involved. It says that God works miracles in our midst that we don't expect. For people stuck in a functional, rationalistic view of God, this message is hard to swallow. What Müller taught me is that if I became a person of prayer who tried faithfully to expect God to bless my ministry and life, God *would*, even if the blessing wasn't always what I expected or envisioned. I began to see a possibility for the mainline churches: they could become houses of prayer through which God's Spirit blew, blessing their members, ministry, and mission. They would face struggles and tests, but if congregations did their best to believe and have faith that God could make the impossible possible, even if that faith was imperfect, wonderful things could happen. As I look back at 20 years of ministry since I first read about George Müller, I can confidently say that I have never been disappointed. When I've asked, I've received, although not always in ways I anticipated. When I've sought, I've found, although not always in ways I expected. When I've knocked, surprising doors of opportunity and possibility have always been opened, even if what was behind these doors was not what I had envisioned.

My faith in God as Power was confirmed in 1997 when I read Rick Warren's book *The Purpose Driven Church*. As a nonevangelical pastor, reading Warren's work felt heretical, but in it I found ideas missing in much of the mainline church. Warren has helped thousands by offering a vision of how to create a church of purpose, but what I found most helpful and enlightening was the story of how he started the Saddleback Valley Community Church in Orange County, California.[2]

In 1979, as Warren was finishing up his last year of seminary, he felt called to start a dynamic new church for the unchurched. He spent time in prayer, sincerely seeking God's will. Afterward, he put a map of the world up in his living room and began praying with his wife for God to show them where they were to start this church. For six months they prayed, and slowly God's purpose became clearer. Using a process that included prayer, faith, and demographic studies that showed the locations of the largest populations of unchurched people, they eventually discerned that they were called to plant a church in southern California, specifically in a town called Saddleback Valley. In 1981 Orange County was the fastest-growing area of the country. Warren sensed that God was calling them to go there.

Being a Southern Baptist, he decided first to contact the Southern Baptist director of missions in Orange County, a man named Herman Wooten. The young minister called and said, "My name is Rick Warren. I am a seminary student in Texas. I am planning to move to south Orange County and start a church. I'm not asking for money or support from you; I just want to know what you think about that area. Does it need new churches?"

Wooten's reply clearly revealed how God as Power responds when we prayerfully act according to God's purpose and presence. Warren's call had interrupted Wooten as he was writing a letter that said, "Dear Mr. Warren, I have heard that you may be interested in starting a new church in California after seminary. Have you ever considered coming to Saddleback Valley in south Orange County?" God's purpose, presence, and power were clearly evident.

Finally, after more research and several visits to Saddleback Valley, Warren and his wife, by now parents of a four-month-old baby, packed up their belongings and drove to California, praying along the way. They pulled off the freeway and stopped at the first real estate office they found. They walked in and met a real estate broker, Don Dale. Warren said to him, "My name is Rick Warren. I'm here to start a church. I need a place to live, but I don't have any money." Dale laughed out loud and said he would see what he could do. Two hours later, Dale had found them a condominium to rent, with the first month's rent free, and Dale had agreed to become the first member of Saddleback Church.

From there the church grew in response to prayer. Another church in the area agreed to sponsor them. A man they had never met agreed to pay their rent for two months, and people they didn't even know sent money to help them, often in the exact amount they had prayed for. From these humble beginnings, Saddleback Valley Community Church grew from a few members to a congregation of 5,000 that has a worship attendance of 10,000 every Sunday.

The important lesson I learned from Warren is not how to build a 5,000-member church. That is his calling, not mine. What I learned is that when we respond to God's purpose and rely on God's presence, the Spirit's power flows through everything we do. I learned that God wants to bless our churches, but too often we reject the power of the Holy Spirit. So nothing happens. I've also discovered in my own church that when we pray, amazing things happen in our midst—events that could come only from God.

RECAPTURING PENTECOST

Forming a church filled with the Holy Spirit was Jesus' promise. It is the power of the Holy Spirit that truly distinguishes the Christian faith from most others. While Jesus was alive, he taught his followers to follow the will of God, love others, and be Christ's servants in the world, but that was only the foundation of what was to come. His real focus was on opening them to the power of the Holy Spirit. Especially in the Gospel of John, we hear Jesus teach his disciples about the power of the Holy Spirit, a power that would allow them to preach, teach, heal, and perform miracles in the name of Christ. The disciples experienced the truth of Jesus' teaching on the day of Pentecost. We are told in Acts that after Jesus ascended to heaven, his followers gathered and waited in faith for the coming of the Holy Spirit. Before ascending, Jesus said, "But you will receive power when the Holy Spirit has come upon you" (John 1:8). So they waited. And then it happened. The power of the Holy Spirit came upon all of them on the day of Pentecost. This power filled their souls and gave them the passion and power to give their lives completely to God. From that moment on, they manifested God's power in their lives.

They preached with a power and a voice that was more than their own. They were able to live in the unity of the Spirit. They healed the sick. They had visions. Amazing things happened as the church grew and spread. It is clear from the events recorded by Luke in the Acts of the Apostles that the power of the Holy Spirit was available to all who had faith, and sometimes, as in Paul's case, even grabbed hold of people unawares. The breath of the Spirit transformed the church from its dogmatic, legalistic roots into a vital faith that connected people with God, allowing God's power to flow through their lives.

Unfortunately, over the past 2,000 years our denominations, with some exceptions (Quakers, Pentecostals, and charismatics), have slowly pushed the Holy Spirit to the margins, limiting the Spirit's power by emphasizing functionality, hierarchy, organization, and adherence to tradition. We are guilty of this omission in our modern mainline churches. To what extent do we expect or invite the Holy Spirit to act? To what extent are we open to God's power, to God as Power? To what extent are we willing to have God's power flow through what we do, bringing blessings, miracles, and transformations?

Our churches are meant to be churches of power. God's original intent was that the divine purpose and presence be manifested in works of power in which God blesses us and the world through us. But this cannot happen unless we, as spiritual leaders, make a crucial decision to let God's Spirit work in our midst. If pastors are not open to the power of the Holy Spirit, the power of the Spirit will be limited in their churches, for the Spirit of God generally enters only in a limited way those churches that remain closed to the Spirit. If lay leaders will not open up to the Spirit, their churches will become stale and dry as God stands outside, looking in. The Spirit generally will not blow through closed doors and windows.

UNDERSTANDING THE HOLY SPIRIT

To become a blessed church, a congregation must become a place that is open to the Holy Spirit; but to do so means understanding the nature of the Holy Spirit, for the Holy Spirit is the least understood and appreciated of the three persons of the Trinity (especially by mainline Protestants). It helps to look at what Scripture has to say about the Holy Spirit. What we get in Scripture is not a complete picture but a glimpse of Spirit experiences. We discover that the Holy Spirit is the person of God, the power of God, that affects the world, transforms life, and showers grace and providence on those who are sincerely trying to open their lives to God. This is no aloof and distant God, but God who is immersed in the world and actively present in every moment and detail of life. This is God who blesses, saves, and becomes apparent in miraculous events.

When we open our hearts, minds, and souls to the Holy Spirit, it fills us with the life of Christ. We become living bodies for the Holy Spirit to become incarnated in flesh. We live at the same time both in God's kingdom and on the earth. We may live the same physical life that all other creatures live, but we simultaneously live in God's realm. This life in two realms gives us the potential, however imperfect, to follow God and live according to God's plan, even if we don't understand completely what it is or where it will lead.

For example, the Holy Spirit filled Jesus and led him into the desert at the beginning of his ministry, even though Jesus didn't fully understand why (Matt. 4:1–11). That time in the desert was a crucial time of preparing Jesus for his ministry. The Holy Spirit opens people up to whole new ways of living that make them one with God and open to a renewed life and a deeper truth (John 3:1–9; 14:17–31). The Holy Spirit sets us free from the power of sin that corrupts and tempts us to seek our own will over God's (Rom. 8:1–17). When we pray, it is not only we who pray to God, but also the Holy Spirit praying within us (Rom. 8:15–16). The Holy Spirit also cultivates in each of us unique gifts that allow us to incarnate Christ in our own ways and spread God's blessings throughout the world as we bear God's fruit (1 Cor. 12:4–11; Gal. 5:16–26). Finally, it is through the power of the Holy Spirit that we become united and share in the unity of the Spirit (Phil. 2:1–5).

Ultimately, the Holy Spirit leads us all to a mystical truth: God is before us, in us, with us, and through us, blessing us and life around us whenever we are open to the power of the Holy Spirit. The potential impact of the Holy Spirit on the life of our churches is amazing. The practical message of the mystical truth cited above is that our churches can be places of blessing and power where God works miraculously to heal, save, and transform lives as we come to union and communion with God and one another. This is not an idealistic pipe dream but a reality when we become open to the Holy Spirit in our midst. Of course, it's only a reality when people are willing to become open to the Spirit.

I want to explore how we can become more open to the Holy Spirit so that our churches can become places of unity and community where people glimpse God's mind and manifest spiritual gifts for the blessing of all.

UNITY AND COMMUNITY

Many churches today are fractured and fragmented as conflict reigns. A friend of mine once said that the most wonderfully loving and the most hate-filled people he had ever met were all within the church. I know many pastors who have been unfairly and cruelly skewered by members of their congregation over matters that amount to nothing, and more than enough laity who have been terribly abused by their pastors. I see the power of this division taking place in my own denomination, the Presbyterian Church (USA). It is filled with passionate people on the left and the right who are so consumed with their own vision for the church that they sow seeds of division everywhere. Chronic conflict is not the vision God had for the church. Christ did not create the church so that it could be a community divided against itself. The church was created to be a place of united community in which Christ's love and God's Spirit reign. What happened? The church became closed to the Holy Spirit.

In most of our denominations, unity in the Spirit has been replaced by a striving for purity of practice and doctrine. In some places fights erupt over practice: who preaches the right way, who offers the sacraments the right way, who plays the right kind of music, who uses the proper order of worship, and who engages in the right kind of ministry and mission. In other places fights erupt over theological belief: who has the right view of Christ, who is more righteous, and who has the right view of Scripture. These kinds of arguments kill the Spirit. Unity cannot be found through right practice and belief. Unity can be formed in a church only when the Holy Spirit is present. Eberhard Arnold, the founder of the Bruderhof movement—a community of Christians in Germany who opposed the evils of the Nazi movement and later immigrated to North America to escape Nazi oppression—has said:

> Full community, full agreement, is possible! It is possible through faith in God, in Christ, and in the Holy Spirit. . . . This unanimity is only possible because of our faith that God uses His Spirit to say the

same to each individual. Mutual persuasion does not do it. God does
it, speaking to us through the Holy Spirit.[3]

The Holy Spirit wants us to be united, but we cannot create this unity
solely through our own powers. It comes only as we collectively open
our hearts to the Holy Spirit. Plenty of books are available that teach
group process, conflict resolution, and systems approaches, offering a
vision of unity grounded in the insights of psychology, family systems,
and organizational research. I have been influenced by many of these
theories through my training and work as a counselor and social worker.
I recommend that any leader become versed in these theories. They
can offer new insights and information on how to deal with conflict.
Still, true unity and community in the church can come only through
the power of the Holy Spirit, which binds hearts and minds together.
Psychology, family systems theory, and organizational theory can take
us only so far.

Unity in the Spirit emerges when we, as leaders and a church, are
willing to put aside our own egos to accept the power of the Spirit
working in our midst. When moderators and other leaders of congregations, boards, committees, task forces, and teams encourage their members to become open to the Holy Spirit by putting aside their own egos
and desires to seek only God's will, Spirit begins to sow unity and
community. As Eberhard Arnold says:

> Only if we have willing, sincere, and open hearts will we find una-
> nimity in our convictions. We have never found it disturbing when
> people have come to us representing convictions that differ from
> ours. On the contrary, that is more fruitful than if we had no chance
> to hear opposing ideas. We believe that a free exchange of ideas can
> help people to recognize the truth, thanks to a Spirit that does not
> originate with us human beings. Then, no matter how diverse our
> opinions may have been, through the ultimate truth we will all be
> united. . . . A united conviction can never be produced by forcing
> anyone to comply. Only the Holy Spirit with His power of inner
> persuasion leads people from freedom of opinions to true unity.[4]

I have seen this kind of unity work in our own church. The members
of our church session hold a variety of opinions and generally feel free
to express their own views and insights. Discussions can range widely as

we explore various options and ideas. Still, it is when they are asked prayerfully to let go of their own expectations and desires and to do what God wants that an amazing unity emerges. It is not just a unity in which we all choose one option to avoid conflict. Instead, through prayer we often discover new options and possibilities that we did not consider at first. When pride and a need to have decisions go "my way" are put aside to allow the Spirit's power to work in our midst, we discover an amazing creativity and openness to possibility. Putting pride aside requires something important from me, though. I must be willing to let go of my own desires and wants. I have to be willing to let go of my own plans whenever I sense through my own prayerful discernment that the Spirit may be talking through others.

For example, early in my ministry at Calvin Church we were faced with a growth problem. We were becoming so full during our second Sunday worship service (about 80 percent of capacity) that we were running out of seats and parking spaces. As most church-growth experts report, when a congregation exceeds 80 percent of capacity, growth stalls because of a perceived lack of space (recently some researchers suggest 70 percent due to the increase in the number of cars families are driving to worship). We had to find a way to get more people to come to our early service, which averaged 20 percent of capacity. We invited members to come together for a meeting to discern possibilities. We looked at a lot of options, but in the end it was the suggestion of one member that held sway. He suggested that we do what was done in his previous church, which was to have the children's education program begin halfway through our first service so that children would be in worship for the first part of the service and then go to Sunday school after the children's sermon. Besides offering us a new alternative, this proposal addressed the complaints of many parents who wanted a way to worship without always having to spend sermon and communion time telling their kids to be quiet.

When our worship committee met, I was very much against the change of schedule. I was involved in adult education on Sunday mornings, and the change would kill our Sunday adult-education hour and my engagement in it. As I argued against the change, the chair of the committee stopped me and said, "Graham, maybe you need to consider that this is something God is calling us to do. Maybe you are being called to lay aside your teaching for the sake of the church." I was stunned, not because he had crossed me but because he was right. I could sense the Holy Spirit speaking through him. And so we changed, and it was wonderful for the church. Our two services shifted to seating around 50 and 65 percent of capacity, respectively, and both are growing—an outcome that has given us room for growth without the need to build a new sanctuary. When we are open to the Holy Spirit, a new kind of unity forms that is grounded in God's call and possibility.

A few years later we went through a small discernment process again and sensed the call to return to the previous worship schedule because we sensed the need to reintroduce the Sunday morning adult-education program. We were pleasantly surprised that not only did the numbers hold, but both services were able to remain at about 60 percent capacity each.

DIVISION AND DISUNITY

While a deep unity comes through the work and power of the Holy Spirit, there is another power that does not want unity in the church: the power of the demonic. Talking about the demonic is very difficult in the mainline church because while we believe in God and God's intervention in life, belief in the demonic seems archaic and childish. Growing up, I was never much of a believer in the demonic, and I basically held the view that belief in the demonic was naïve. Still, the more I have become involved in a ministry of prayer and spiritual formation, the more I have seen this darker force at work in the church. Whether you call it the demonic, the power of division, or the dark side of the force, something out there does not want the church to be unified in the Spirit as a community of Christ. There is a divisive power in our world.

I was given a great awareness of the power of the demonic by a series of lectures given by Adrian van Kaam that I heard while I was studying at Duquesne University for my doctorate. The demonic had never been mentioned in any class I had taken in seminary. In fact, the topic was avoided. When I heard van Kaam, who had an appreciation for the reality of it because of his Roman Catholic faith and from his experiences, I knew he spoke of something real that threatened the unity of the church, but only if we let it. Basically, the demonic is a force whose only real power is to sow division through our fears. It has no real power of its own, and it's not something to be feared. We just need to be aware.

The demonic is a force, energy, or entity that seeks to pull humans away from God and to prevent people from loving God and experiencing God's grace in their lives. According to van Kaam, the demonic works through two means: demonic possession and mini-obsession. Demonic possession is extremely rare and was exemplified in the 1972 film *The Exorcist*. When a person is possessed, her mind is either partially or totally overwhelmed and invaded. I have never witnessed a possession myself, and I hope I never will, although I have met people who have experience with possessions. They occur only in rare circumstances, usually when families or individuals become open to the demonic through their own extreme dysfunction or by dabbling in satanic practices. According to van Kaam, the purpose of possession is to blind people to the possibility of demonic mini-obsession. Possession attracts such attention that people become blind to how the demonic is working through mini-obsessions to sow division in the body of Christ.

It is through mini-obsessions that the demonic works to set Christians against one another. A mini-obsession occurs when a seemingly *minor* psychological obsession over something relatively small becomes so strong that it gets blown out of proportion in a way that creates fear, anger, and anxiety. It is important not to confuse a mini-obsession with obsessive-compulsive disorder. The disorder is an almost incapacitating psychological illness that can be treated through psychotherapy and medication. A mini-obsession does not incapacitate or otherwise interfere with a person's ability to function in everyday life. Rather, it causes a person to become so obsessed with an issue, event, ideal, or ideology that all who do not agree are regarded as the enemy.

For example, a mini-obsession may be at work in the church when a person or group has a legitimate concern to address but in the process, the member or group becomes so obsessed with it that the matter begins to bring division into the body of Christ. People may obsess over the church budget, a mission of the church, the use of contemporary or traditional hymns, a perceived slight by the pastor, abortion, homosexuality, or orthodoxy. Whatever the focus of the obsession, they become so consumed with it that they make it a church-dividing issue, forcing people to take sides. In their minds, all who take the side opposite their own are wrong, evil, or, ironically, in league with the devil. They believe that they are bringing unity by defending a moral, ethical, ecclesiastical, or even political principle, but the way they go about their defense creates conflict by giving rise to anger and defensiveness.

Probably the most obvious mini-obsession dividing the church today has to do with the whole issue of homosexuality and ordination. This serious and important topic should be discussed, prayed over, and resolved. Yet in many denominations and churches it has become a dividing issue as people acrimoniously attack one another's character and faith in their efforts to win the battle. People who agree in 95 percent of the areas of their faith can become sharply divided against one another in this one area. As a result they become suspicious of others' motives as well as the genuineness of others' faith. As one person, reflecting on the acrimonious fights in my own denomination over the issue, said to me, "The demonic is having a field day over all of this. Look at how we attack each other in the name of Christ." I've certainly experienced this division that has dominated my denomination throughout my entire ministry career, and that has led to the splitting off of many churches within my denomination.

The demonic gains entry into our lives through our pride and ego. It uses human pride by leading humans to see themselves as more and more self-sufficient, apart from God. For example, with the issue of homosexuality, the entry for the demonic is the pride of those on the right and the left who believe that they are so right that they quit praying and seeking God's will and a pathway to unity in the matter. They believe that their reading of Scripture, their theological acumen, and their moral stance are so unassailable that anyone who disagrees must be immoral or evil.

The demonic also can gain entry by hooking into existing conditions, such as negativity, cynicism, envy, hunger for power, problems with authority, and the reactivation of earlier traumatic experiences such as child neglect and abuse that lead to distrust of others and "acting out" in divisive ways. I've seen these manifested on a congregational level many times, even in my own church. One pastor who came to me for spiritual direction struggled with a woman who was plagued with most of the conditions cited above. She was an extremely negative and cynical person who had problems with authority, served on most of the committees in the church, and constantly hungered for more power. Over the course of a few years, she falsely accused the pastor of embezzling funds (including surreptitiously building a $70,000 home library), verbally attacking her in public (even though witnesses to the event all said that the pastor had treated her respectfully), and purposely acting against the constitution of the denomination (despite the fact that she couldn't say how).

In spiritual direction we discussed how the demonic had been using her and how to overcome it. This pastor wanted to defend himself by verbally attacking and accusing the troublesome woman in front of the church board. I shared with him van Kaam's theories on overcoming demonic mini-obsessions, which I believed this woman clearly had. Van Kaam says that we overcome mini-obsessions and the demonic by becoming aware of their power and increasing our openness to God in faith while also diminishing our own prideful desires to defend ourselves or to attack others. In other words, we overcome it through prayer and faith and humility.

We cannot overcome the demonic purely by human powers because the demonic revels in human power and works. If we try to fight the demonic with outward power, human power, the demonic twists our efforts and causes us to become equally as obsessed as our enemy, thus consuming us in a corresponding mini-obsession. Eventually the desire to attack the demonic tears us away from God and leads us into sin. If the pastor had attacked the woman, using his position of authority as a pastor to crush her, he would have relied on human powers, not on God as Power. He could have become as much a pawn of the demonic as the woman, creating an even greater division in the church, by forcing people to choose sides.

We overcome the demonic by following Jesus' guidance: "So make up your minds not to prepare your defense in advance; for I will give you words and a wisdom that none of your opponents will be able to withstand or contradict" (Luke 21:14–15). The pastor and I developed a strategy that he would respond to this woman with faith, hope, love, and prayer—a counterintuitive response. The pastor would not respond defensively and attack her but would respond in love and patience while also asking the board of his church and the denomination to get involved. The pastor would trust in God and let God take care of him.

What he experienced was clearly the work of the Holy Spirit. The more he responded in faith and love, the more she accused him, but the accusations were becoming more preposterous. The congregational council became involved. Seeing how she was trying to hurt the pastor and divide the congregation, council members surrounded the pastor and insulated him from the attacks. Eventually, they brought a case against her to the synod (the regional Lutheran authority), and the synod had to step in and reprimand the woman while telling her that she could not be involved in any committees of the church for six months. She was also prohibited from accusing the pastor in public. Violating this edict would lead to her excommunication—an extreme punishment in most denominations. Throughout, the pastor simply trusted and prayed, letting the council care for him and the church. Ultimately, the pastor discovered that the Spirit does work and take care of us, even in the face of the demonic. As of this writing, the woman has left the church to go elsewhere.

In the end, we can overcome division and live in unity only through the power of the Holy Spirit. The Spirit wants unity in the church, and only the Spirit has the power to overcome the power of darkness that sows seeds of division and disunity.

GLIMPSES OF GOD'S MIND

As we become more open to the power of the Holy Spirit, we receive an amazing gift. We increasingly gain glimpses of God's mind. What it means to glimpse God's mind is hard to explain, and people can easily manipulate others by falsely claiming that they've glimpsed God's mind. You've witnessed this behavior by people who falsely report hearing God's voice as a means to gain power, money, or influence. Others become so pridefully convinced of their own righteousness that they assume whatever they want must be what God wants and their thoughts must be God's thoughts. Despite the reality of manipulative and self-righteous people, people of deep faith do get glimpses of God's mind through the power of the Holy Spirit.

Rufus Jones, a Quaker spiritual writer, has said, "God is always revealing himself, and that truth is not something finished, but something unfolding as life goes forward."[5] We are never able to capture in our conscious minds God's whole plan for creation, the world, or us. Even if God revealed this plan, it would not make much sense to us because

God's plan is like an eternal tapestry woven beyond our ability to com-
prehend all at once, and much of this tapestry has yet to be completed.
Our concerns in life constitute a tiny thread of that tapestry, and much
of life is spent trying to find that thread and to discern its meaning.

The questions for us are these: How do we first discover the thread
that pertains to our life, and second, how do we understand it in the
context of the tapestry of all of life? In other words, how do we gain a
glimpse of how we are to live according to God's plan and purpose for
life? Many people expend much mental energy in trying to figure out
their lives and how they are supposed to live. They work hard at this
task, but discerning God's plan is not so much a process of hard work as
it is a process that begins with relaxing and trusting in God. It continues
through faith, humility, and prayer (as almost everything spiritual does).
Churches, and especially their boards, can glimpse God's plan when
they collectively put aside their egos, demands, and expectations simply
to seek what God wants. God then gives these glimpses as gifts.

I need to make a really important point here because the ability to
be a church of spirit depends upon it. Most people reading this book
will be coming out of the Protestant tradition, where the model of faith
is to be grounded in Scripture, reflecting Luther's and Calvin's emphasis on *sola scriptura*—by Scripture alone. So the model we all have in
the modern Protestant, and even evangelical, churches is to look for
answers in Scripture—to be really grounded in what the Bible says.

It is crucial for us to be grounded in Scripture, but running to the
Bible looking for guidance, ironically, is not the biblical model. Very
few people in the Bible looked to Scripture for specific guidance. Certainly Noah didn't, nor did Abraham, Isaac, Joseph, Moses, Joshua, or
the biblical judges because there was no Scripture for them to run to.
While Jesus knew Scripture (at least the Old Testament—he was living
the New Testament), as did his disciples, they rarely ran to Scripture for
guidance. The biblical model is not to run to Scripture, but to run off to
the desert, to a mountain, to a garden, to a lonely place, or to a private
room to pray and seek God's will. And the reason they ran off to these
places was to struggle in solitude so that they could let go of their own
pride, ego, and selfishness in order to be more truly open to the Spirit's
guidance. That's the model Jesus follows in the Gospels. Remember, it
was the Spirit that led him into the desert after his baptism (Matt. 4:1).
Going off in solitude to pray was also the model the apostles and early

Christians followed in Acts. The Bible is clear that seeking glimpses of God's mind by seeking God's guidance in quiet prayer is our model. And the church has been built over the past 2,000 years upon millions of people gaining glimpses of God's mind, as flawed as most may have been.

You have had these glimpses, as have most people in most churches. Unfortunately, it is easy to ignore them. The ones who discover God's power at work in their lives are the ones who have had a sense, however small, that God was calling them to act and then responded in faith. For example, in 1998 Calvin Presbyterian Church embarked on a capital campaign to raise $250,000. We glimpsed *the possibility* that God was calling us to create the conditions for growth by renovating our sanctuary and much of the church. Many in our congregation were hesitant and reluctant because this church hadn't participated in any capital campaign in more than 50 years. Still, we stepped forward in faith.

In fact, acting prayerfully in faith was so important to us that in choosing a fund-raiser, we rejected our denomination's program and used a nondenominational one that emphasized Scripture, prayer, and faith. The denomination's program focused on teaching us how to approach members in a functional way to help them figure out what they could afford to give. We went with a group that would teach us prayerfully to lead people to ask what God was calling them to give. This group would teach us how to put faith and response to God's grace at the center of the campaign. In the end, we raised more than $330,000, which was pure providence: that was exactly how much we finally needed, since our costs for renovation were higher than anticipated, and our plans changed during the campaign as we sensed God offering us other opportunities. For example, a house next door to the church that went on the market could house much of our youth and education program. God had given us a glimpse, and when we acted in faith, God provided exactly what we needed, no more and no less. When we glimpse God's mind and act in faith, God as Power can work in wonderful ways in our lives, both as individuals and as communities of faith.

SPIRITUAL GIFTS

A hot topic among many growing (and trying-to-grow) churches has been spiritual gifts. The term "spiritual gifts" comes from 1 Corinthians 12:4, where Paul says, "Now there are varieties of gifts, but the same Spirit; and there are varieties of services, but the same Lord; and there are varieties of activities, but it is the same God who activates all of them in everyone." Over the past decade or so, more and more churches have used "spiritual-gift inventories"—forms that members of a church fill out and that identify what spiritual gifts they have that can be used in service to the church. The reasoning behind the inventories is that somehow we can categorize and organize spiritual gifts so that people can be matched with particular ministries of the church. The identified gifts range from teaching, leading, organizing, building, fixing, and singing, to accounting, praying, visiting, and mission. The idea is a good one and is one that could benefit most churches. Some of these inventories are relatively helpful, but they raise a problem. They focus more on the functional aspects of ministry, such as one's physical and psychological skills and abilities, but they don't identify anything spiritual such as depth of faith, openness to God, ability to discern God's voice, and other spiritual attributes. The lack of focus on the spiritual is ironic since they are "spiritual" gift inventories. The inventories take something (a spiritual gift) that is given by the Holy Spirit and is unique to each person and then try to categorize the gift in a standardized way by identifying it according to function. Having taken the inventory, a person may be identified as having a "spiritual" gift for finance, teaching, cleaning, or something else, but the inventory doesn't reveal the true calling of the Spirit. Such instruments assume that a person's functional skills are the same as her calling. What happens if a person has functional skills in teaching, but God is calling her to reach out to the poor, a ministry for which she may have no apparent skill? That's what happened with Mother Teresa in the story recounted in chapter 4. If she had taken a spiritual gifts inventory, it probably would have identified her as having a spiritual gift for teaching and organizing, but it would not have disclosed her calling to help the poor. Spiritual gift inventories can be helpful, but we must take care not to assume that functional gifts are the same as spiritual gifts.

By their very nature, spiritual gifts arise out of God's special call to each of us, a call that is also bound to God's call for all churches and the universe. Typically, people become increasingly aware of their gifts as their relationship grows with the God of purpose who calls forth these gifts, with the God of presence who creates the need for them, and with the God of power who cultivates and nurtures them.

In addition, another movement that has grown in recent years has been the missional church movement, which is a great movement because of its focus on helping members of the church become less focused on themselves and more focused on how to serve others. Still, the missional church movement easily slips into functionality. Since the focus is on getting churches to engage in mission, the emphasis can easily shift to doing activities that reach out beyond our church doors rather than on prayer that leads to reaching out. Again, the biblical model is not on just reaching out. It is on immersing ourselves in prayer and responding to the call of the Spirit. Read through the Gospels and the book of Acts. You'll notice that whatever mission Jesus, the disciples, his followers, the apostles, and the early Christians embarked upon emerged out of spiritual experiences first. Mission is a response to guidance discerned in prayer.

The more a church becomes open to God as Power, the more spiritual gifts and missional callings are discerned. They emerge organically in each person and in response to God's purpose for him. I am not suggesting that spiritual gift surveys and programs should never be used. Nor am I suggesting that all mission must be ratified by some sort of "come to Jesus" spiritual experience. What I suggest is that as our churches becomes more open to God's purpose and presence, people will emerge to serve in the church according to their real spiritual gifts and missional callings—gifts and callings that may not show up in surveys or be typical church missions. People will answer God's call to serve in the church in ways that are right for them, not necessarily in the ways we think are right for them. A person identified by a spiritual gifts survey as a teacher may find her ministry in building a website. A lawyer with personnel and financial experience may hear a call to develop spiritual retreats. A mathematics teacher, who would be identified as strong with finances, may become involved in church drama projects. A discerning approach allows the Spirit to work in our midst to raise the right people with the right gifts for the right ministries and missions.

The more we trust in the power of the Holy Spirit, the more it allows us as a church to break free of the functional categorizing that afflicts so many mainline churches and traps them in a cycle of functionalization (described in chapter 2)—a state that can lead eventually to dysfunction and to what I have called *disfunction*. We become much more open to all sorts of potentials and possibilities. We become more creative as we willingly take faith-based risks, allowing the power of the Holy Spirit to work in our midst.

PROVIDENCE

One of the greatest experiences I have had as pastor of Calvin Presbyterian Church is the privilege of witnessing and experiencing God's providence at work in the church. This is perhaps the hardest facet of becoming a blessed church for Christians to accept because of our functional approach and our unspoken expectation that God will remain distant and uninvolved in our congregations. Plainly put, when we have faith and trust in God's power, amazing providences (what some people might call coincidences, but which people of faith know are not coincidental because they come from God—what might be called "God-incidences") take place in our midst.

William Temple, archbishop of Canterbury early in the 20th century, once remarked about these kinds of providences that, "I notice that when I pray coincidences happen. When I stop praying, coincidences stop happening." This is exactly the experience I have had at my church and in my life. God works to bring about coincidences, providences, and miracles. The more prayerful we are, the more events both unexpected and unexplained seem to happen to bring about blessings.

Here's an example of how God as Power can work in our midst when we humbly pray and expect God to work. Walt Kallestad, senior pastor of Community Church of Joy in Glendale, Arizona, experienced this providence in his church. Community Church of Joy was, at one point in the early 1980s, a 200-member church in a suburban, blue-collar area of Phoenix. Today it is one of the largest Lutheran churches in America, with more than 10,000 members. As the congregation slowly grew, its members seriously sought God's will in prayer. What they discovered was a call to move the church farther out into a developing area of

Glendale where they could build a church complex on more than 150 acres. They prayed for God to show them where to go. Eventually they found a tract of land that seemed to be exactly what God wanted. They had little or no money. But they had their prayers.

They prayed for God to reveal the property God had chosen for them, and soon they found a perfect spot. But would the people sell? They initially focused on one farm of five acres that was key to the project. Kallestad drove up the narrow dirt road belonging to the owners and found a run-down trailer. He knocked on the door, and slowly the door was opened. According to Kallestad:

> An elderly man dressed in farmers' bib overalls stood in the doorway. I introduced myself and explained that I was the pastor of Community Church of Joy. I explained that many at the church were praying about his orchard, wondering if God would provide a way for us to buy it and build a new center for mission with a worship center, a Christian school, a seniors' center, a place for youth, and much more.
>
> The old gentleman grabbed my arm and pulled me in. He told me his name was Scotty and asked me to follow him to the kitchen table where his wife, Ruthie, was sitting. As I entered the kitchen Scotty said, "Reverend, please tell my wife what you just told me."
>
> So I told Ruthie about our dream of purchasing the land in order to build a new center for ministry. Ruthie started to cry. I noticed Scotty was crying, too, large tears running down his grizzled face.
>
> Trying to regain composure, Scotty eagerly said, "Reverend, my wife Ruthie and I moved to this land forty years ago. Five acres of these orchards belong to us. Nearly every day for the last forty years we walked around our orchard holding hands and praying that one day there would be a great church built here.
>
> I lost my composure and joined my tears to theirs. It was one of those holy moments when you sense the mysterious moving of God's spirit.[6]

Afterward God's providence continued to work. Even though they had an agreement to buy more than 150 acres, they still had to finance the purchase. They secured a bank loan of $9 million but were told that they still had to raise about $3 million on their own. As the time drew closer for them to produce their part of the deal, they were $2 million short. Kallestad describes what happened next:

One day as Community Church of Joy's leaders were in my office talking and praying about that seemingly insurmountable goal of $2 million, the telephone rang. It was a trust officer from a local bank, calling to inform me that a 102-year-old client of the bank's had recently died and left a bequest for Joy in her will. He paused for effect and then told me that this woman was a devout Catholic and had never been to Community Church of Joy. Another pause, and he went on to explain that although she had never worshiped at Joy, she had heard stories about what we were doing for the children. The needs of the children, it seems, were a special passion of hers. Believing that God was working through our church to meet our needs, Gladys Felve left over $2 million for the mission purposes of Joy![7]

This is the kind of thing that happens when we are open to the power of the Holy Spirit working in our churches. I have experienced many similar occurrences in my own church, although not to the extent that the Community Church of Joy did. What I do know is that at Calvin Presbyterian Church, we try to be open to the Holy Spirit in our meetings, worship, and all other aspects of our congregation's life. God responds through all sorts of miracles and providences. Over time, the blessed church becomes a place where these kinds of providential occurrences are accepted, expected, and anticipated. In other words, these kinds of divine coincidences don't surprise people anymore because they happen so often.

God wants our churches to thrive and to be places of deep love, grace, and the power of the Holy Spirit. God wants our churches to succeed, but for that to happen we have to believe it, be open to it, and depend upon it in faith. A man once said to me: "God never sets you up to fail." I've discovered the truth of this promise. When we trust in God and rely on God in faith, believing and acting on that faith no matter what obstacles appear before us, God comes through. Our part is to trust and act on that trust. When we do, God doesn't let us fail.

BECOMING A CHURCH OF POWER

So how does a church set out to become a church of power? It does so by taking three steps that are like turning on a fan: "plug in," "click on," and "bask in the breeze." First, we need to *plug in*. This means that we have to be mindful of connecting with the power of the Holy Spirit through prayer. As pastors, our primary responsibility is to pray. It's amazing, though, how strongly both pastors and laity can resist making prayer a priority. In fact, one pastor told me about a time he was in the sanctuary praying. The church secretary came in and interrupted him, announcing the arrival of a member who was waiting for him. The pastor told her he was praying and couldn't meet with the man for at least 20 minutes. After the pastor had finished praying, the member confronted him in his office, saying, "How dare you keep me waiting while you pray! Your job is to be available to me when I need you, not to be off at leisure praying." It's amazing that people can think prayer is leisure. For me, prayer is hard, but it is also the foundation of everything I do.

Prayer opens us to these kinds of divine coincidences. Obviously, in the life of every church, even in those that are struggling and dying, all sorts of providences are given—family, home, food, health, meaningful work, friends, and more. Still, prayer opens us to more miraculous gifts that go beyond the blessings God bestows on us every day, providences that reveal how wonderful God really is.

Prayer opens the door for Christ, who stands knocking. I know that I can sense a difference in my church between the times when I am more prayerful and the times when I am not. I have a PhD in spiritual formation, I have been trained in all ways of praying, and I am adept at many, but I still struggle with prayer. I struggle to make the time for it. I struggle with distractions when I pray, and with the feeling that I don't know what I am doing. No matter how much training I get or how much expertise I gain, I'm still a novice in prayer. Yet when I pray despite my inadequacies, providences happen, and when I don't, they don't. As a pastor I have to make sure that I set a discipline of prayer in which I try my best to be centered in God and then pray for the church, its members, my family, and myself.

One of the greatest boons to the ministry of Calvin Church was the prayer group we started within the church. The days and times have changed, as have the members, but for more than 20 years, one morning a week, a group of 5 to 11 members have gathered to pray for the church, the staff, the members, and the world. I believe that in many ways they are the hidden heart of the church. This group has kept the church connected with God, and through it the power of the Holy

Spirit has remained strong in the church. I believe that these kinds of prayer groups are as responsible as anyone else for opening us to the power of the Spirit. I also believe that any church that forms a similar group can similarly become more open to the power of the Spirit. If you would like to begin a similar group in your own church, you can find a process in appendix N, "A Guide to Creating a Prayer Group, with Covenant."

While prayer is the way we plug in, we *click on* through faith. Our faith, our surrendering trust in God, turns on God's power much as turning on a lamp in a house fills the room with light. When we turn on a lamp, we trust that the lamp will work. If it doesn't work, we are momentarily befuddled. That's how strong our faith in lamps is. When we have a similar kind of faith in God, then God as Power can flood us with grace and blessing.

It's not enough only to pray. Many churches and Christians pray, but they pray without faith. In other words, they pray, but they are not really trusting that God can work. They pray much as we might wish on a star or read a horoscope. They don't believe something will happen. When we click on, we not only believe that something will happen. We act in faith, *knowing* that something will happen.

The first thing we need to do to "click on" as a church is to act in faith. When we act in faith, we trust that God will do something. We haven't yet seen the results, we've had nothing but a glimpse of a possibility, but still we trust. To trust, we have to let go of our fears about "what if": What if God doesn't come through? What if this idea is just our own? What if we trust and nothing happens? Instead, we trust and allow the power of God to begin to work. The distinction that separates people like George Müller, Rick Warren, and Walt Kallestad from most of us is that they had a solid, if not audacious, faith that God would act despite the obstacles. God does amazing things for those with faith. As Jesus said, "Truly I tell you, if you have faith and do not doubt, not only will you do what has been done to the fig tree, but even if you say to this mountain, 'Be lifted up and thrown into the sea,' it will be done. Whatever you ask for in prayer with faith, you will receive" (Matt. 21:21–22).

When I refer to amazing things, I'm not necessarily referring to numerical growth. Some churches won't grow numerically, no matter how blessed they are, because that isn't their calling. But what does happen is that they experience God's blessings in other ways, such as creative mission, a loving environment, or a transforming impact on the surrounding community. We also need to be aware that having a strong faith and trust in God's power does not necessarily bring an end to all difficulties in a church or a ministry. If we are engaged in a difficult situation, it is not automatic evidence of a lack of faith, prayer, and discernment. God sometimes calls people of faith to ministries that are full of suffering and difficulty. Most of the people of the Bible were called precisely to such ministries. Not everyone with a strong faith will experience exuberant blessings and growth. Still, the people of faith, prayer, and discernment who are called to these ministries often have the ability to experience God's blessings amid the turmoil by noticing the subtler blessings God gives them to keep them going and to make small inroads.

To many people, the providential response to faith exemplified by Walt Kallestad and Community Church of Joy sounds impossible, but God makes the impossible possible. With God all things are possible: growth in the midst of decline, healing amid disease, stability amid turmoil, and more. To experience these occurrences in our churches, we have to have the courage of faith to trust and "click on" God's power. We have to have the courage to dream God's dreams and to act on them in faith. If we don't, all we will have is the power of God's potential, not God's power making that potential a reality.

Finally, when we have plugged in and clicked on, we can *bask in the breeze*. Whenever we plug in and click on the power of the Holy Spirit, our churches begin to experience God's Spirit blowing through everything we do, much as we sit in front of a fan on a hot day and let it cool us. When we bask in the Spirit's breeze, we become a church that learns to expect God's power to work through everything we do. We cease being anxious. The church becomes a place of joy and laughter as we do our work in faith and power. Decisions lose their ability to stress us because we know that God will make everything okay if we pray and have faith. Because we witness God's power working everywhere in great and small ways, our congregations become places of power, of the Holy Spirit.

POWER AS A PATH TO PURPOSE AND PRESENCE

The more we become blessed churches of God's power, the more we also become blessed churches of purpose and presence. There is a wonderful Trinitarian concept called *perichoresis*. It means in part that even though we can experience and form a relationship with each person of the Trinity, we still experience and relate to the other two persons through that one person of the Trinity. This is possible because even though we experience the persons of the Trinity as distinct, the three are really experiences of one God who can be experienced in three different ways. The three persons of God are three personal relationships we have with God. The Creator and the Holy Spirit are in the presence of Christ. Christ and the Creator are in the power of the Holy Spirit. And the Holy Spirit and Christ are both in the purpose of the Creator. While we can relate with and experience each one separately, we cannot separate them.

What does this truth mean for us on a practical level? It means that the more we try to become a church of power, the more we also become a church of purpose and presence because the purpose and presence that are in the Holy Spirit lead us to do so. It also means that when we are intent on becoming a church of purpose, we also experience God as Presence and Power in our midst; and as we become a church of presence, we will discover purpose and power. Ultimately, in becoming a church of one person of God, we become a church of all three.

In a church of power, the leaders sincerely try to discern God's will for the church, and that church simultaneously becomes a place where people experience Christ and the power of the Holy Spirit, even if only in small ways. The church's pastors and leaders try to reveal to others Christ in their midst. They also end up helping people to discern their own life's purpose and to discover more explicitly God's power working in their lives. As the church's pastors and leaders seek ways to become more open to God's power, they simultaneously create the conditions in which the church and its members become more aware of their purpose and know that Christ is in their midst making possible the realization of that purpose.

REFLECTION QUESTIONS

1. To what extent do you sense that your church is truly open to God's power?
2. To what extent do you sense that your church is willing to experience the power of the Holy Spirit?
3. What events in your church have demonstrated the power of the Holy Spirit to you and other members of the church?
4. What concrete things can you do to open yourself and your church to God's power and to steep the church in a relationship with God as Power, with God the Holy Spirit?
5. What steps can your church, and especially your leadership, take to become more open to the Holy Spirit?

Part III

Leading a Church to Blessedness

Over the years, I've had both the privilege and the burden of helping pastors and their congregations strive to become blessed churches. I've been blessed to share with them this vision for what can happen when we allow God's purpose, presence, and power to transform us and our churches. The challenge is figuring out how to help these churches take the most practical steps toward becoming blessed churches. Having pastored my own church into the possibility, it can be hard to remember what it was like at the beginning and to remember how much courage it took to attempt a different way. When I instituted changes at Calvin Church, there was no real model. And I was convinced that denominational bigwigs would come down and proclaim that we must stop praying, and we must return to the real gospel: *Robert's Rules of Order*. I had to adopt a simple approach: "God, I will do my part if you do your part. I will try to help them open up to you in prayer. I'm asking you to respond and lead this church to experience you."

Most churches and church leaders are so caught up in a functional style of ministry and life that they are scared to change their ways. Ironically, they aren't sure that they can really trust God. They worry that a more prayerful approach will cause members to leave. They are so nervous about making fundamental changes to how they organize and operate as churches that they tend to be really tentative. Even if they envision what taking steps to become a blessed church might mean for them, it's hard for them to figure out the practical things they need to do to lead others to follow this vision. The grand ideas are great, but most church leaders don't know where to begin at a practical level.

Becoming a blessed church begins with leaders—pastoral and laity—who are willing to help their churches move toward new horizons. In the mainline church we've been doing things the same way for so long that adapting to a new era is really difficult—especially when the leaders of many of our churches are older and remember a golden age when being a church was much easier. Back then the culture supported church, and churches grew easily just by following a simple plan that a retired pastor described to me: "We played the normal church music, sang the normal hymns, preached the normal sermons, and visited people. People just came. We didn't have to think about the unchurched, technology, and changing our music and preaching styles." Today's church leaders need to adopt a different approach because what we are doing isn't leading to either health or growth.

Becoming a blessed church requires leaders who genuinely want their congregations to bear the love, grace, and life of Christ in their midst. They yearn for it because they are tired of the kind of life present in far too many churches. The problem is how to get people to want to go there.

Yearning is not enough. Leaders need to take certain practical actions that will lead their churches to blessedness. They need to be "spiritual" leaders who motivate people to seek and do God's will. Evangelical writers Henry and Richard Blackaby describe this as "moving people on to God's agenda."[1] Today's church leaders need to offer healthy leadership, grounded in practices that lead people to spiritual health. They need to be able to help members become comfortable in and competent with discerning God's will. They need to develop programs that help leaders and members grow in spiritual awareness and openness. They need to create processes that overcome natural human resistance to change and that enable both immediate and long-term discernment.

Ultimately, leading a church to blessedness means living and leading in such a way that God's purpose, presence, and power flow through everything. This means adopting an approach to church leadership and life that makes the leaders and the church available to God's guidance. Claude King, who with Henry Blackaby wrote the book *Experiencing*

God, tells how he discovered this alternative way of leadership—a way that relied less on his own efforts and more on God's grace.[2] After graduating from seminary in 1984, King felt the call to become a tent-making pastor who would plant new churches while supporting himself financially through a secular career.

To prepare himself, King studied all the books he could on planting and growing churches. He spent time envisioning what these churches' worship and life would be like. He spent 18 months developing a step-by-step "business" plan. He worked hard, did all the right things, and nothing happened. He was unable to start a new church. No one seemed interested in his plans. He still felt called to plant churches, but his field remained barren. So he took a job as an editor for the Baptist Sunday School Board. The job frustrated him for six years because it confined him to a desk and prevented him from doing what he felt called to do. Meeting Henry Blackaby turned things around for him. Blackaby taught him that God's mission begins in prayer and faith, not in our own plans and deeds. He mentored King to adopt a prayerful, rather than a typically professional, approach.

Eventually King had the opportunity to serve as a volunteer in a local organization devoted to starting new churches. This time he and his colleagues grounded their work in prayer. Instead of spending an inordinate amount of time developing plans, they spent time in prayer, asking God to guide them. They visited local churches and encouraged the members to join them in praying for God to lead them in a mission of starting new churches to reach the unchurched. In contrast to their earlier efforts, they offered no plans or timetables, just an invitation to pray. To their amazement, after three months they had a list of 14 towns or groups that were interested in starting new churches. Where did these people come from? People just started coming up to King, saying that they were interested in a new church, not knowing that he was interested, too.

Afterward, King reflected on the difference between leadership grounded in human plans and actions and those grounded in God:

> God allowed me to follow my *own* plan in Georgia, and I failed
> miserably. He had an important lesson to teach me, and I chose to
> learn the hard way. I found that I could not plan or even dream how
> God might want to do His work. I found that my relationship to God
> was of supreme importance. I learned to love Him more dearly, to

pray more faithfully, to trust Him fully, and to wait on Him with anticipation. When he was ready to use me, He would let me know. Then I would have to make the necessary adjustments and obey Him. Until then, I would watch and pray. His timing and His ways always would be best and right.[3]

Ultimately, leading a church to blessedness begins and ends with leadership that recognizes that it all begins and ends with God. The next three chapters are devoted to helping you discover ways to nurture leadership within your own church. In chapter 6 we will look at the whole topic of discernment—how to do it personally, and how to do it communally. The focus is to build from an individual understanding toward a communal understanding of how to seek and do God's will.

A quick note about chapter 6 and how it relates to the missional church movement that is popular today. You'll notice that I have not included a chapter on mission. The reason is that if you look biblically, prayerfulness always precedes mission. Look at Jesus' life before he embarked on his own mission. He spent a month in the desert in prayer (Mark 4:1–11). Prior to his healings, sermons, and even crucifixion, he went off to pray. The apostles, in the book of Acts, always began their efforts in prayer. In the Old Testament, notice the extent to which Abraham, Joseph, Moses, the judges, Samuel, David, and the prophets are rooted in prayer before action. And then notice what happens when people like Saul, David, and the kings of Israel and Judah act without prayerfulness. Biblically, prayer precedes mission.

My conviction is that when mission is rooted in prayer and discernment, it naturally leads to ministry and mission filled with blessings and providence. Mission that excludes them often leads to frustration and burnout. Looking at Calvin Church, I rarely preach, write, or teach about mission, yet we are one of the most missionally active churches you will find. The reason is that we have one requirement: listen prayerfully for what God is calling you to do, and respond. This has led us to have an incredibly active and diverse mission and ministry in our church—one that has led us to do everything from offering a preschool; creating an after-school program; supporting members going on mission trips to Africa, Central and South America, and throughout the United States; creating a sizable special mission fund to help people in crisis; supporting the local food cupboard and meals for the homeless; hosting Narcotics Anonymous; and so much more. They happen because we seek God's will in prayer first. God then offers us opportunities to serve.

Chapter 7 explores how to create programs, especially small group programs, that nurture prayerfulness and openness to God in a way that spiritually deepens a whole congregation.

Finally, chapter 8 explores why churches resist changes that can actually make them healthier, and then it offers strategies for overcoming the resistance. This includes a strategy for transforming a church by including teams in the transformation process. It offers a strategy that shares the leadership and as a by-product nurtures prayerfulness and discernment.

6

LEADING A CHURCH TO LISTEN

For more than 30 years I have made trying to listen to God central to my life. During my late teens and early 20s I realized that we could hear God if we tried. I was clearly aware of God answering me during my freshman year in college. I was facing a decision. I had planned to go to that college, Roanoke College, for only one semester. I had been told by the admissions office at the University of Virginia, which was my clear first choice for college, that if I received a 2.25 GPA or above for my first semester at another college, I would be accepted by Virginia for the second semester.

By mid-November it was clear that my grades were going to be above their threshold, so what was stopping me from transferring? I was ready to go, but something deeper nudged me to pray over my decision. So I stood on a hillside, looking out at the distant mountains. I thought deeply about what to do and then prayed, asking God whether or not I should transfer. Silence. Then I felt something. I had a sense of deep peace, and it was a peace connected to the realization that I was where God wanted me to be.

Looking back, it's clear that this was the right choice. Certainly I would have received a good education at the University of Virginia, and my life would have turned out fine if I had gone, but I was able to do things at Roanoke that I never would have been able to do at Virginia.

I wanted to eventually be a therapist, and the opportunities to prepare for that career were greater at Roanoke. For instance, I was able to declare my major in psychology at the end of my freshman year rather than waiting until after my junior year at Virginia. This allowed me to take one-third more psychology classes. I volunteered at a local VA hospital, visiting geriatrics with mental disorders. I was a resident assistant of a dormitory, being trained in how to deal with difficult residents. I was able to be a teaching assistant for several classes. I was able to do a six-month internship as a Roanoke County probation officer with youth, which gave me training as a therapist. In addition to counseling preparation, I was also able to play on a national championship lacrosse team, which has influenced my understanding of how to get different people to work and sacrifice together toward a common goal. All of those were opportunities I probably wouldn't have gotten if I had transferred. They helped shape who I am, and I was available to all of them because I took the time to try to listen for what God wanted for me rather than what might make more rational sense if I had reduced my decision to simple pros and cons.

This experience confirmed in me that we can hear God when we pray. That doesn't mean that we'll receive an immediate, or even clear, answer each time. It does mean that God is active in our lives, when we are willing to invite God. I've often said to people that in general, God is a polite God who doesn't typically barge into our lives uninvited. A reason so many people believe that God doesn't exist is that they haven't experienced God. They don't believe that God can be heard, so they never really try to listen. This is true of churches as well as individuals. I heard God because I believed that God could speak to me in that decisive moment. First we have to believe, then we hear.

LISTENING SO WE CAN HEAR

I'm not sure that most mainline churches—their pastors, leaders, and members—believe that God can be heard in decisive moments. I've already explored one of the fundamental problems of the mainline church, which is that we can be so rooted in functional ways of decision making that we don't create room for God's Spirit to speak. Ironically, we'll say that we are scriptural and that we are rooted in the biblical example, but then we don't follow that example. We proclaim ourselves to be founded in the principle of *sola scriptura*, which means "by Scripture alone." We believe in grounding ourselves in Scripture for our theology, our structure, and our beliefs, but then we miss something glaring in the biblical model. We're missing the fact that the biblical model is not of people running to the Bible for answers. It is going off to lonely places to pray so that God can be heard.

Don't get me wrong in what I'm saying. A lot of Christians, when they hear me say something like this, assume I'm diminishing the Bible's authority and suggesting that we shouldn't root ourselves in Scripture. That's *not* what I'm saying. I'm saying that in the Bible few figures run to Scripture for guidance, either because there was no Scripture at the time to follow (i.e., Abraham and Moses) or there was no New Testament to run to, only the Old Testament (i.e., Jesus, Peter, Paul). The biblical model is people going off somewhere lonely and private, or gathering with others, to listen for God in prayer.

It was this lonely listening that led Abraham to leave the comfort of the city to follow God as a nomad. It was lonely listening while in slavery, and then in prison, that led Joseph to be able to interpret dreams and serve the pharaoh as vizier. It was lonely, holy listening that led Moses to hear God not only in the burning bush but on the mountain, in the desert, and in Egypt. The judges went to God in prayer and heard God speak personally and through signs. The prophet Samuel heard God personally as a child and then again through prayerful listening throughout his life. David heard God, and Elijah heard God, as did Elisha, Jeremiah, Isaiah, Ezekiel, Daniel, and all the other prophets. Jesus heard the Spirit speak, and it led him throughout his life as he followed into the desert, on long journeys, up mountains, onto plains, and to his crucifixion. Jesus constantly prayed to the Father before deciding anything. The book of Acts is filled with examples of early Christians and apostles seeking God's guidance in community and in solitude. The biblical example is that God speaks to us when we seek God's guidance.

This doesn't mean that Scripture is unimportant. It is vital. In fact, it teaches us that we can hear God in prayer. The biblical model demonstrates that being rooted in Scripture teaches us how to listen to God, but we have to actively seek God in prayer if we are to hear God.

PURPOSE AND CALL

Hearing God, individually or as a church, means setting a spiritual foundation for discerning God's *call*. We have to create the conditions for discernment by trying to live according to our purpose. If we're to create those conditions, it helps to take a step back to understand the difference between *purpose* and *call*.

The apostle Paul talks about purpose and call in his Letter to the Romans. He says, "We know that all things work together for good for those who love God, who are *called* according to his *purpose*" (8:28—emphasis mine). Every person, every church, every group, and every living entity has a purpose and a call, or more accurately, a purposeful life filled with calls. God has endowed everything with a purpose. I'm not just talking about spiritual things here. God endows everything with a purpose that is their reason for being.

Our purpose is so deep it's manifested genetically through our DNA. Think about the activities and things you naturally gravitate toward. Did you grow up as an athlete, or did you grow up as someone who liked intellectual pursuits? If you liked intellectual pursuits and are a klutz athletically, how would you respond if I told you that your problem was that you never worked hard enough on sports? If you had only applied yourself and practiced harder, you could have been a great athlete, right? Wrong. You know that it wouldn't have mattered how much you practiced, you would still be a klutz. The reason is that you weren't genetically endowed to be an athlete. It wasn't part of your purpose. How we are built is part of our purpose.

Where we grow up influences our purpose, as does our family, our ethnicity, our economic status, our cultural identity, and so much more. Everything about us shapes our sense of purpose. This is not only true for humans, this is true for trees and flowers and plants. Their genetic packaging determines how they will grow, but so does their climate zone, their soil, where they are planted, and so much more. Every congregation also has a purpose. I already gave an example of a church recovering its purpose in chapter 3 when I told the story of the church that was led to discern God's call for them—whether to close their doors or try to keep them open—and then heard God calling them to start a new church development. They never answered the primary question of whether or not to close their doors but instead sensed a call to start a new, separate church somewhere else. Afterwards, when a member studied the history of their church, she found that this church had been a frontier church early in the 1800s and had been responsible for starting over 20 Presbyterian churches in their region. By spending time in discernment, they had recovered their original purpose to be a church that starts new churches.

So what is our purpose? Our purpose is to live out our purpose. Doesn't that make everything clear? No? It shouldn't. We can never quite figure out cognitively what our purpose is. It's too deep. It's too wrapped up in our genetics, our family origins, our ethnicity and cultural identity, our educational level, our aptitudes and capabilities, and so many other attributes difficult to ascertain. So how do we live out our purpose if we don't really know what our purpose is? That's the struggle of living out our purpose, whether as a person or a church. We can't describe it, we can't define it, but we generally know whether or not we are living out our purpose in life.

How do we tell if we are living out our purpose? We gain awareness of it as we respond to God's call—or, more accurately, the accumulation of God's calls over the years. It takes experience. Part of what Scripture, and especially the Christian spiritual tradition, teaches is that God constantly calls us. It's not just episodic, such as when a person feels called to ministry or pastors seek a new "call" to a church. Calling is constant. Some calls are major life-changing callings, while others are more minor.

When I reflect on my life, I recognize a number of major callings. I was called to be an athlete. It was part of my genetic makeup and for many years my passion. I was a hockey player, a lacrosse player, a racquetball player, a tennis player. As long as you put something in my hand—something to hit or catch with—I was in my glory. Playing sports helped shape me. I was especially attracted to team sports, and that shaped me in so many ways, such as learning to work cooperatively with others, to sacrifice my ego for the team, and to take criticism without being crushed by it.

I wasn't called to be solely an athlete. I was also called to be a counselor. From the age of 15 I had a passion for studying psychology. As a teen I read every book on psychology I could get my hands on, even if most of it went over my head. I was a psychology major in college, received a master's degree in counseling, and worked for a number of years as a therapist with teens, adults, couples, families, groups, and more. I also was called to be a pastor (despite my massive complaining and resistance). I was called to study spirituality intensively for my PhD. I was called to become a writer, a teacher, a spiritual director, and a mentor. I was called to be a husband, a father, and a friend. All of these callings came together to help me better recognize my purpose in life. God was calling me to every one, but at the same time, they were callings in consonance with my deeper purpose. As a result, I've become much more aware of what my purpose is. And I'm much clearer about when I'm living according to my purpose and when I'm not.

How has responding to all of these callings helped me understand my purpose? It's still difficult to succinctly articulate my purpose since purpose is ascertained more intuitively than cognitively. What I can say is that I now know that my purpose is to help people live a more consonant life in greater openness to God and in partnership and community with others. My passion is helping people to come together in ways that help them build more meaningful, balanced, and healthy lives relationally, physically, mentally, and spiritually.

As stated above, it's not only people who have purpose. Churches do, too. Yet it's only as churches respond to God's call that they recover their purpose. I realized a number of years after coming to Calvin Presbyterian Church that I had helped it recover a sense of its original purpose. Calvin Church was started in 1845 in an area dominated by people of German descent. Religiously there were Lutherans, Harmonites (a sect of Lutherans following an end-times preacher named George Rapp), Mennonites, and German Reformed. People of Scottish and English descent were misfits in this heavily German area where people still spoke German. Calvin Church started as a place for these misfits.

When I came to Calvin Church, I focused on our listening for God's calling, and it has led us to attract a different set of modern misfits. Our immediate region ranges from heavily conservative evangelical to fundamentalist, and we've attracted people who felt as though they had no place in these churches. Some simply thought differently and resisted the strong theological dogmas of these groups. Others had grown up in these kinds of churches and had felt judged. Others simply saw themselves as "spiritual but not religious" and dismissed these other churches as being "religious but not spiritual." They found a home in our church because we've been a church that reaches out to people who don't feel like they fit into the typical Christian culture.

To sum it all up, the more we respond to God's call, the more we live according to our purpose. The glitch is that we've all been given a precious gift, which is the freedom to choose. It's not a total freedom. I don't have the freedom to suddenly become Chinese. I don't have the freedom to jettison my upbringing. I don't have the freedom to completely change who I am. But I do have the freedom in any moment to choose whether or not to live according to God's purpose or to forge my own purpose. I am free to reject what God has created me to be by seeking a different kind of life. I did that for a while. In my early 20s, after burning out while working as a therapist with teens in a psychiatric hospital, I decided that I would no longer care about others. I was going to seek a career focused on myself. I was going to make money, become successful, and not have to worry about the welfare of others. It didn't last long. I was miserable. My purpose involved caring, and a life of not caring caused me to become lost for a while.

In fact, many, many people who forge their own path end up being miserable. Not all, but a tremendous number do. In my vocation I meet these kinds of people all the time in counseling, among addicts, among the generally angry and cynical, and among the chronically shallow. Their lives never seem to give them deep satisfaction.

So once we try to forge our own purpose, does that mean that God no longer calls? God always calls. The question is whether we listen. Many people who have forged their own paths do listen to God, and it leads them to quite dramatic experiences as they snap back to their original purpose. We know these experiences. We call them "conversion" experiences or "born-again" experiences. We can hear the dramatic transformation in the stories they tell about their lives: "I was spending my life chasing women/men, spending my evenings drinking or taking drugs, and living a miserable life. Then something happened. I realized that there was more to life than satisfying my urges and seeking pleasure. God wanted me to live a different kind of life."

What I find interesting about people who have had these experiences is that God often uses what they've learned while forging their own path to actually fulfill God's original purpose. In other words, they are able to use the experiences they had while following their own path to help others who have gone astray. This is the wayward youth who becomes a youth director, the alcoholic who becomes an AA sponsor or drug and alcohol therapist, the former corporate millionaire who starts Habitat for Humanity (Millard Fuller), or the formerly self-focused engineer who now runs missions to build filtered wells for African villages.

I believe that many, many of our modern churches have forged their own paths for too long. I believe that this is a primary reason so many congregations struggle. They were originally started with a strong purpose to reach out to the people of their community, whether they were farmers, immigrants, or people moving into new suburbs and developments. Over time they stopped being other-focused and became self-focused. They no longer wondered what they were called to do and started doing what they'd always done. Their focus became more on how to make their members happy while ignoring the need to be a church for others. The way for these churches to recover their purpose is to once again seek their call, which leads them back to their purpose. That takes courage, and too few modern mainline churches have the courage to ask together what God is calling them to do. So even if they do believe God can be heard, they don't generally feel comfortable listening prayerfully with others.

THE CULT OF INDIVIDUALISM THAT KILLS DISCERNMENT

For good and for bad, modern North Americans are committed to the cult of individualism. We have become so individualistic as a people that we suspect anything that reeks too much of community. For example, look at our suspicion of institutions. People complain about government and religion, thinking that all institutions are bad. They say that they don't like organized or institutional religion. They say that they are "spiritual, not religious," suggesting that the real problem today is the plethora of religious institutions. They suspect institutions because they believe they breed bureaucracies that stifle initiative and force conformity—all considered to be evils in today's world.

They have a valid argument. Many of the problems the mainline church faces are connected to our seeming love of institutional religion and bureaucracy. We love our traditions, rituals, and rites as well as our organizations and meetings. That doesn't mean we really do, but any-time we create a community, some sort of institutional rules have to be implemented. And in many ways our institutional ways can be mill-stones around our necks, inhibiting creativity, risk taking, and a willing-ness to courageously seek God's calling.

Churches are no different from any other organization. Over time all organizations create some sort of institutionalized structure. What's ironic is that these people who eschew organized, institutional religion have little problem with other organized institutions. They send their children to private or public schools, and even when they homeschool, they use curriculum developed by those institutions. They work for, buy products from, and participate in events held by corporate institutions. They watch professional or collegiate sports that are all part of institu-tional leagues. They watch films and plays produced by institutional filmmakers and theater groups. They may complain about institutions, but it's mostly religion and government that seem to be targeted for being institutional.

So they seek spirituality on their own. Ironically, they cobble togeth-er their own spiritual beliefs from an amalgam of beliefs plucked from all the major religions while ignoring one of the key facets of all relig-ions. They create a fusion of different religious approaches and prac-tices, trying to get to the essence of all religions, but what they miss is that all of these religions emphasize community as a primary spiritual necessity. No major religion sees the individual as self-intact, and no religion emphasizes individual discernment over communal discern-ment.

Digging into a short history of discernment in the Christian tradi-tion, it's very plain that discernment was always communal, even in Christian movements that emphasized individual spiritual exploration, such as the Desert Fathers of Scete in Egypt. These third- and fourth-century men (and later women) imitated Jesus' experience of being led by the Spirit into the desert after his baptism (Matt. 4:1–11), and spent days, weeks, months, and sometimes years in solitude in the desert, seeking to transform themselves by grappling with their own nature by trying to turn themselves over completely to God. They were individu-als, but they were always part of a community, returning regularly to share the wisdom they gleaned and mentoring other monks and nuns.

Despite their seeming individualism, they were communal and followed Jesus' example. Jesus created a community of 12 disciples. The early church was passionate about creating more and more communities of faith, and the early apostles virtually always discerned in community. For example, early on in the church, the apostles gathered together to discern who would replace Judas as apostle:

> So one of the men who have accompanied us throughout the time that the Lord Jesus went in and out among us, beginning from the baptism of John until the day when he was taken up from us—one of these must become a witness with us to his resurrection. So they proposed two, Joseph called Barsabbas, who was also known as Justus, and Matthias. Then they prayed and said, "Lord, you know everyone's heart. Show us which one of these two you have chosen to take the place in this ministry and apostleship from which Judas turned aside to go to his own place." And they cast lots for them, and the lot fell on Matthias; and he was added to the eleven apostles. (Acts 1:21–26)

Many people get tripped up on the "casting lots" part of this passage, but casting lots was actually a common practice in the ancient world when trying to decide between two seemingly equal options. It wasn't letting chance decide. It was allowing God to use the lots to decide. The point is that they gathered in a community and discerned together God's will. Later we find a similar kind of communal discernment as they choose Paul to be an apostle:

> Now in the church at Antioch there were prophets and teachers: Barnabas, Simeon who was called Niger, Lucius of Cyrene, Manaen a member of the court of Herod the ruler, and Saul. While they were worshipping the Lord and fasting, the Holy Spirit said, "Set apart for me Barnabas and Saul for the work to which I have called them." Then after fasting and praying they laid their hands on them and sent them off. (Acts 13:1–3)

Again, they were in community as they fasted, prayed, and sought God's will. This same theme of communal discernment has persisted throughout Christian history. Whether we are talking about the early Christian church communities or the early monastic communities, communal discernment has always been a theme. In fact, much of the

Protestant Reformation was focused on setting up intentional communities of faithful people who could read Scripture together in their own language and discern together God's will based on Scripture, which explains our belief that all discernment begins in the Bible.

Unfortunately, in today's environment, even when discernment is a part of church life, it's treated as something private and personal. The whole field of spiritual formation has tended to treat spirituality as personal and private. We haven't done a good job of finding a way to bring spiritual practices into the life of congregations and instead treat these practices as something people learn while on retreat, in a seminary class, or on their own. Spiritual direction, which for thousands of years was a practice done in monasteries for people living in community, now is done mostly one on one.

The impact of this on the modern church is that we don't necessarily see discernment as something central to the life of congregations and communities.

DISCERNMENT AS CENTRAL TO LIFE OF THE CHURCH

Looking at the early church through the lens of the book of Acts, it's clear that prayerful discernment together was an essential part of the church. So why has prayerful discernment been so absent in the modern mainline church? Throughout the years as I've done many seminars and workshops on bringing discernment into the decision making of the church, I've heard a number of explanations for why being prayerful isn't so necessary.

Some have said that God gave us rational minds so that we wouldn't have to run to God all the time for help with decisions. Thus, God gave us our minds, God wants us to use our minds, so when we go to God in prayer for help with decisions, we're diminishing God's creation. Others have said that prayerful discernment is fruitless because God is so busy running the universe that God can't possibly care about the issues of a church. Unfortunately, thinking like that actually goes against the example of Acts, where the apostles and followers constantly sought God's will for things as profound as choosing new apostles and as simple as choosing those to serve meals.

The real problem for many in the mainline tradition isn't that they believe God wants us to use our rational minds more than praying. The real problem is that we've become so uncomfortable with prayer. We don't feel like our words are flowery enough, our knowledge of prayer is great enough, and our confidence in prayer is high enough. How do we listen together for God in prayer when we are so thoroughly uncomfortable with prayer? How do we listen together when we are so individualistic?

Individualism creeps even into our communal discernment. We are so used to voting only our own consciences during church meetings ("All in favor, say 'aye'") that we don't really appreciate how discernment can work in a group. We need a model for group discernment. One of the best models for discernment is embedded in the work of a 19th-century German philosopher named Georg Hegel. Hegel was curious about how new ideas and greater truths are discovered. He recognized that there was a dialectic, a certain pattern of dialoguing about ideas, that leads to new ideas. Many since his time have called this the "Hegelian dialectic."

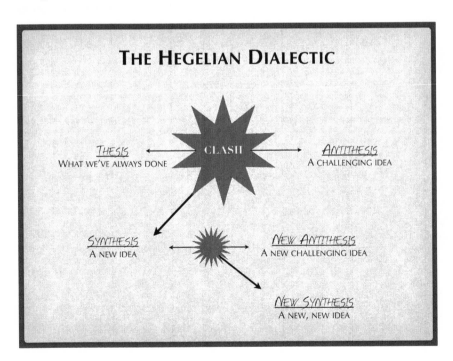

He recognized that over time people embrace a particular fixed understanding of the way things are, which he calls a "thesis." In the realm of churches, a thesis might be that the organ is the standard musical instrument for worship, that sanctuaries should be stripped of all statues and symbols because they promote false idols, or that pastors should always wear robes during worship. Eventually an "antithesis," or challenging idea develops: rock music can be used to worship God, sanctuaries should look more like auditoriums, and pastors should wear clothes that make them more relatable.

The problem is that anytime an antithesis is introduced, it creates a clash or conflict between the two sides. If people can stay in the clash long enough, engaging in dialogue, they can eventually reach a "synthesis," which is a hybrid of the old and new ways of thinking: we should mix traditional and contemporary styles of worship, we should use projected presentation slides to project artistic photos of crosses and inspirational art, and pastors should wear casual clothing. The synthesis is a unique combination of ideas that creates something new. The synthesis I just described is the emergent worship movement, which is a hybrid of traditional and contemporary elements. Thus, discernment seeks God in the old, God in the new, God in the clash, and God in whatever emerges.

This dialectic isn't just something for churches. It is foundational for democracies as new ideas are developed out of the clashing dialogue between competing political parties. It is foundational for technological advancements as old forms of technology are challenged by new ideas and new synthesized possibilities are developed.

This kind of dialectic is essential to communal discernment, and it breaks apart a fallacy that many people have about how God works. It is common for people on opposite sides of theological or liturgical issues to say, "God is either for it or against it! God can't be for both." Looking at the history of church growth demonstrates that this isn't true. For example, God is either a Catholic or a Protestant, God can't be both. Really? Seems that God is in both and that the Protestant Reformation didn't strip the Catholic Church of God. God is either for the organ or against it. Really? Seems that many people encounter God through either traditional or contemporary worship or a hybrid of both. God is either for pastors dressing one way or another, but God can't be for both. Really? Seems that God can be preached regardless of pastors' garb.

What I don't think people recognize is that when we try to discern together, God may actually be speaking to us through the thesis, the antithesis, and the synthesis. God calls us to enter the clash because God is also in the clash. True prayerful discernment means listening to those defending a thesis while paying attention to the possibilities of the antithesis, realizing that perhaps God is calling us to uniquely integrate traditional and contemporary elements. God may not want us to just scrap the old to create the new or to hold onto the old while ignoring the new. God is often in the clash of the ideas, guiding us to develop a synthesized approach that integrates the traditional with the new.

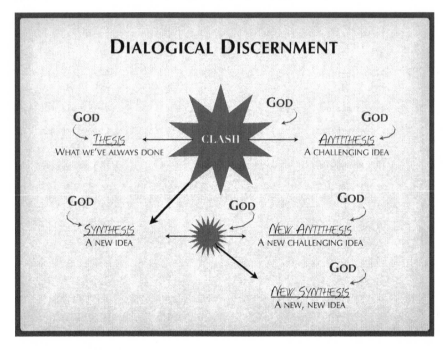

This is a difficult perspective for those who are committed to a black-and-white, this-or-that way of thinking. It means accepting that God's creation is ongoing, so creativity is ongoing. The history of Christianity is not of a church that was created once and then statically remained the same. Christianity has constantly grown and adapted while constantly integrating new ideas. That's true whether we are talking about individual churches, denominations, or the Christian movement as a whole. Why else would God tolerate so many different forms of Christian expression, from Catholic, Protestant, Orthodox, and Coptic to Pentecostal and Evangelical as well as a thousand other forms in between?

Simply put, discerning as a group, community, or church requires being able to listen to how God may be speaking through all points of view. It requires listening to what others say and considering the possibility that God may be speaking through them. It means listening to ourselves and considering the possibility that God may be speaking through all of us. It means listening to all possibilities and considering whether God may be calling us to integrate a synthesis of all these ideas, a synthesis that is unique to our place, time, and situation.

The role of pastors and church leaders is to guide the church to discern. As pastor and moderator of our church board, I take very seriously my role of listening to all sides and helping the board members listen to one another while also being aware of leading them to possible synthesis.

For instance, we had an issue several years ago where we were considering whether to hire a new percussionist in January 2014 for $5,000 per year. A member of our board was adamantly against the hire because she felt it would move us too far away from traditional music. Others felt that this was an important step toward reaching out to younger people. One of the dissenting board member's argument was that $5,000 in one year for a percussionist was too much to add to our budget, especially in light of other increases proposed. The board seemed to be ready to move on despite her reticence.

I stopped them and said, "I think you aren't listening to the possibility that God may be speaking through her. Perhaps she's offering us some wisdom we need to pay attention to. Perhaps it would be better to start the percussionist in June, so we would have only a $2,500 impact on our budget. Also, it may be good to consider the percussionist to be provisional for six months so that we can assess whether this has been a good move for us." In the end, the board unanimously accepted that synthesis and felt as though that was the avenue God was leading us down.

Of course, in some churches pastors aren't moderators of their boards. In those churches moderators are chosen from the board members to serve as a council president. I've mentored and consulted with a number of these pastors as they've expressed their frustration with not being able to moderate the board and institute toward a more discerning approach. With them I've still stressed that they have the authority to train council presidents, to guide the board in adopting a more discerning agenda as found in appendix B, and in guiding the board to be more discerning. I've also stressed that they have the spiritual authority to still listen and summarize points of view and to encourage the board to seek a discerning consensus in listening in one another's ideas to what may be from God. Even if a pastor isn't the moderator, there are many options that these pastors have to train for, plan for, encourage, and guide discernment.

PRINCIPLES OF GROUP DISCERNMENT

Discernment as a board or group requires discerning leadership. It does not happen simply because people want to discern. It especially requires having a leader who guides the process. This is why it is so important to have spiritual leaders on the board rather than merely functional leaders. Functional leaders squash discernment in favor of majority rules. They declare, through their method of board leadership, their preference for shutting God out of the process. They prefer a functional process they already know, despite its shutting God out, than a process they have to learn, even if it genuinely seeks God's will. We're a functional culture, so functionality is always the baseline.

To overcome functionality, leaders need to be aware of certain issues if they are to lead a church in discernment. First, the leader's role *isn't to discern for the group but to set the context for discernment*. While the leader can certainly express her opinion, she can't use her authority to manipulate the board or group to adopt her point of view. True communal discernment requires the expression and consideration of all points of view. The spiritual leader aims for that. There is no one standard technique for cultivating a variety of opinions. Some leaders like to go around a table and ask each member to share his or her opinion. Others, like me, simply allow enough time in a discussion for a free flow of opinions. What matters is that the leader takes seriously that she is the guardian of discerning dialogue and encourages members to share. So the leader has to try her best to let go of her own prideful and egoic need to have her will be done in order to cultivate the listening for God's will.

Second, the leader *helps to clarify the issue*. The leader makes sure that when a recommendation or motion is presented, it is as clearly articulated as possible. I should mention that in our church, we do not start discussions with motions. We start them with recommendations. We allow the dialectical discussions to lead us to listen for what God may be saying in one another. Then as consensus seems to develop, we articulate that into a motion that is then voted upon. This process leads us into the clash of ideas where a synthesis can be discerned. I see my role as helping the person making the recommendation to be as clear as possible, helping him to articulate all the thinking that has gone into it. I make sure that everyone is clear on what is being recommended. I also make sure that everyone is clear on what the eventual motion is to be presented, prayed over, and voted upon.

A key technique for guiding a board through the clash is simply summarizing what people say, especially when what they've said is complicated. Often disagreements occur not because people disagree, but because they don't always understand what people have said. A good moderator will try to succinctly summarize what a person has said, saying something like, "I think what I've heard you say is . . ." Then she makes sure that she has grasped it and articulated it before encouraging responses.

Third, the leader *creates an environment for free exchange of ideas and thoughts*. I've mentioned this a number of times before, and I'm repeating myself here. Yet it's important to stress that the leader is responsible not only for helping everyone share her or his opinion but also to diminish conflict over opinions when they arise. Many issues evoke strong emotions on all sides. So a good leader isn't afraid when people become emotional, but he is able to help them to calm down and re-center once emotions become tense. Generally, if it seems like emotional conflict is arising, I will gently but firmly stop the discussion and say to the board, "We're starting to get a bit hot over this issue. I'd like us to take a minute of silent prayer to regroup and re-center ourselves so that we can listen for God in one another." Then I will give them about a minute or two of silence. Almost always the dialogue is then able to continue with a much more discerning spirit.

Related to this, the spiritual leader works to keep personalities and emotions in check in order to facilitate faith over fear. With so many issues for church boards to consider, especially if a possibility represents a radical change, fear can overcome faith. Many church boards, especially in struggling churches, feel a constant state of survival anxiety. They worry about their church declining and dying, and they fear that anything new might fail and actually accelerate the decline. They begin to give into fear. The good leader helps them return to faith. In fact, this may be the key contribution of a pastor on boards where others moderate. They may not have the authority to call for votes, but they do have the spiritual authority to call members to faithfulness and to act with courage in the face of fear and anxiety.

Finally, the spiritual leader *encourages prayerfulness, especially against functionality*. Every church, every board, and every group will eventually slip into functionality over time. It's inevitable because functionality is the way of the world. Most members are steeped in careers and organizations that have fully adopted functional approaches to decision making. So when in doubt, church leaders will slip back into what they know. Spiritual leaders encourage others to remain open to the possibility of hearing God rather than slipping into a mere human way of making decisions.

THE PROCESS OF DISCERNMENT

Ultimately engaging a church, a board, or even ourselves in a process of discernment is like the process of nurturing a plant to grow. It requires three things: *preparing the ground for growth, selecting and planting seeds*, and *cultivating the growth*.

Starting with the need to *prepare the ground for growth*, it's important to recognize that discernment by individuals, groups, and congregations requires an environment that nurtures discernment. It reminds me of my lawn this summer. Over the course of the past eight years, we have built an addition onto our house, replaced a failing retaining wall, and had to have numerous trees removed. The constant construction vehicles along the side of our house stripped the topsoil off of a significant part of our lawn, leaving behind shale stones and scraggly grass. I've had to have massive amounts of nutrient-rich topsoil placed over that area while running the sprinkler almost every other evening for a month to get new grass to grow. In other words, I had to create a good environment for the grass to grow.

Preparing for discernment is a similar process. We have to prepare the ground for it. Just because we want to discern doesn't mean it automatically happens. As pastors, this means that we have to take courses and workshops on prayer and discernment that help us to understand it, but it also means that we may need to see a spiritual director to guide us. And we have to practice discernment in our personal and professional lives, and not just in the big areas of life. We need to be prayerful in our sermon preparation, asking God to guide us to discern what God wants to reveal to us through Scripture, and then asking prayerfully how God wants us to communicate this to others. We need to be discerning regarding the direction of our ministries, the decisions we make in our personal lives, and so much more. We need to be discerning in making personal decisions unrelated to ministry.

The struggle for modern mainline pastors is that even though we may have taken a few classes on spirituality in seminary, we typically are not in denominations where discernment is part of the lifeblood of our decision making. Most mainline denominations rely on functional methods using the guidance of *Robert's Rules of Order*. Discernment is not our normal practice.

At the same time, we need to prepare our congregations for discernment by teaching them how to discern as members and as groups. This means offering classes on discernment, developing small groups that teach discernment, and preaching about discernment in sermons. It also means training leaders in discernment. One way we do this at Calvin Church, both in our board and all of our committees, is that I have created what we call "Committee Studies" that we distribute to all the committee chairs and to the board each month. Everyone uses the same sheet. It is a one-page sheet with a prayer that everyone says together, a quote from a Christian spiritual writer on a topic related to discernment, and reflection questions. If you would like to use these for your own church, I have created a three-year cycle of studies that can be found in the "resources" section of my website: http://www.ngrahamstandish.org. They are available free to download and use. The authors quoted vary from ancient to modern, from evangelical to progressive, and from Protestant to Catholic and Orthodox.

A second part of discernment is *selecting and planting the seeds*. This means that we have to pay attention to what *may* be God's voice emerging from life around us and to consider where it may be leading. A seed can be a thought, a comment said to us, a feeling, a phrase, a possibility. It can come from reading Scripture or a book, watching a film, watching a television show (although I have my doubts that God speaks much through most reality shows), or having a conversation with a friend. It can be a thought that comes into our head (which can include a remembered passage from the Bible or the verse of a hymn), a Facebook post, a blog, or anything else that God may speak through. Just because we think we hear something doesn't mean it comes from God. We have to take time to consider whether this is good seed or weed seed.

Much of discernment is intuitive, which means it brings together our cognitive thinking, our emotional connection to a possibility, and our spiritual awareness. One of the struggles of discernment is we can't really approach it from only one perspective. For example, discernment isn't like rational analysis, where we simply think about it cognitively. We need to also include an emotional component, where we also "feel" whether something is right or not. At the same time, we can't approach discernment from an emotional perspective alone because emotions alone can mislead us. This is one of the struggles of discernment. It is very easy to passionately want a certain outcome, which can skew our discernment when we confuse our passions with God's voice. So many abuses of religion have occurred over the centuries from people who confused their passionate desire for something with God's call. This confusion has led to religious conflicts between Protestants and Catholics, Muslims and Christians, and within denominations. It has also led to the rise of cults, where a charismatic person has mistaken his or her desires with God's calling.

Each of us also has a deeper part of consciousness that actually connects us with God. Our brains seem to be wired for spiritual awareness.[1] Debates may rage in scientific circles over whether this means that God is simply a neurological concept created by our biological brain structure, or the creator of such a brain structure to house our consciousness, but for our purposes it indicates that we are wired to connect with the divine. So a part of us is always deeply spiritually aware.

Completing the circle, even though discernment requires an emotional and spiritual awareness, there is also a cognitive component. We
need to bring reason into our discernment as a way of making sure we
aren't just deluding ourselves emotionally and spiritually. There are
many cognitive approaches to discernment, but I find the theories of
Adrian van Kaam to be among the best. He says that when discerning, it
helps to always keep in mind four questions—what he calls the four Cs:
Is the possible directive from God *congenial to our purpose*? Is it *compassionate to others*? Do we *have the competence* to do it? Is it *compatible with our situation*?[2]

Beginning with the question "Is it congenial to our purpose?"[3] we
ask whether the possibility is in harmony with our natural and spiritual
inclinations. In other words, if I respond to this possibility or if our
church responds to this possibility, is it true to who we sense we most
deeply are? For instance, if we live in a rural area far away from a city,
does it make sense to try to take part in an inner-city ministry? Probably
not. But there are ministries in our own area that may fit with our
purpose—with who we sense we are. For an inner-city church, homeless ministry may be fully congenial with the church's purpose.

Second, if we do what we sense we're called to do, "will it be compassionate to others?" For most ministries and missions, this will be the
easiest to answer, although there is a caveat. We have to also ask whether it is compassionate to us, too. Will doing this not only be compassionate to those we reach out to but also be compassionate to our families,
our members, and ourselves? For instance, does it require so much
time and effort from one person that it may cause burnout? Will it
cause friction within a family? Will it require more time and energy
than we can handle?

Third, if we follow this call, "do we have the competence?" And if
not, can we gain the competence? Whenever I think of this I think of
Mother Teresa, who was the headmistress of a wealthy private girls'
school in Calcutta when she embarked on her ministry to the poor. She
had competence in educating children but not with reaching out to
poor children on the street. So she worked to gain the competence. She
managed to find a supply of rice and would go out into the street every
day armed with a bag of rice. To every child whom she taught to read
and to write the alphabet using a stick to write in the dirt, she gave a

handful of rice. She may not have had full competence at first, but she had enough that she could build the competence.

Finally, is the calling "compatible with our situation?" In other words, if we do it, is there a high degree of probability that it will work in our particular context? For instance, we may feel like it is congenial to our purpose to teach English as a second language, it may be compassionate, and we may have the competence, but if there is no one within 100 miles to teach it to because we live in an area without immigrants, it's probably not compatible. We have to ask whether it seems like the right fit with our situation—do I have the financial means, does it work with my family life, can the ministry work in our area, and so forth.

Ultimately, if we sense that we are called to do something, it seems to be connected with what we sense of God's will, and it seems to pass the four Cs, we can be pretty sure that we are being called to something. How do we tell? This is what leads us into the third part of discernment: *cultivating growth*. Ultimately, cultivating the growth of our discernment means nurturing faithfully what we've discerned by carefully letting it grow into concrete actions. In other words, we apply what we sense we're called to do in concrete ways.

What we discover is that if what we sense really is from God, things will seem to work out. This is not 100 percent guaranteed, but generally both providential and normal circumstances occur that allow what we've done to work. Even though this is the case, we do need to be careful to make sure we don't confuse responding to a call with procuring certain results. We have to learn to distinguish between our part and God's part. When we discern, we are simply discerning what we are called to do. We are not discerning what will happen as a result of what we are called to do.

For instance, this past year we felt called to nurture and support one of our members to start an after-school program in our church for children between the ages of 12 and 16. It was a wonderful program aimed at an at-risk population of teens who might otherwise be home alone each afternoon—a time when teens are most likely to engage in risky behaviors. The kids who were involved in it made a significant amount of progress under the care and tutoring offered them, and because they were no longer just sitting at home alone for hours on end until their parents came home. Unfortunately, the local school system would not bus children to our location, even with parental permission, which meant that at best we never had more than four students. Meanwhile, after really developing the program in our church, the program was able to start a branch of the program in a nearby school system where the school was completely supportive. They now regularly have 10 students each day, with more interested. From a rational, analytical point of view, the program at our church could be viewed as a failure. From a discerning point of view, it was a great success because it made a difference and eventually worked elsewhere. We focused on what we were called to do and let God create the results.

FINAL THOUGHTS ON DISCERNMENT

Creating a discerning congregation sets the conditions for transforming a congregation, just as it has the power to transform us. When we are willing to genuinely seek God's will and live according to our purpose, as individuals and as a church, it has the ability to completely change the way we live and the way the church lives.

Discernment isn't easy, though. That's why so few churches embrace it. It requires a kind of humility that says to God, "Here I am, Lord." It is willing to put aside what we clearly want in order to discern what we fuzzily and provisionally believe God wants. We walk by faith and not by sight, but we also discover in faith tremendous things taking place because we were willing to take a leap of faith in following a call. It's exactly this kind of discernment that the restructuring of board meetings suggested in chapter 3, and demonstrated by appendix B, accomplishes. It also provides a different way of being a church, a way that is more in consonance with the original church.

7

LEADING A CHURCH TO DEEPEN

Becoming a blessed church isn't just a matter of being a church that listens for God's call and follows faithfully. It's also about being a church that promotes a deeper spiritual life among members. Unfortunately, a great part of the modern mainline church has ignored much of the Christian spiritual tradition.

I became aware of how much spirituality is ignored when I first entered seminary. The main reason I decided to go to seminary was to receive training in spirituality so that I would know how to deal with spiritual issues that often arise in the course of counseling. I was motivated by experiences like the one I mentioned at the beginning of this book, when a young man I was counseling saw Jesus in the window, which led to a healing experience for him.

In my counseling training, I had been taught to ignore spiritual issues, but I didn't want to ignore them. So I thought that getting my master of divinity while simultaneously working on my master in social work would prepare me to address spiritual issues. It didn't.

I don't want to lambast seminary training in general because most seminaries have very good programs and do a good job of teaching biblical understanding, pastoral care, and Christian theology. The problem is that if we listen to the people who have left the church but who haven't opted for the atheist or agnostic route, they often proclaim themselves to be "spiritual but not religious." They are pointing out that we've lost our connection with a deep Christian spirituality in the modern mainline church and that we no longer dip into our rich spiritual,

mystical tradition. Mainline Protestants only vaguely know the names of
great spiritual writers from our history: Athanasius, the Desert Fathers,
Dorotheus of Gaza, Benedict of Nursia, Guigo II, Meister Eckhart,
Hildegard of Bingen, Julian of Norwich, Catherine of Genoa, Thomas à
Kempis, Jean-Pierre de Caussade, Brother Lawrence, Thomas Kelly,
Thomas Merton, C. S. Lewis, Catherine Marshall, Evelyn Underhill,
Teresa of Avila, Henri Nouwen, Elder Thaddeus of Vitovnica, Father
Arseny, Richard Foster, and so many, many more.

These are all writers who aren't so much interested in figuring out
the nature of God or of life but rather in understanding how we experience God, hear God, allow ourselves to be guided by God, and serve
God throughout all of life. In other words, they've tried to discover and
teach how to live by the first part of the Great Commandment: "Love
the Lord your God with all your heart, and with all your soul, and with
all your strength, and with all your mind" (Luke 10:27). The modern
mainline church has been much more focused on theological thinking,
trying to articulate a theology of orthodoxy, social justice, morality, ethics, and other topics that have less to do with an encounter with God
and more to do with an understanding of God. In short, our approach
has emphasized thinking *about* God more than connecting *with* God.

This emphasis on a more speculative theology is a relatively recent
phenomenon that grew out of the Enlightenment. Prior to the 18th
century, theology was rooted as much in the experience of God as it was
in trying to understand the nature of God. Prior to the Enlightenment,
great theologians rooted their theology in their experiences of God and
the divine, whether it was through worship, prayer, Scripture, or art.
They then tried to develop a theology based on those experiences. The
focus wasn't so much on understanding what was going on in heaven. It
was more on understanding how to lead people to an experience of God
in this world. That's changed. Through the Enlightenment, the emphasis on rational, analytical thinking has disconnected much of our theology from a foundation in spirituality.

A great example of this is found in how we talk about the Trinity.
When asked to describe the Trinity, many Christians use the metaphor
of water, with it being one substance found in three states: ice, steam,
and liquid. They compare the Trinity to that, where we find one person
of God in three persons. Like water as ice, God is incarnated physically
as Christ. Like water as liquid, which is the basic source of all life, God

is the source of life as Father. Like water as steam, God is invisible and pervasive as Spirit. That's a great description, but it is a description stripped of all spirituality. There's no experience in the explanation. It tells us nothing about our relationship with the Trinity, nothing about how to experience the Trinity, nor how to form a relationship with God as Trinity.

The Trinity is very much a spiritual concept telling us how we experience God. We experience and relate to God much like a father, the ideal parent, who gave us life, who always loves us, and who does what's best for us. We experience and relate with God as Christ, who is the incarnation of God in the man, Jesus, and who is also experienced in all of creation. In other words, we experience Christ in nature, in others, and in ourselves (John 1:1–3). We experience and relate with God as Spirit, who is everywhere all at once—"who is above all and through all and in all" (Eph. 4:6). This understanding of the Trinity leads to a spiritual theology of God, not just theological speculation about the nature of God.

We've lost touch with the spiritual side of Christian faith because we are unfamiliar with the mystical writings of Christianity. I wasn't exposed to many of the great spiritual writers in seminary. I discovered them first on my own and then through my doctoral studies. I once said to someone that seminary was like being given an overabundance of food with no water to wash it down. It was nourishing, but I couldn't digest it because it was too dry and too much to chew. My exposure to the great spiritual writers gave me living water that allowed me to finally digest everything else I had learned, while allowing me to finally be fully nourished by the theological food I had been given years before.

Reading the works of these mystics helped me recognize that church could be done a different way, a way that was in keeping with the more spiritual focus of the original churches. These writers helped me understand that if churches aren't focused on helping people to experience God, they just become a religious institution. The Christian mystics were focused on leading people to a tangible, transformative encounter with the Trinitarian God. And it is these writers who've helped me realize that leading people to an encounter with and experience of God has to be our main mission.

GROUNDING IN A SPIRITUAL SMALL GROUP MINISTRY

As a result of the evangelical movement, many modern churches have recovered the discipleship movement exemplified by the original disciples. Most people don't know what the word "disciple" means. It is grounded in the Latin word *discipuli*, which means "student." Jesus' disciples were fundamentally students while they were with Jesus. After his resurrection they became apostles, which is a very different word. It comes out of the Greek word ἀπόστολος, or *apostolos*, which means "sent one" or "messenger." While they were with Jesus, their focus was on learning and being trained to eventually spread the Gospel. They weren't just learning theology. They were learning to connect with the Father, and it's this spiritual rootedness that was the foundation for their later apostolic missions.

Having read the mystical writings of Christian history, I developed a belief that our church could create a small group, discipleship ministry focused on deepening people spiritually. I looked at many of the evangelical churches and saw that while they took seriously the call to "make disciples of all the nations" (Matt. 28:19), often the materials they used were targeting Christians only at the most basic, seeker level. In other words, most of the materials they used were written for new Christians, not those who were Christian and were looking to grow deeper. I realized that creating a small group program based on exposing people to great Christian spiritual writers could really help a church become religious *and* spiritual.

Thus, at Calvin Church most of our small group programs are based on reading the works of Christian mystics. This poses a bit of difficulty because these mystics cover a 2,000-year history, and they don't tend to write in a modern style. Finding good translations for many of the works is really a key task, as is deciding which books are useful and which aren't because the language and the writing style are too complex and archaic (for a list of suggested books, go to appendix O, "Bibliography of Writers in Spirituality and Spiritual Theology").

Ultimately, the focus of grounding a small group program in the writings of Christian mystics is to expose people to ideas reaching beyond our own day and age. The modern church movement, whether we're talking about evangelicals or the mainline church, has a tendency to expose people to a very limited range of theological and spiritual thinking. For modern evangelicals, that means reading Bible studies, books, and curriculum written from a mostly conservative 20th- and 21st-century perspective. For modern mainliners, that means reading Bible studies, books, and curriculum from a modern moderate to progressive perspective. While each movement may also include the writings of a founding thinker (Martin Luther, John Calvin, Menno Simons, John Wesley, George Fox, or others), the range of thinking remains somewhat narrow spiritually.

Exposing members to the writings of Christian mystics means getting them to read the works of writers from the *ancient period* (the founding of Christianity roughly until the Renaissance), the *classical period* (the Renaissance through the Protestant Reformation), the *modern period* (roughly from the time of the Reformation to the early 20th century), and the *contemporary period* (from the beginning of the 20th century until now). It also means exposing people to different Christian traditions. We all tend to stay in our own comfort zone theologically and spiritually, staying with materials that are contemporary and familiar to our own tradition. Reading the mystics helps us integrate a much greater spiritual perspective.

At Calvin Church we will choose contemporary resources that reflect our own tradition, but we also want people to be formed by the collective wisdom of writers from many eras and ages.

WHAT IS THE PURPOSE OF A SMALL GROUP?

Small group ministries have become very popular in churches across the country. As I noted earlier, they have become especially popular in the large evangelical megachurch movement that has been a growing force in Christianity. Many of these large churches actually began as small groups that grew into worshiping churches. They understood something that has taken more mainstream denominational churches years to accept, which is that many in today's population feel adrift and alone and are seeking answers to life's questions. Worship services provide an opportunity to grow spiritually, but they don't necessarily allow people to engage in discussions and form relationships that are also part of the Christian experience. Small groups take what is begun in worship and then offer people weekly opportunities to build their faith.

This focus on small groups isn't new. Jesus' disciples were a small group. The early monastic movement was a movement of bringing a small number of adherents together to create small group communities. Martin Luther and John Calvin encouraged families and small groups of Christians to read the Bible together. John Wesley, the founder of the Methodist movement, used a "method" of Christian growth built on small groups.

Small groups ultimately are part of a church's overall adult education program, offering a more intensive program of growth than typical Sunday adult education classes. Sunday morning classes and courses help people to understand the life of faith and the life of the church better, but they are designed mostly to help people grow intellectually. Small groups do much more. They help people grow in mind, heart, and soul by engaging people at deeper levels. The discussions help people change their lives as they listen to the Spirit's voice and guidance in one another.

Today, small groups range from those that meet to do simple Bible studies to groups that meet to discuss the most complex theological concepts. The program at Calvin Church is designed to move back and forth between a study and discussion of the Bible and a more in-depth exploration of the teachings of great Christian mystics and modern spiritual writers.

ONLOOKERS, FOLLOWERS, DISCIPLES, AND APOSTLES

What we offer in our education program, which includes small groups, is what we call a "program in adult spiritual formation." While that's a complex term, it basically means that our program aims to help adults grow "spiritually" by helping them "form" a life that is always becoming more mature. In short, we want to help people form a healthy life psychologically, relationally, and spiritually. Ultimately our program is based on trying to stretch people beyond their comfort zone so that they can be stretched to grow.

A number of years ago we noticed that there are basically four kinds of people who are attracted to the life of any church. We've called them *onlookers*, *followers*, *disciples*, and *apostles*. We loosely based these types on whom we imagined gathered to listen to Jesus as he preached the Sermon on the Mount. We based our insights on how the Monty Python comedy team portrayed the Sermon on the Mount in their film *Life of Brian.*[1] In the film, the camera rests on Jesus as an intimate crowd of 30 or so listen intently. It then pans out, letting us see other small groups gathered at different distances, listening intently, but not wanting to get too close. The camera finally rests on a group about 100 yards away. They are listening, but they mishear the words. So instead of hearing "blessed are the peacemakers," they hear "blessed are the cheese makers." They then have a heated debate over why Jesus would bless the cheese makers and not others.

We realized that these people represented three of the four kinds of people who are part of a church: *onlookers* (what are usually called "seekers" in evangelical churches), *followers*, and *disciples*. Typically, onlookers avoid being involved in a church, other than attending worship every once in a while. They are definitely reluctant to become part of small groups. Followers and disciples are more committed, although their levels of participation are not the same. We try to create group and educational experiences that attract onlookers, followers, and disciples and help them to grow deeper so that onlookers become followers, followers become disciples, and eventually disciples become *apostles* (a fourth category of Christian explained below). So what do the different categories mean?

An *onlooker* is a person who is attracted to a church but is reluctant to commit. In *Life of Brian*, these are the people standing far away, debating the blessing of the cheese makers. Jesus was constantly surrounded by onlookers. They were the ones who showed up to hear Jesus preach, who appreciated what he said, and who then went home, saying, "I like what he said about love. I'm not sure I agree with everything he said, but I liked it. I'll have to hear him again if he comes back to town." They heard Jesus, but what they heard didn't necessarily change them.

Church onlookers aren't invested enough to really embrace the Christian spiritual message, but they periodically like to hear the message. They may like the church, the members, the worship services, the preaching, and the music, but they don't make the connection between a commitment to the church's life and the spiritual quality of their own lives. They'll call themselves Christian, but they don't really believe that regular church attendance is essential to living a good, loving, and spiritual life. Faith for them is a concept but not a life.

Creating small group experiences for these kinds of people is extremely difficult. So the focus for us is to try to create worship, a church environment, and periodic events (concerts, plays, guest speakers, and short-term classes) that might encourage them to want more.

Many of these onlookers recognize the need for something more in life. Either turmoil in their lives or changes they are going through lead them to periodically seek something spiritual to make their lives better. Onlookers are a step beyond those who show up only for Christmas and Easter. Those really aren't onlookers—they're "tagalongs." They show up simply because it's what someone does on these holidays. Tagalongs are really tough to reach because they see worship as no more (maybe even less) important than Thanksgiving dinner, New Year's Eve, Memorial Day picnics, and the Fourth of July (at least if we're talking about American ritualists). Onlookers periodically do recognize that something is missing in their lives, so they will seek answers. The trouble is that they often look like hummingbirds going from flower to flower. They look for answers to their seeking questions anywhere that looks fruitful, seeking answers in worship, in a series of self-help books, or in anything else that promises to fill the gap.

Like people suffering in the desert, onlookers can confuse mirages for true spiritual water. They are most likely to either become enamored of New Age ideas or fall for black-and-white, simplistic, legalistic Christian ideas. They are seeking answers to their problems, making them easy prey for anything that makes sense, even if it is false. Jesus was surrounded by people like this who either flirted with the surrounding religions of the time or were attracted to the rigid Jewish system of the time. They were people like the rich lawyer who walked away disappointed when Jesus told him to sell all and follow him (Luke 18:18–30). When seekers are surrounded by healthy Christians who introduce them to a healthier faith and practice, they can be stretched to become followers who take spiritual growth, prayer, and service more seriously.

A *follower* is willing to commit to Christ and to placing Christian faith at the center of her or his life. Followers are generally committed to serving God in the church. They attend worship regularly, pray on a regular basis, try to love others as best they can, and want to learn more so that they can grow in their faith. They believe that they can be God's hands and feet in the world. In Jesus' time, these were the folks whom Jesus sent out to teach and heal. They were not as committed as the disciples, but they served Christ. Luke's gospel says, "After this the Lord appointed seventy others and sent them on ahead of him in pairs to every town and place where he himself intended to go. He said to them, 'The harvest is plentiful, but the laborers are few; therefore ask the Lord of the harvest to send out laborers into his harvest'" (Luke 10:1–2). They had regular jobs and families, but they still committed a lot of time to serving Jesus in his ministry. Many of the most committed church leaders and workers would be considered followers. Over time, followers can become disciples if they are willing to grow. Small group programs, classes, and retreats give these people the opportunity to grow deeper as disciples.

A *disciple* is a Christian who has committed her or his life to deep learning about God and the Christian life and to taking an extra step that says, "I will put Christ first in everything." In the beginning there were only 12 disciples around Jesus, but the circle grew after Jesus ascended to heaven and the apostles (who had been disciples) took on disciples around them. These were the people who were willing to change everything about their lives in order to grow deeper in their knowledge and their openness to the Spirit. Ultimately, all of us are called to be disciples, but not all of us say "yes" to that call. Our small group program is geared to lead people to this kind of commitment in the end, although it certainly is not a requirement at our church. We don't actually put particular people into these categories. We just shape our programs around encouraging people to enter these phases of faith. So we intentionally expose people to deeper Christian thinkers in order to stretch them spiritually, just as Jesus constantly stretched his disciples.

Not all people will move from follower to disciple, but many do. They not only become staples in different small groups, every retreat, and every class, but sometimes they go on to seek more education at the seminary level or through parachurch organizations that aim to stretch people to grow deeper. These are people who are hungry spiritually and know it. Over time, they can grow into apostles.

The ultimate goal for any Christian is to become something like an *apostle*. I don't want to sound too grandiose. I'm not thinking of the term "apostle" in the way many denominations do, which is that the apostles were the founders of the church. I am sticking more closely to the definition I shared earlier: "sent ones." They have deepened. They have learned. Now they have a passion to serve. Some become pastors. Some go on mission trips or become missionaries. Some have a ministry of praying for others. Others have their own unique ministries that they feel called to.

The disciples eventually became apostles. To be an apostle literally means to be sent out by God to change lives and the world. It means being a spiritually deep person of commitment, devotion, love, and service. Not all can become apostles, for not all will be willing to make that level of commitment. No program can teach a person to become an apostle. Only God can call apostles. Our hope, though, is that over time people involved in our small group program will sense that apostolic calling to be God's "sent one."

CREATING A SPIRITUALLY GROUNDED SMALL GROUP PROGRAM

Our small group program at Calvin Church is designed to lead people to grow from whomever they are and from whatever level of faith they have to a deeper level of maturity. We recognize that most group participants are at the follower and disciple levels of faith and commitment. So when we start a group, we begin at a follower level and over time encourage the group members to dig deeper into a life of faith. The initial resources might be more general, meaning that we would start with a Bible study or a spiritual book chosen because it is easier to understand. An example of this might be Richard Foster's *Celebration of Discipline*,[2] which explores different kinds of spiritual disciplines. Over time we encourage them to use books and resources that stretch their understanding of the spiritual life. This means stretching back into history to books by great mystics with translations that can be more readily understood by modern readers. Over time we will also expose them to great spiritual writings from other Christian traditions so that they come to know that there isn't just one Christian spiritual approach to God, despite our tendency to tribally defend our own traditions. Eventually we introduce members to difficult topics such as suffering, miracles, the faith journey, growing in spiritual maturity, understanding the nature of God, justice, compassion, the nature of following Christ, and a whole variety of topics that are part of the struggle of the spiritual journey.

Our small groups typically use books as the basis of their discussion. We gravitate more toward books that have stood the test of time rather than toward popular Christian books. Choosing noncontemporary books can be a difficult track to take because it means choosing materials that stretch people who are resistant to stretching spiritually. At times we have created groups that use more popular Christian and spiritual writings as their foundations, but what we've noticed is that they rarely last longer than a year or two. When the material they choose doesn't stretch them, the group slowly dies. The slow death isn't apparent because initially it looks like people are just busy elsewhere. What's clear is that they no longer make time for the group. Other things get in the way. And then they stop coming as the group atrophies. Any group will slowly die unless people experience some sort of week-to-week, month-to-month growth. If there's no stretching, what makes it any different from a gathering with friends?

Over the years we've had a number of people want to start a small group, but who resisted this deeper spiritual growth. None still exist, and some that we have now are shrinking. Meanwhile, the groups we've had that have met the longest (between 15 and 18 years) are those that have emphasized constant spiritual growth. These are also the groups whose members have had the biggest impact on our church and its overall spiritual depth.

THE PRACTICE AND DISCIPLINE OF SPIRITUAL READING

Growth through a small group takes place as people engage in three disciplines that open them to the voice of the Holy Spirit: *spiritually reading the material, turning the reading into prayer*, and *discussing it with others*. Our small group practice is grounded in the ancient practice of *spiritual reading*. As I already noted, the reading materials are selected to explore topics that lead members to grow spiritually. Reading the materials spiritually and prayerfully teaches members to hear the voice of the Holy Spirit speaking to them through their readings. In essence we've been trained in *informative* reading, not *formative* reading. When we read formatively, we read to be formed, transformed, and reformed by God. When we read informatively, we read to get information that will help us with a task, project, or intellectual understanding.

Reading formatively and spiritually is not a contemporary practice. We have all learned to read analytically, critically, and ideologically—to read informatively. For example, if we graduated from high school, college, or graduate school, we've learned to read analytically to understand an author's point but to also critically figure out what's wrong with the author's point. We've also learned to read ideologically, reading in a way that focuses on whether or not we agree or "like" what we've read. Much of Internet reading is ideological and emotional as we search for blogs and articles that correspond to what we already believe. So conservatives we will gravitate toward conservative sites. Liberals will gravitate toward liberal sites. Racists will gravitate toward racist sites. Conspiracy theorists will gravitate toward conspiracy sites. Spiritual reading allows our reading to become prayer by inviting God to form and transform us through our reading.

How do we practice spiritual reading? It begins with a belief that when we read the Bible, devotional materials, or spiritual books, God can speak to us personally and communally through the author. Reading the Bible spiritually helps us discern God's voice more fully in our lives. Instead of sitting down and reading briskly so that we can get the information into ourselves quickly (e.g., how we would read for a test, when doing research, or when reading something critically and analytically), spiritual reading is slow, reflective, and prayerful. We read in a way that helps us discover God's voice in the passages.

Too many people read intellectually, trying to "figure out" what a book or passage is saying. They spend so much time trying to understand it intellectually that they never really hear God speaking through it. For example, when reading the biblical creation stories, too many people focus on whether or not they are literally true. Spiritual reading asks us to put those concerns aside for the moment in order to ask, "What is God saying to me through these stories? What is God saying about why the universe was created? What is God saying about what our relationships with God are meant to be like? How are we to live in relationship with all creation?" When we read prayerfully, God slowly answers these questions.

The actual practice of spiritual reading includes the following but can be adapted as people see fit or agree upon:

- Setting aside a certain time, in a quiet place free of distractions, for prayer and reading—usually 20 to 30 minutes, but it can be longer.
- Centering ourselves in a minute of silence.
- Asking God to guide us as we read.
- Reading only a small portion at a time that can be reflected upon rather than trying to read a whole chapter or as many pages as possible.
- Reading slowly, ready to grapple with the reading and intentionally pondering over a passage rather than trying to figure it out. Figuring out the passage is a secondary concern. The primary concern is listening to what God may be saying to us through the passage.
- Pausing, reflecting, and praying over what we have read. This means that we may read as little as a paragraph but decide to spend our time pondering and praying over that small portion.
- If we disagree or don't understand something, asking God to help us. If we continue to disagree, letting it go rather than dwelling on it. We are discerning what God has to say, so we are focusing on what's right in what we've read, not on what's wrong.
- Offering our concerns to God in prayer, thanking God for guiding us, and closing in silence.

There is a discipline to spiritual reading that goes beyond the practice. These have to do with what we do internally to prepare ourselves to be spiritual readers.

First, we have to *read humbly*—to willingly putting aside our egos, biases, and expectations in order to open up to God. This is not easy to do because our egos are invested in certain ideological, theological, and spiritual beliefs. Our belief systems guide us on how we approach God, how we see life, and how we interact with others. Reading humbly means doing our best to put these aside temporarily so that they can possibly be transformed. So for that time of reading, we are completely open to the possibility that we may be wrong. We try to listen for what God is telling us instead of confirming what we already believe. We recognize that at first we will generally resist the truths that God wants to reveal to us, and that the truths that will set us free are probably the truths we'd rather not hear.

A second facet of the discipline of spiritual reading was stated earlier, but it bears repeating. Are we willing to *read and reread*? Prayerful reading involves rereading, dwelling, reflecting, and praying so that we can discover deeper messages. We have to be willing to keep going over the same material so that it can form us more deeply.

Third, *stress quality over quantity*. Don't read that material just to "get it done," but try to dwell on it in order to discover what it says for our lives. So, if we are reading Scripture, we place ourselves in the Scripture by asking: "What is the basic message of God in this passage? How does the message of this passage affect my life? How do I implement what I am hearing in my life?"

Fourth, *be patient and trusting*. Are we willing to stay with the passage even if we don't get any great ideas or insights and even if we don't entirely understand what we've read? Trust that God is speaking through the words we are reading, recognizing that sometimes God speaks in very subtle ways. Patience gives subtle messages the space they need to grow.

Next, *wait upon God to disclose God's mysteries*. God always works and speaks in mysterious ways because God inhabits the realm of the eternal. God isn't confined to our time and space, nor to human logic. God is more patient and gentle than we are. So insight and inspiration generally comes with time.

Sixth, *remember that the Bible and other spiritual writings are meant to be read over and over again*. Spiritual reading values not only dwelling on passages of Scripture but also rereading passages and books. For instance, there are books for me, such as Thomas Kelly's *A Testament of Devotion*, that I have spiritually read at least 12 times over the past 25 years. Each time, I discover God speaking to me through the book with insights and inspirations I missed the previous times. This equally applies to Scripture. Nobody ever "knows" the Bible completely, even if they pretend they do. It is written in a different way from modern books. As we read each passage, we read knowing that in the future we will get other opportunities to explore it more and to hear God speak in different ways. When reading Scripture spiritually, each reading is only provisional. No insight is permanent because each time God will reveal more, building on what we understood before.

Seventh, *encourage readers to pray over the materials.* It's not enough simply to read the materials. We need to pray over what we've read and reflect on it. God uses the readings to speak to us not only through the author but through our own thoughts and reflections.

Finally, *discuss the readings as a group.* Our approach to prayer and spiritual growth is typically so individualistic that we forget the importance of community to the Christian life. Being part of a spiritual reading group helps us recognize that God doesn't speak through only the readings and our reflections. God speaks to us as we grapple with, question, and clarify our insights and inspirations through our group discussions. It is amazing to me how often people will read a chapter of a book for a group, feel as though they got nothing out of it, and then find their minds and spirits opened up in brand new ways through the discussions.

Ultimately the point of spiritual reading is to turn our thinking into prayer and reflection by letting every part of the process create an avenue for God to speak, guide, and transform us. For a printed guide to give to others when starting a group grounded in spiritual reading, you can find a brochure that contains a guide to spiritual reading in the "Resources" section of http://www.ngrahamstandish.org.

LEADING A SPIRITUALLY GROUNDED SMALL GROUP

As is clear, the discussions for the group each week are based on the week's readings. In the introduction to the group, the leader should stress reading the material over the course of a week and not only immediately prior to group meeting, as people tend to do.

In constructing the group, weekly meetings are always preferable to biweekly or monthly groups. Monthly groups are appealing because the commitment level is lower, as it is with biweekly meetings. The downside is that if people miss one monthly meeting, they've now missed two months before the next meeting. If they meet biweekly, missing one meeting means missing a whole month before the next meeting. People lose connection, and the group usually falls apart within a year.

In going through the books for the group, it is best to take it one book at a time and one chapter at a time. Again, our tendency is toward informative reading, so members will gravitate toward assigning larger chunks of a book so that there's more material to discuss. For example, I've seen monthly groups that read a whole book in a month because they are worried that having too little to read will limit discussions. They don't trust that the Spirit can speak through smaller amounts of material.

Also, as a rule of thumb, I tend to make sure that when moving to a new group book, we select an author coming from a different era and/or a different denominational tradition from the previous book. I might follow up a modern Protestant spiritual writer with a Catholic writer from the 19th century and then follow that up with a 20th-century Eastern Orthodox writer. The point is to keep the group from falling into the rut of always reading the same kinds of books that keep offering the same kinds of insights in different ways. If the group is willing to stay together, there is always another resource and another direction for the group to go.

The leader should introduce a new book to the group prior to the completion of the present book (except in the case of the first book, which should be introduced in the first session). Each book should be divided up into a reading schedule that goes chapter by chapter (when the chapters are normal in length) or even cut down if the chapters are overly long. The optimum number of pages to read each week is between 10 and 20 pages.

As we prepare to introduce a small group to others, it's important that we set the proper foundation, which is prayer. The leader needs to pray that God will send the right people for the group and trust those that God calls. The goal is always to let the group be a work of the Holy Spirit. As group leaders, our ultimate responsibility is to facilitate the work of the Spirit.

The ideal group size is between six and eight members. Since there is always attrition in small groups, it is best to try to start with a group of 8 to 12 members. If a group grows to more than 12 members, we can divide the group to create two new groups, although groups that have been established will resist this. Over time a large group, unless it is very time-limited to something like eight weeks, will shrink to a size closer to 12. Also, the group should always be open to new members. Closed groups will atrophy over time.

How do we initially invite people to become members of the group? The obvious way is an open invitation in the church bulletin, newsletter, and e-mails for people to join the group. Although a public invitation is important, the reality is that most groups grow best through personal invitations to people within the church whom you sense may be hungry for spiritual deepening. This can be friends whom you already know as well as those you think may be interested. This often means opening the group to people who are not members and who may never become members but who have a spiritual hunger.

The first group meeting should be a general introduction to the group, with time especially spent giving members a sample of what will take place (unless you've assigned a chapter of a book or some other reading ahead of time). For instance, during the first session you might want to have a copy of two or three pages (try to pick interesting ones) from your chosen book for people to read and discuss. At that meeting you can hand out copies of the chosen book or resource with a schedule of reading.

Where should you meet? It all depends on what kind of people you expect to attract. Meetings can be held in coffee shops, homes, or the church. Gain a sense of who you are inviting and what kind of context for discussion is best for them. If you are doing the group as an out-reach, meeting in a church may be intimidating. At our church we have a variety of settings. Our Thursday morning men's group meets at a restaurant in a local Marriott. We've had a young adult group meet in the town's coffee shop. We had a "Faith on Tap" group that met month-ly in a local restaurant after their dinner service was mostly finished. We've had groups meet in our church conference room but also in the living room of a house the church owns next door. We tailor the setting to the degree to which potential members feel comfortable with meet-ing in a church versus other venues. We also have to choose a time that is conducive to who we are trying to attract. This is becoming more and more difficult because people have become busier, most couples have both partners working, and people are more mobile in terms of travel and work times. This can be the most frustrating part of starting a group.

What is the best length of time for a group? I've found that for a group that wants spiritual depth, it should typically meet for about one-and-a-half hours but with the option for people to leave guilt-free after an hour. Longer than that time and it begins to wear people down and cause them to feel trapped. Shorter than that time and there usually isn't enough time to greet, socialize a bit, and then discuss.

The aesthetics of the venue are important. If it is possible, create a spiritual aesthetic that may include placing cloths or materials on the table that reflect the liturgical season or somehow create a more spiritual atmosphere. For example, in our conference room we have pictures of ancient Celtic crosses on the walls as well as a swatch of quilted, embroidered, or artistic cloth on the table representing the liturgical color of the year, and we place candles in the center of the table, which we change periodically. We gravitate toward tea candle holders that have three votive cups in some arrangement that symbolizes the Trinity.

We will often give five to ten minutes for people to settle in by inviting them to chat about what's going on in their lives. Then we move into the discussion. When leading the discussion, the focus of the group is to get the participants eventually to speak both in depth and in practical and personal terms. We are not trying to get them to tell us their dark and dirty secrets but to get people to reflect more deeply on what God is saying to them about their lives. Most people, when talking about spiritual matters, will typically try to talk theologically and abstractly and to avoid talking about things spiritually and personally. Our point here is to get them to talk more personally about what they are hearing God saying to them through what they've read in a passage and then to discern how to apply what they've heard in their lives. Thus, the leader has to help the participants gravitate away from surface, abstract talk to more in-depth, personal, spiritual perspectives (e.g., "What I hear God saying to me is that I need to be willing to let God change me from the inside, and to do that I need to be more open to listening to God, especially when I don't want to hear God").

We move people into depth by combining ever deeper questions with a sensitivity to the pitfall of trying to drive people too deep too soon. By the end of the meeting, people should be talking more deeply on their own. As the group grows over time, the members will learn to do this themselves. There are some differences, though, between how a men's group and a women's group might typically gravitate toward depth. Men usually don't have sustained, in-depth discussions. They generally pop in and out of depth. So they may talk in-depth about something but then relate it to sports. That may lead to a short discussion of the local football or hockey team and suddenly jump back into the in-depth discussion, only to pop out again to talk about a video they saw on YouTube. Meanwhile, women tend to talk more relationally. Their in-depth discussion may last longer, and they are more likely to talk personally by telling stories about themselves. The struggle for them is that they may often take longer to go into an in-depth discussion and may end up avoiding the in-depth discussion by venting more about what is going on in their lives, thereby turning the group into something closer to a support group. In mixed-gender groups, men tend to dominate the discussions more, although that's becoming less the case as more and more women have developed the confidence to share their thoughts in mixed company. Ultimately these are tendencies, not certainties. Each group has its own characteristics, yet they are tendencies to be aware of.

The kinds of questions we ask are important, especially if we ask questions that lead into depth. I'm not a big fan of bringing in prepared questions because they can actually restrict a group that wants to grow deeper by asking questions that may not fit the flow of the discussion. Still, I recognize that some leaders need these prepared questions because they give a sense of security. So good questions for the beginning of each group meeting are: "What did you hear God saying to you in our passage this past week? What words or sentences really struck you? Did anyone struggle with any parts of the passages?" If no one responds or it seems like people are floundering, we can get it started by saying, "Let me tell you what hit me this past week . . ."

As the group progresses, we want to ask open-ended questions that lead people deeper: "What does this say about what God is doing in your life? What does this say about your relationship with God? What does this say about what God is calling us to do in our lives?" Toward the last third of the meeting, it's helpful to lead people to think more pragmatically about what they've discussed by asking questions such as, "So what does all of this mean in more practical terms? How do we take this and apply it in a realistic way in our lives? How do we implement this in our lives?"

Groups can be ended in any way, but I've always found that creating a circle of prayer helps. Clasp hands and form a circle. Have the leader begin by saying a prayer. When finished, she or he squeezes the hand of the next person. If that person wants to say a prayer, she or he does so. If not, she or he squeezes the hand of the next person. Continue this until it comes back to the leader. The leader can close by inviting all to share in saying the Lord's Prayer together. During this time, encourage people to offer prayers over concerns mentioned in the sharing time.

ISSUES IMPACTING THE GROUP

A number of sticky issues arise in every group in terms of *how long the group should go on*, especially if it's struggling, *what to do when a member dominates*, and *how to deal with conflict, attrition, and disagreements over beliefs or with the author's beliefs.*

Starting with how long a group should last, it's important to recognize that every group has a life span. Some groups have a longer life span, others a shorter one. We have one group that has been meeting for 18 years and is still healthy. Another is still healthy after 14 years. That doesn't mean that either group still has its original members. The second group has many of them, but not the first. Typically, the longer the life span, the healthier the group. Or, more accurately, healthy groups tend to have a longer life span. Ensuring a long life for a group normally entails making sure that resource materials are chosen (as said earlier) that will gently push people to grow spiritually without being too complicated. Also, the group should always welcome new members as long as they agree to the conditions of the group.

Finally, the leaders should periodically check with the members to see whether the group is still helping them to grow. This doesn't have to be a formal process. It simply means talking to the group about whether the books we are using are working to help people grow spiritually.

Other factors tend to cause groups to die sooner. They include factors such as *becoming too insular*. All groups are initially resistant to bringing in new members. Having a group that doesn't welcome new members isn't necessarily a death knell for a group, but it inhibits the health of the group by barring new voices and causing the group to potentially form into a clique. This isn't just true for groups. Churches can suffer from insularity. Sometimes a group can become closed and remain healthy, but only with good leadership that guards against the group becoming a clique or a social group.

We also face a struggle when *one member dominates the group in a negative way*. It's not uncommon for a few people in a group to have stronger voices than others and for them to be the ones typically to introduce the issues and ideas to be discussed. To have a few stronger personalities be more vocal in a group is generally a normal and healthy thing, as long as those stronger personalities offer the opportunity for others to talk. It becomes a problem when one person becomes a negative force, either by offering persistent cynical comments and complaints or by causing the group to focus on her or his problems (in essence, treating the group like a therapy or problem-solving group). What do you do when a person dominates in a negative way? It can be very tricky, but usually there are two effective strategies.

The first is subtler. The leader needs to be aware of when the person is about to "go off" and then work to gently bring the group back to the topic at hand. One way of doing this is simply saying to the domineering person, "What you are saying is really important, but I don't want to lose sight of our discussion. What we were talking about was [summary of the topic]. Does anyone else have anything to say on what we were talking about?" Another way is to gently talk to the person privately about the need to let others speak. The latter is more difficult because it creates conflict. If you are considering it, you have to be ready for the person to become angry with you and possibly to leave the group in a huff, or to stay in the group but be undermining in a certain way. For instance, the person may say something, look at you, and say, "So . . . is that an okay way of saying it, or am I being too disruptive?" while smirking or saying it in a mocking tone. Our response, whatever it is, has to be one that treats the person with respect but remembers that the health of the group is more important than the issues of the individual. Certainly the person's health is important, but an individual shouldn't be given the power to kill a group. This may also mean asking the person to stop coming to the group, which can lead to greater conflict.

Another issue is conflict between members that threatens to disrupt the group. It is rare that this happens, but when it does it can cause problems. The best way to deal with it is simply to talk to each person privately and tell them your concerns that their conflict will disrupt the group. Invite them to deal with their issues privately.

Over time the group will also have to *deal with attrition*. Most groups shrink over time as members deal with real-life factors such as family or work needs, commitments to other organizations or groups, and a need to slow life down. This is normal. When a person drops out of a group, it is helpful if the leader has a private conversation with the person to make sure that the problem is not with the group itself, such as resources not being helpful, conflict within the group, or struggling with her or his faith. Inviting new members to join overcomes natural attrition. Each time the group starts a new book or study is a good time for the group to consider inviting at least one new member to join the group.

A serious problem that arises in any group occurs when *there are disagreements over beliefs*. At some point in every group's life there comes a time when people with strong theological beliefs clash. This can be a positive situation in the end, but it does require firm and gentle group leadership. When leaders join in the argument, picking one side or the other, it usually backfires. A better way of handling the disagreement is to see it as an opportunity for spiritual growth. If the leader can summarize both positions and then ask whether there is a way both can be true or both reveal the Spirit's guidance, then it can lead to growth. Consider saying something along the lines of, "What I hear you saying is [summary of the first person's beliefs]. And what I hear you [the other person] saying is [summary of that person's beliefs]. Is there a way that the Spirit may be leading us to another insight rather than it being just one or the other?"

Members will also *disagree with the beliefs of the author* of the resources we are using. This is healthy. It is rare to find a book or resource that has all the right answers for everyone, no matter how much the author, or those who like the author, may believe that she or he has all the right answers. Disagreements are only a problem when the discussions are always about what we disagree with. It's okay for people to say that they disagree with something, but the leader should always refocus the discussion on what the author says that's helpful. For example, a leader might say, "Yeah, it is hard to agree with this. But what do you agree with and find helpful?"

AN ORGANIC RATHER THAN ORGANIZATIONAL APPROACH

Over the course of the past 50 or more years, all churches, but especially the mainline church, have developed an approach to structuring the life of the church based on common practices of the corporate world. We've talked about this more in-depth in other chapters as we've talked about creating a more spiritual approach to leadership, decision making, and program development. When it comes to forming small groups, our congregation has looked for a different way to create groups that are more spiritual. One way we've developed that is to emphasize an organic small group and education program rather than an organizational one.

Our spiritual groups are organized, but we try to be more organic in our approach, looking for what is growing or can grow. So in addition to creating groups based on spiritual reading, we also form groups based on movements we see growing in the church. We look for where people have interests that seem to intersect with spiritual growth. We look for potential seeds of spirituality and nourish them to bear fruit.

For example, we've created prayer groups for people interested in praying for the world, the church, and others. We've created a science and spirituality group for those interested in grappling with the connections between religion and science (rather than engaging in the debate between religion and science). We've created a near-death experience group for those who are interested in reading accounts of and discussing near-death experiences. We've created groups around those interested in viewing and discussing religious miniseries such as *A.D.: The Bible Continues*. We've started groups around Beth Moore Bible studies, Dave Ramsey's *Financial Peace University*, contemplative prayer, women's issues, and anything else that gathers interest and seems to help people grow spiritually. We don't worry as much about whether the programs are conservative or liberal, evangelical or progressive. Our focus tends to be whether there is an interest in it and whether it will help participants grow in faith. We do make sure, though, that the groups aren't polarizing by pushing a particular dogma that could divide the church.

A final way we have developed spiritual groups revolves around the meetings in the church. As mentioned before, each month we generate what we call a "Committee Study" to be used by every committee, task force, and the governing board. The sheet has a prayer to be said together, a quote from the writings of a spiritual writer that has to do with aspects of leadership and listening to God, and discussion questions. The point is not only to train every leader in the church in discernment and spiritual growth but to turn every committee, task force, and the board into a small group so that all of our leaders grow spiritually. To find the three-year cycle of these studies, go to the resources section of http://www.ngrahamstandish.org.

FINAL THOUGHTS

Leading a church to deepen takes intentionality. Most modern mainline churches struggle with how to deepen members of a church, and they struggle because they have learned a more informative, functional way of educating its members. We've often been trained to teach church members information about the Christian life without necessarily focusing on formation in the Christian life. It is very easy to teach people facts and data about the Bible without actually helping them to be formed by the Bible. That happens, for instance, when we do a Bible study on Jesus, teaching people about his birth, his life, what he taught, his death, and his resurrection while never actually using Scripture to help people connect with and experience Christ in their lives.

A more formative approach uses the same information but in the service of leading people to discover Christ's voice and guidance in their lives. It would use Jesus' parables as a way of listening for how God is calling them to transform their lives. The focus is on how to use biblical information in the service of spiritual formation rather than using biblical information to teach people religious information. One of the significant problems of our culture is that we've taken such a rational, functional, informational approach to all education, teaching people analysis rather than discernment.

Creating a small group program rooted in spiritual formation overcomes this informational style of teaching.

8

LEADING A CHURCH THROUGH TRANSFORMATION

The challenge of leading a church to become a blessed church is that churches resist change. That's not the same as saying that they don't want change. Nor is it the same as saying that church change is impossible. It merely recognizes that while most churches generally know that they need to change and believe that they want change, it is human nature to resist. It's also human nature to be constantly baffled by people's resistance.

Resisting new ideas, new realities, and one another is a constant fact of life—we resist making new friends, learning new skills, adopting new political ideas, accepting changes in cultural values, listening to our parents, and making new commitments. It's not that we don't want anything new. We like surprise, but we like safe surprises. We'll like a new song if it comes out of a genre we already embrace. We'll resist a new song from a completely new genre unless that new song somehow feels slightly familiar.

The struggle in transforming a congregation is that they not only resist change, but they can become quite hostile to us as we try to lead them through change. We think we're leading them to where they said they wanted to go, but then we experience the sniping, the backbiting, the gossip, and the outright criticism and attacks.

Psychologist Greg Lester, a leading writer in the area of personality disorders and understanding human behavior, says about resistance:

We want others to be rational, decent, and sensible. We want them
to be able to see the obvious, to know their impact on and to understand us. We expect them to see the world as we see it. But people
often don't. They surprise us. They do things that don't make sense
to us. They do things that are so opposed to the way we think things
should be done we end up wondering how anyone could do them.
We wonder how they could say some of the things they say. We end
up confused about why people seem so difficult.[1]

Why do people resist change, sometimes in rude and insensitive
ways? Resistance is part of our human biology. It's part of the human
survival instinct built into our brains and bodies. As Lester says, "Because biology has survival as its basic task, its priorities are very simple.
The importance of any function or any action is determined by its
ability to assist in survival. Activities most likely to ensure living are the
activities it will favor. If there is a choice between several possible
actions, the one most effectively serving the purpose of staying alive is
the one it will generate."[2]

It's not only individuals who have a survival instinct. Congregations
do, too. No matter how spiritual they want to be, their survival instincts
can lead them down the very same nonspiritual, conflict-laden paths.
This is especially true if they have been in long-term decline. So why
don't churches in decline, but that still want to survive, reach out and
grab for the transformational changes we suggest, which will help them
survive? They don't because the survival instinct is concerned only with
how we will survive in the short term. Biology doesn't naturally lead us
to think about how we will survive for years to come. It's instinct, not
reason. Our instinct is to protect ourselves against new ideas, even if
they could help us survive in the long term. Why will a wounded animal
bite us, even if we are trying to help it? The answer is that when
something is in survival mode, it isn't able to consider long-term welfare.

Even using this book as a tool for transformation won't prevent
survival instinct from rearing its self-protective head. It's not only the
congregation as a whole that acts on survival instinct. Powerful people
within a congregation also do, which means that sometimes leaders
recognize the need for change, but particularly influential members
lead a resistance movement.

I saw an interesting example of this prior to my publishing the first edition of *Becoming a Blessed Church*. I was increasingly being invited by local church boards to talk about how to spiritually transform their churches. A local Presbyterian church's pastor asked me to do a one-hour presentation for his church's board, followed by 30 minutes of questions and answers. The pastor of the church had hoped that this would spark them to become more prayerful in their approach to ministry and mission.

So I gave my talk and discussed how Calvin Church had been transformed. I received a very good response, with many of the elders on the board commenting on how this could really open up the church in new ways. I left feeling pretty good about myself. Several weeks later I spoke with the pastor, and he told me about what happened after I left. After a 10-minute discussion of my ideas, an elder chimed in. He was the biggest contributor to the church and a perennial board member because of his influence. He said, "If you do this . . . if you follow what that guy said, I'll quit the board and I'll quit giving to the church." With that, he walked out. The board sat in stunned silence. Eventually they decided to go forward with changing the way the board operated and to do so in a more prayerful way, but it was painful.

Why did he threaten them? Because he felt threatened. He was one of the most powerful men in a smaller congregation. The church rarely made significant decisions without consulting him. Creating a style of leadership where decisions are made prayerfully, seeking Christ's voice rather than his voice, evoked his survival instinct, threatening his power. My guess is that if he were asked to explain rationally what his objections were, he wouldn't have been able to do so. He was reacting on instinct rather than rational thought.

Lester points out that our survival instinct kicks in when ideas threaten us, and they do so because humans aren't quite like animals. Animals apply their survival instincts only to physical threats to their food, territories, and bodies. Our instincts certainly kick in when we are threatened physically, but they also do so when our beliefs and values—what Lester calls "concepts"—are threatened. He says that to us, concepts "are real, but only in human brain wiring. We refer to them by such names as meanings, principles, values, beliefs, standards, and interpretations. We can do to concepts all of the things we do to any 'things.' We can identify them, share them, exchange them, keep them, change them, and lose them. They exist in the brains of human beings, referred to through the use of language, and applied to sensory events and objects."[3]

So why did this elder become defensive over the possibility of having a more spiritually grounded, prayerful board? Because these ideas threatened his power, his influence, and his survival as the most powerful man in the church. He may not have actually been the most powerful man, but in his mind he was. A growing church threatened this power because new people with new ideas might erode his influence. It was better to be powerful in a declining church than to be just another person in a growing church.

Many modern mainline churches are in survival mode. They resist steps toward thriving because trying to thrive might threaten their ability to survive, especially if new attempts to grow go horribly wrong. They fear the unknown. This is the reason that it's much easier to start a new church and adapt it to a rapidly changing culture than to transform a mainline church, especially if it has been in decline. My own denomination, the Presbyterian Church (USA), recognizes this reality. For many years it has tried to get established, declining churches to revive, but recently it put its resources behind a new initiative that doesn't threaten anyone's survival. It's called "1001 Worshiping Communities," and it is an attempt to create a "movement in the Presbyterian Church (U.S.A.) to begin 1001 New Worshiping Communities. Using new and varied forms of church for our diverse and changing culture. Forming new disciples of Jesus, transforming our denomination, and impacting our world."[4]

The Presbyterian Church and other denominations have realized that it is much easier to start a new church, seeking people who have little or no resistance to change (even if they may have resistance to Christianity), than it is to transform a church stuck in survival mode.

Transforming an existing congregation requires tremendous skill in making people feel safe, especially if our suggested changes can't guarantee success and may lead to failure. Churches fear failure because failure can potentially lead to a quicker death. In other words, if we try to do something and it fails, then it may mean failing *permanently*. The more decline a church has experienced, the more it will fear future decline and resist change.

Declining churches can especially fear risk because over time their risk takers have left the church, leaving behind the loyalists and traditionalists who love the way the church had been. Meanwhile, newer churches attract risk takers who are eager to try new ministries and missions. This is why adapting to newer technology is much easier in new churches: new churches attract members who have embraced newer technologies already and aren't intimidated by them.

This fear of failure also explains a significant difference between the ways evangelical churches, whether nondenominational or Baptist, have approached the issue of starting new churches versus the ways mainline denominations have approached it. Typically, Baptists and nondenominationals have taken the attitude that seeds of new churches should be scattered wherever possible, whether a well-developed plan exists or not. If they get three churches to take root out of 10 attempts, they consider themselves to be doing well. They hope to bat .300 by being successful 30 percent of the time. In mainline denominations, we approach every church plant as though it must succeed. We want to have every effort hit a home run. If each attempt isn't successful, it feels like a failure, especially for a denomination in decline. The reality is that most entrepreneurial efforts in anything fail. To be entrepreneurial means to court failure in process of seeking success, and reviving a church means being entrepreneurial.

MAKING CONGREGATIONS FEEL SAFE

As I said earlier, churches need to feel safe if they are to be transformed. Good leaders intuitively get that, recognizing that when a congregation feels safe, it will naturally subdue its own survival instincts and become open to possibility. The conundrum for pastors is that while most churches want their pastors to lead them, they are still anxious about the pastor's new ideas, especially if they suspect that the pastor is going to leave in a few years.

I experienced this apprehension in my first years at Calvin Presbyterian Church. When I came to the church its condition mirrored its decades-long decline. The carpet in the sanctuary was worn and wrinkled from age. Weekly I watched older people trip on the wrinkles. The lighting was dim, rooms were dirty, wallpaper sagged, paint was peeling, and the church in general was dirty. They had a custodian, so floors were cleaned and vacuumed, but there was an accumulation of material that never got thrown out. The mantra of many in the church, at least as some members articulated it to me, was that spending money to upkeep the church was selfish. Money should go to mission, not buildings. I didn't agree. I believe that the whole church is mission, and just as we keep up our houses, we should keep up our church so that it is inviting to visitors and the community. For example, if our worship space is dingy and uninspiring, how does that help make worship a mission to reach out to people and help them encounter Christ?

One of my first ideas was simply to do a massive cleanup of the church. The cleanup filled to overflowing a 42-cubic-yard roll-off dumpster (the kind that goes on a tractor-trailer). The next year we filled a similar one to two-thirds full. How does an idea like this help a church feel safe? It was a simple transformation of the church that required little money but that led to a great feeling of success. Many walked around the church the next day, commenting on how wonderful the church looked.

The cleanup energized people and got them thinking about other things we should do to upgrade the church. For example, people suggested repainting walls, replacing carpets, refinishing flooring, upgrading lighting, and improving our sanctuary sound. Intuitively I knew that this put me in a conundrum: I could spearhead multiple efforts to raise money for each of these, spurring project after project. Or we could create a comprehensive plan. Yet if we created a plan but it seemed like it came from me and my hand-picked team of members, it would evoke the congregation's survival instinct.

So I asked our board to create a task force to work with me. This small task force eventually suggested embarking on a capital campaign to renovate our sanctuary and look for ways to expand the church as it grows (I'll talk more about this task force later). When they proposed the campaign to our board, one of our board members argued vociferously against the renovations and the campaign in general because of fears that I would leave in the middle, leaving the church in debt with no leader to guide them in paying off their debt. This woman's argument was, "My father's church had a young pastor like Graham who had all sorts of new ideas. He got them to do a capital campaign. And then he left. It's been eight years and they are still in debt, and it's caused them to shrink." Her vote was to do nothing. I assured her that I had no intention to leave them in debt, but she was still afraid. Ultimately I had to help her feel safe by guaranteeing that I would stay for at least the three years of the capital campaign, although I also emphasized that embarking on a campaign needed to be an act of discernment and faith, and that fear and anxiety over time would kill our ability to listen.

This member really reinforced the reality that when we lead a congregation through transformation, we need to build up trust as much as possible. We have to pay attention to how safe a congregation feels with change. In the discussions over the capital campaign, the other elders did their best to talk about the benefit of the change to the congregation and its mission as well as making rational arguments about the need for the campaign. It wasn't until I made my guarantee that the last holdout felt safe enough to agree.

Why did it take my guarantee? Most leaders, when they try to make a congregation feel safe, often focus their attempts in the wrong direction. They think that pointing out the future benefits will get the congregation to jump on board. They think that talking rationally about the need for change will help people overcome their fear. It doesn't. The reason has to do with leading an elephant down a path. What?

In their groundbreaking book, *Switch*, entrepreneurial writers Chip and Dan Heath talk about how to turn around organizations.[5] They say that successful turnarounds are a matter of getting a *rider* to lead an *elephant* down a *path*. They use this metaphor to demonstrate what most leaders do wrong in trying to transform an organization. Most leaders either focus on passionately explaining the *path*, sharing their vision of what can be. Or they focus on explaining rationally the need for change—speaking to the *rider* (the leading figures of the congregation) about why we need to go down that path. What too many leaders ignore is that an organization is like a huge elephant, and it is instinctual like an elephant. If the elephant doesn't trust the rider and the path, it's going nowhere.

The elephant is the embodiment of an organization's emotions and passions. The elephant is fear, hunger, anxiety, wariness, confusion, and more. If the elephant is skittish, it won't matter how much we convince the rider or envision the path. We won't be going anywhere without the elephant. Good leaders (the riders) help the elephant feel safe. Our congregations are like elephants. If the path seems safe and the rider is caring, they will go down the path. If the rider is abusive and the path seems dangerous, the elephant will stay put. And if the rider gets too aggressive, or even too insistent, the elephant can become quite dangerous. The real task is to make the elephant feel safe, help the rider understand the path, and encourage the rider to guide the elephant down that path. In other words, *it is to make sure the congregation feels it can trust the leaders to help them envision a path and then lead them down that path.*

What does this mean in practical terms? It means that in times of transformation we need to find ways to validate the congregation by rooting our actions in praise and encouragement rather than criticism. Unfortunately, fear of either conflict or failure can sabotage a church moving down a transforming path. I've been surprised over the years at how many pastors and church leaders choose one of two paths. Either they fear conflict so much (they fear the elephants so much) that they never try to lead a congregation down a path, or they fear failure so much (a fear of the elephant's power) that they force the congregation down a path and bully it when it resists. Our church has seen the damage of the latter. We've come alongside another Presbyterian church, Trinity Presbyterian Church in Butler, Pennsylvania, after a previous pastor bullied them, causing a 200-member congregation to shrink to fewer than 30 members over three years. In essence, the rider whipped the elephant to walk down a path it never understood.

The process of making a congregation feel safe can be nurtured by enlisting the trusted members of the congregation to help us. In other words, we seek the help of those who are already trusted. A huge mistake many pastors make is to propose changes in a congregation, all in the sake of positive transformation, without enlisting the help and leadership of the members who are already trusted. In other words, they point out a path, and then try to keep the elephant on their own, despite the fact that the elephant may not trust them. Good leaders point out the path by articulating a vision, but they also allow the congregation's trusted and experienced riders (the trusted leaders of the church) to take them down the path.

TRANSFORMATION THROUGH TRANSFORMATIONAL TASK FORCES

In chapter 2, I mentioned an experience I had as an associate pastor in a growing church, where I witnessed firsthand how a growing congregation with everything going for it could let its big elephants keep it from going down a truly favorable path. We think of growing churches as a good thing, and that congregations would naturally want to take a path that leads to growth. The dilemma is that when churches grow, they also enter unsure areas where they have no experience. Often there is no guidebook, and they have to make decisions they've never faced before—the hiring of new staff, renovating or expanding a building, starting another worship service, changing a service's music, and so much more.

Our church badly needed to expand our building to accommodate a growing ministry. The senior pastor had asked a real estate developer in the congregation to work with him to envision how we might expand. The elders quickly accepted the proposal, recognizing what a good plan it was. The sticky point was what side of the building to build the project on.

Several of the strongest members of our board, who represented the elephants of the congregation, argued that it should be built on the other side of the church from the proposed area, in a grassy field bordering on a busy road. The developer had proposed building on an existing parking lot bordering five acres of woodlands that could be expanded, which actually made more rational sense. What was obvious was that the objecting members resisted because they weren't consulted ahead of time. They really didn't care that much about the side of the building, but it was their way of saying, "We should have had more say!" They were being overly sensitive elephants who felt disregarded and ignored.

I also suspect that they weren't quite sure about growing. What if this attracts too many new members with new ideas that push the congregation to do things in new ways rather than how they've always done it before? What happens if we no longer feel as though we know anyone anymore? These are all issues we've dealt with over the years at Calvin Church. We currently have 550 members, which is an increase over the 200 that were members in 1996. In that time, though, we've done over

110 funerals, and easily 50 members have moved away or left the church, leaving only about 40 members remaining from 1996. In other words, the church has really added 510 new members over 20 years, creating a virtually new church. Anticipating this amount of change can be scary for a congregation that's declined and has become comfortable with sameness. Change makes elephants nervous.

Returning to the story of the other church, it remained split over the ensuing months. They reminded me of a Dr. Seuss book, with star-bellied and bare-bellied sneetches arguing over who was better, or the north-going and south-going Zaxes refusing to give ground.[6]

So a task force was created to research the problem in depth. By the time the task force was ready to complete its work, I had left to finish my PhD, and the senior pastor had left, frustrated over the continual battles with those who wanted control no matter how it might impact growth. Their paralysis over which side to expand led to a return to decline.

Since then the congregation dropped the expansion project, and it has struggled through a number of pastors, seeing its congregation dwindle from about 525 members down to a little more than 150. Reflecting on the incident, I learned a lot about keeping the congregational elephant always in focus. The senior pastor was a tremendous pastor. He was the best mentor I could have worked with, and every congregation he has served has grown healthier and larger. In his work with that congregation, he had done all the right things, and it led to growth. Still, something was different this time, something that taught me an important lesson about congregational transformation: *congregational trust is the biggest factor in congregational growth*. Churches will follow leaders, especially pastoral leaders, but only if they feel as though the path is safe and will lead to good things. As someone once said, "If the elephant don't want to go down that path, we ain't going down that path."

RENOVATING THE SANCTUARY

During my first few years at Calvin Church there was a push to upgrade the church. Remembering my experience as an associate pastor, I was very aware that doing anything to upgrade the church could lead to conflict because everyone had his own opinion.

LEADING A CHURCH THROUGH TRANSFORMATION

I didn't want to end up experiencing what we did in my previous church, so I decided that the best course of action was to reverse what my senior pastor had done. He had put together plans for expansion and, when conflict arose, created a task force to deal with it. It occurred to me that perhaps this process could be flipped. I didn't yet cognitively understand the Heath brothers' concept of *rider-elephant-path*, but I understood it intuitively—make sure we focus on trust and safety. We knew the path we needed to walk down, which was renovating and modernizing the sanctuary for a modern population. We also knew how to talk to the rider and explain to anyone and everyone the rational reasons for walking down this path. But the elephant was sure to re- member the 30-year decline that included losing money and savings. The eventual plan to raise at least $125,000 to renovate the sanctuary (and eventually $330,000 for a three-year capital campaign) was a huge, scary, hairy step.

Based on my previous experiences, I realized that the task force should come before the proposal. Also, I realized that loading it with already trusted church leaders meant that *they* could convince the con- gregation of the right path to take, not me. In other words, calmer, wiser members (riders) who knew the congregation might be best at calming the fears of the congregational elephants.

Initially I spoke to the board about the need to renovate the sanctu- ary and to possibly do a small capital campaign to raise the necessary funds. I told them that this would be preferable to upgrading the church one project at a time. I made it clear that this wasn't what I necessarily wanted (which was true—I almost didn't come to Calvin Church because of my dislike of doing capital campaigns) but that it was clear many members were already moving in that direction. I sug- gested that the board create a task force to consider the possibility and to make plans if needed, and then I outlined for the board what I thought the qualifications for serving on the task force should be:

- They would represent the different ages and theological positions of our church (we didn't have a very racially diverse congregation, so racial/ethnic diversity wasn't an issue).
- They would have a desire to seek what God wants for the sanctu- ary, a sensitivity to the congregation's needs, and an ability to work well with others.

- They would have some sort of ability in property, interior design, or at least what seems like good judgment in these kinds of issues.
- They would be willing to serve on a task force for about eight months.
- We would make sure that the majority of task force members were people the congregation knew and trusted already.

Our church board gave me a list of about eight names, ranked from top choice to last choice, and I agreed that I would invite them and explain the process. We wanted a task force of five members. Within three weeks we had our "Sanctuary Task Force" ready to go. In our monthly newsletter, we explained to the congregation what their purpose was, who was on the task force, and what the outcome could be.

I met with the task force initially and did a training session that focused on several areas. I explained to them their purpose (the path), which was to renovate the sanctuary in a way that had three elements: a clear theological purpose underlying it, a clear spiritual focus on helping people experience God through the aesthetics, and a clear functional understanding of what we needed in terms of space, lighting, and sound. I also set the agenda for how each meeting would operate. Over the course of five months they would read articles about worship to give them a foundation for thinking through the theology, structure, and aesthetics of a sanctuary. These included articles on the theology and spirituality of worship, how to create welcoming spaces, and generational studies specifically on how to eventually reach what would become the millennial generation (who in 1996 were between 0 and 15 years old—a topic that is now very popular).

They would also visit other church sanctuaries in the region to get an idea of what's possible. They looked at everything from traditional to contemporary worship spaces. My role was to select the articles to read and suggest sanctuaries to visit. I was part of the task force for the first three months, leading discussions on the readings and helping them to talk through their visits. My focus was simply helping them coalesce their thinking by thinking theologically and spiritually. Their final meetings were without me. I wanted them to own their decisions, with no one thinking that their proposal was really mine masquerading as theirs. I offered them suggestions, and that was part of the mix, but it was their judgment that I wanted to be put forth to the congregation.

They decided to work with a member's niece, who was part of an interior design company and could help them create a plan that embodied the perspectives they had developed. They chose colors and materials that were classic in nature but evoked a more modern look. They filled the sanctuary with complementary colors rather than sticking with the typical Presbyterian style that often strips sanctuaries of color, art, and symbols. It was from insights developed from study and visits, along with their work with a professional, that led to their eventual proposal.

In the end, their suggestions were better than anything I could have anticipated. They were clear theologically and spiritually about the sanctuary, reworking a chancel dominated by a pulpit, lectern, and organ console to become less dominated by word and more oriented toward word and sacrament. They proposed getting rid of the lectern and replacing it with the baptismal font that had been consigned to a corner of the sanctuary. They put the communion table that had been placed below the chancel on the floor (where it was difficult to see above the pews) at the center of the chancel between the pulpit and the baptismal font in a way that created a triangular (Trinitarian) pattern between the three. They also moved the organ console to the side. They suggested that we add theatrical lighting and sound to accommodate a better worship experience and to be adaptable to our drama program, which used the sanctuary once a year. A number of other proposals became part of our eventual renovations.

In the end it was their proposal, not mine. By training the task force but then trusting them to create the proposal, I allowed them to take ownership of the process and proposal, which enhanced their trust in me. They saw me as empowering them to do what was right for them rather than coercing them into what I wanted. The task force made the proposal to the board and then to the congregation, which meant that they ended up leading the congregation through the renovations. I was really pleased with how well this worked. It also gave me a template for future transformations of the church.

A LEGACY OF TRANSFORMATIONAL TASK FORCES

Over the years, this model of using what I call "transformational task forces" (TTFs) has led us through many changes: the restructuring of our session and committee system, the purchase of property next to the church, the restructure of our Sunday morning worship and education times, the creation of a supplemental songbook, an eventual $1.6 million expansion and renovation project (one task force to suggest what we need, another to work with an architect on plans, and another to work on the decor), and the creation of a task force looking at how we might significantly change our worship services to reach out to the millennial generation that is more resistant to church. We've also had many smaller task forces to deal with issues such as creating a more spiritually oriented confirmation class, developing a small group program, and reaching out in mission to Trinity Presbyterian Church in helping them grow again. In each case, the task forces have led the congregation through successful transformations with very little resistance.

Initially, before developing a policy of creating specific, targeted task forces, we had set up a long-range planning task force (LRPTF), much as other churches do. I had been trained to believe that for churches to grow they needed a detailed mission statement and a five-, three-, and one-year plan. So creating an LRPTF made sense. The members agreed to serve a three-year term as it developed plans for the future. After a few years I realized that all of these long-term plans were actually making it difficult to listen for God because our plans were becoming more important than listening for God's call, which might lead us in a different direction. I had two epiphanies regarding long-range planning: (1) *when looking for long-term task force members, we were focusing too little on whether they had the skill to prayerfully consider a particular possibility for the church and too much on whether they would agree to serve a three-year term*; and (2) *when a church makes long-term future plans, it often isn't discerning enough to pay attention to where God may be calling it in the present, nor flexible enough to take advantage of opportunities God may be putting before it.*

This "aha" moment came to me when our LRPTF studied what we might need to do architecturally if we kept growing at our present pace. The task force and the board were meeting with an architect hired to help us look at our future growth. He had suggested that we need to either relocate to a larger site (his top choice) or purchase three adjoining houses and properties, which would allow us to expand where we are. At the end of his presentation, a member of the LRPTF raised her

hand and said, "I have another suggestion. Instead of looking at reloca-
tion and construction, why don't we just ask all those people who want
the church to grow to leave and start their own church?" I was stunned.
I thought secretly, "Wow! If we did that, she and a handful of others
would be left with this big building, and 70 percent of the congregation
would leave with the staff and me." I realized that LRPTFs, by nature
of being long term, don't call forth members who have the targeted
skills to lead the congregation through a specific challenge. They generally focus on getting people who will serve for three years, without
considering what challenges they may be asked to overcome. Targeted,
short-term task forces have the advantage of attracting people with
specific, harmonious talents. Within a year we disbanded the LRPTF.

When it comes to the task of discernment, long-range thinking
doesn't generally allow us to be available to shorter-term opportunities.
I've learned that God often presents opportunities that weren't ac-
counted for. That's not a consistent truth. There are times when we
need to look at the long term because we've discerned a long-term path
as coming from God. But even then a short-term task force can be
created to think long term.

I don't want to make it seem as though the efforts of our LRPTF
were wasted. They still helped us sense a call to follow the architect's
suggestion to purchase the three adjacent properties. Although those
properties had not been bought or sold for a number of prior years, the
three parcels providentially all became available over the next four
years. They were key acquisitions, allowing us to do a major expansion
and renovation 10 years later in 2007.

Since then we have faced a number of major transitions and transformations. We have also created a number of specific transformational
task forces to lead us through them. Each time, the process has led to a
better way of moving forward.

SETTING UP TRANSFORMATIONAL TASK FORCES

In originally setting up these transformational task forces, I was going
on intuition as to how to proceed. Now, looking back on 20 years of
employing them, I recognize some basic rules that are important to
creating healthy and effective TTFs. They are (1) *soliciting members*

who reflect the congregation; (2) *overcoming the curse of knowledge*; (3) *pastor serving as resource coordinator*; (4) *pastor serving as facilitator*; (5) *turning takeaways into proposals*; (6) *the task force as proposing transformations to the board and the congregation*; and (7) *pastor serving as implementer*. Ultimately there is another element that grounds all of these rules, which is that as much as possible in all things, prayerful discernment is the foundation.

1. Soliciting Members Who Reflect the Congregation

Who serves on these task forces determines how well they'll work to discern what God is calling the church to eventually do. So who should be asked to serve on a task force? First of all, they should be chosen to reflect both the different generations in the church and those we may hope to attract to our church. Typically, they are members, but if the church is trying to reach people who aren't in the church, it may want to consider adding those who aren't part of the church but are friendly to it.

Also, it's good to have the task force represent the different perspectives in the church, whether that's theological, ideological, liturgical, generational, financial, racial, gender, or more. The more diversity the better. I have learned a basic caveat that is really important: don't put friends on a task force, especially if it is a small task force. When people who are too familiar sit on a task force together, they tend to form a clique that prevents them from exploring a wider range of ideas. Their friendship makes decision making easy, but it also means that they may share too many of the same preferences. Friends tend to be more tribal and resistant to other points of view, especially if they are friends who represent the way a church has always been. Task forces staffed by people who aren't so familiar with one another end up having to consider one another's perspectives. The point is to make sure that there is enough diversity that cliques are inhibited. A secondary effect is that by bringing different people together, we build up deeper relationships in the church among those who don't know one another. I've seen good friendships develop from these task forces.

2. Overcoming the Curse of Knowledge

One of the primary benefits of these TTFs is that they overcome what Chip and Dan Heath call "the curse of knowledge"—the reality that "once we know something, we find it hard to imagine what is was like not to know it. Our knowledge has 'cursed' us. And it becomes difficult for us to share our knowledge with others, because we can't readily re-create our listeners' state of mind."[7] All pastors are cursed by their seminary education, the "groundbreaking" books they've read, and the numerous conferences they've attended. They forget that their members haven't had this training. They are cursed by their knowledge because they no longer remember what it was like not to have it. Thus, what can seem like such small steps of change for us pastors may feel like leaps across a frightening abyss to our members. TTFs bridge the *curse of knowledge* by exposing members to ideas and concepts that the pastor knows but has a hard time communicating. Having the TTF members spend significant time reading different resources helps them gain knowledge that they are then able to pass along to the members at large when proposing changes. In essence, the freshness of their knowledge makes it less cursed and less likely to establish a chasm between them and church members.

For example, when we created our Future of Worship Task Force to consider how to reach out to younger generations, we had the task force read articles and books on reformed worship, contemporary worship, emergent worship, reaching out to millennials, creating welcoming spaces, and more—all topics I had studied. So each month they read selections from books as diverse as *Emerging Worship*, by Dan Kimball, *Reformed Worship*, by Howard Rice and James Huffstutler, *Turn Your Church Inside Out*, by Walt Kallestad, and my book, *In God's Presence*, a book on transforming worship. We also had them visit eight different worship services in our area that ranged from big-steeple traditional to contemporary, emergent, and Taizé. Being exposed to all of these ideas and approaches allowed the task force to become educated and to gain an understanding that was closer to what I had been trained to understand. But since it was new to them, they would be the ones best able to help the congregation eventually close the gap between what they now knew and what the congregation tended to think.

3. Pastor Serving as Resource Coordinator

One of the great things about TTFs is that the pastor doesn't have to be responsible for generating the ideas. Instead, the pastor becomes the resource person offering educational materials and opportunities to the task force members while letting them generate their own conclusions. Typically, when establishing a TTF, I assemble materials for the members to read and then distribute them once a month. I make sure not to overwhelm them with too much (our curse of knowledge can afflict our choice of readings, too, by giving them too much to read or materials that are too complex for someone without theological and biblical training). In choosing resources, I try to be wide ranging and look at all possibilities. I try to expose them to concepts and approaches that I already know about and perhaps have even been trained in so that our collective knowledge can become relatively equivalent. This may include training them in how to pray and discern if part of their task is to discern.

Ultimately I'm using my training to train them. This is not the same as manipulating them to eventually decide what I want. I genuinely want the Spirit to work through them to lead us to what is right for the congregation. Still, I recognize that as miraculously as the Spirit can work, it certainly helps the Spirit when a deeper level of understanding can open them to a deeper level of guidance from the Spirit. I am in a tradition that values education and believes that spiritual and theological education enable us to discern God better. Certainly there are times and tendencies where we rely too much on education and push God away. That in a nutshell is the problem of rational functionalism mentioned in the beginning of the book—we become so intellectual in our approach that we quit trying to discern. With that said, being a resource person who educates task force members allows them to engage in discussions where we're all on relatively equal footing. It places members in a better place to discern.

4. Pastor Serving as Facilitator

In the actual meetings, my role is not to push particular ideas. I facilitate the discussions in a way that encourages task force members to explore their ideas. For example, our Future of Worship Task Force met each month for two hours. For the first hour the members discussed the readings and shared their experiences of the church visits. I wanted the discussions to be wide ranging. My main focus was the question, "What really hit you or touched you in the readings and/or visit?" I emphasized that no one is "right" or "wrong" in her or his perceptions. This was simply a time to share and discuss.

For the last hour I helped the group members share their "takeaways." These are insights or thoughts that they had from the readings or visits that they believe *might* work at Calvin Presbyterian Church. I might share my own thoughts and insights based on readings or my own previous visits to these or similar churches. As facilitator, I don't lock myself out of the sharing process because I do have insights, and part of leadership is sharing insights. At the same time, my focus in this task force wasn't on getting my way. My focus was on helping them to cull ideas that may be from the Spirit. So I would ask them to share their takeaways, and I would list their takeaways with minimal bias. My main focus was helping them craft the clearest articulation. Periodically I might raise an objection to a particular takeaway if it was obviously impractical, but that was rare.

For example, one takeaway coming from an emergent church in the Pittsburgh area, the Hot Metal Community, was to have a communal meal each Sunday after worship like they did. With two worship services on Sunday, and with a congregation that is very regional, and with a congregation filled with parents of children, our trying to pull off a communal meal would be difficult. Would it only be after our second service? If so, what would we do for our first-service members? With people leaving after worship to get kids to soccer games, go to a Pittsburgh Steelers' football game, or visiting parents, who would stay for the meal? Still, I would make those arguments for only a takeaway that is very obviously not going to work. The real key is simply gathering takeaways that will be revisited near the end of the process. These takeaways become the minutes of the task force meeting and are really the only thing, in the end, that matters.

5. Turning Takeaways into Proposals

The assignment for the last meetings of any TTF is to take all of the monthly takeaways collected over the life of the task force and then turn them into a proposal for the church board and the congregation. My role is to help the group to turn the takeaways into practical plans that can be implemented over time. Generally I follow a basic process:

1. Have the members review all of the takeaways on their own and highlight the ones that they sense prayerfully might work the best in our church.
2. Ask the members to reflect on the takeaways and see whether they are sensing possible syntheses that can be built on their previous insights.
3. During subsequent meetings, using a consensus process prioritizing those takeaways that seem like they may both work the best and be our calling. This means doing the messy work of having the members come to an agreement on what they sense together is best. "Together" is the key word. A split task force is no good. I always push the idea that a split group splits off the Spirit.
4. Create a solid list of proposals that distills all possibilities to those that seem to fit with our church culture, our vision, and our community.
5. Spend the last meeting refining the proposals and turning them into well-articulated proposals that include a rationale for why. The rationale can include an explanation of why we sense God wants us to do this at Calvin Presbyterian Church.
6. Finally, turn the set of proposals into a written, comprehensive proposal. The pastor's role is to becomes the scribe, or to at least work with someone else who acts as scribe, writing up the proposal into a format that can be handed out to the board members and a congregation in written or presentation form.

6. Task Forces as Proposing Transformations to the Board and the Congregation

When it comes time to make the proposal to the board, and eventually the congregation, the members of the TTF make the proposal. They are the trusted ones. As pastor, my role is simply to make sure that they get a fair hearing. I neither advocate for their proposal nor defend it. But I do clarify when necessary, helping to make clearer a proposed point or rationale. To be able to do this, I have to be able to put aside all the time and effort I've put into the task force, to put aside my pride and ego investment in the proposal, and to only make sure the proposal gets a fair hearing. This builds trust in me with the board and congregation because they don't see me as having an agenda nor as being the force behind the proposal.

I also push the idea to the TTF members that they need to overcome their own curse of knowledge by remembering that neither the board nor the congregation has had their training or experiences. They have to reflect back to how they thought before the task force and steep their proposal in an awareness that they are speaking to people who are what they used to be.

If the board agrees to the proposal and decides to implement it, I then ask them to join the TTF in presenting the ideas to the congregation. Thus, we end up with both a trusted task force and trusted leaders being the ones to propose to the congregation, not the pastor(s). Again, my role during the congregational proposal is to clarify, not advocate. If the leaders of the church cannot persuade the members, then it tells me that either the proposal isn't ready, the time for it hasn't yet come, or the congregation is just too resistant (which may mean that I have to reconsider my future as a pastoral leader in the congregation).

7. Pastor Serving as Implementer

My final role, if the proposal is accepted, is to be the person responsible for making sure the plan is implemented properly. In some ways I become the institutional memory of the church by being the one who remembers the proposal over the ensuing years and who keeps bringing the board back to the need to implement the proposals—especially if the proposals can't be implemented all at once. Board members may change, the task force may go away, but I am the one left making sure the proposals become practice.

My role is also to help the board, church committees, and teams figure out a process for implementing the proposal. For example, I helped the board think through the process of hiring a proposed percussionist for worship. We worked on what the cost might be. We settled on $5,000 per year. We worked on whether to start in January or June, with the advantage that June would cut the cost in half for the first year. I worked with the music staff to put together a job description. I also helped think through who would make the final decision.

FINAL THOUGHTS

Ultimately the point of TTFs is to lead churches through transitions and transformations in a healthier way that allows church leaders to lead the congregation rather than to put pastors in a position where they are more likely to be resisted and criticized. As pastors, this way of doing things calls on us to have a different role—to be teachers, resource persons, facilitators, and implementers. It allows us to let leaders lead members while we become leaders of leaders.

The real focus is to help a church overcome its natural resistance by creating a process that increases participation, that considers a wide range of possibilities, that narrows those to practical proposals, and that creates a high level of trust. As mentioned in the beginning, churches resist because they don't trust. They worry about their survival. But if those leading them through transformation are also part of the survival concerns, they can really help the congregation move from mere surviving to thriving. They can also lead the church from analysis that excludes God to discernment that embraces God.

APPENDIX A

Assessing the Church's Spiritual Openness

SUGGESTED USE

1. Invite the leaders of the church to take this assessment home with them and to spend time prayerfully reflecting on the questions and answering them on a separate sheet of paper.
2. Gather the leaders together on a Saturday morning or weekday evening to discuss what they have discerned individually in prayer. You are encouraged to add a short time of worship and/or a short Bible study based on Proverbs 3:5–6 (focusing on what that passage is saying about what the emphasis of leadership in the church should be).

   - Form discussion triads and set appropriate time for leaders to discuss their answers honestly and humbly. Invite them to formulate new answers to the same questions on a separate sheet of paper.
   - Gather the triads together and set an appropriate time for a large-group discussion of their discernings. Have each group present its assessment of the church.
   - Invite the whole group to answer the questions again together and to craft an overall assessment of the state of the church.

3. Follow up with another Saturday session to discuss concrete ways to increase prayerfulness, discernment, spiritual vibrancy in the church, and faith.

DISCUSSION QUESTIONS

Prayerfulness

- To what extent are people in the church comfortable with prayer? Do they generally make public and private prayer a priority in their lives?
- How comfortable are the lay leaders with prayer, especially in making prayer a priority in their lives during times of confusion and crisis?
- How comfortable is the pastor with prayer, especially in making prayer a priority in her or his ministry?

Discernment

- To what extent do members seem to give priority to prayerfully seeking God's guidance through prayer and Scripture?
- To what extent do the leaders, pastoral and lay, give priority to seeking God's guidance through prayer and Scripture in their lives and ministries?
- To what extent do the leaders of the church board and committees encourage the board and committees to spend time in prayer seeking what God wants instead of simply going with majority rule?

Faith

- To what extent would you say that the members of your church have a strong faith in that they are willing to trust God in all situations and circumstances, especially in times of crisis and turmoil?
- To what extent would you say that the leaders of the church act in faith during times of crisis and trouble, and to what extent do they trust mainly in their own powers and abilities?

Spiritual Vibrancy and Integration

- To what extent would you say that your church seems spiritually vibrant?
- To what extent do you believe people sense God's purpose, presence, and power working in their lives?
- How strong is the spiritual dimension in the church; that is, to what extent do spiritual concerns lie at the center of all decisions and determinations of the church and the leadership?

APPENDIX B

Sample Session Agenda

Calvin Presbyterian Church
Zelienople, Pennsylvania
Sample Session Agenda for [Insert Date]

Lighting of the Candle and Time of Centering

Prayer of Blessing

Holy God, bless us this evening so that we will be doing your will in everything we do. Help us to put aside our pride and ego that seeks only what we want so that we can be filled with your Spirit that leads us to want what you want. Hear us in silence as we center ourselves and ask you to guide us this evening . . .

Gathering Chant

Prayer of Praise

Eternal God—Father, Son, and Holy Spirit:
You have called us to be spiritual leaders of your body, this church.
Help us to surrender our hearts and minds to you;

To humbly seek your voice;
To boldly do your will;
To compassionately share your love;
To faithfully be your servants;
And to reverently lead your people
Bless all that we do,
So that we can do what you bless.
In Christ's name we pray. Amen.

Session Sharing (good news or concerns)

Monthly Study

Receptions, Approvals, and Special Concerns

- Clerk Considerations
- Committee Considerations
- Staff and Pastoral Considerations

    - *Issues with the confirmation class*

- Votes of reception and approval:

    - *Approve minutes from the [insert month] session and congregational meetings.*
    - *Receive the Financial Report for [insert month].*

- That the following Special Mission Project funds be approved:

    - *$400 for a family facing eviction.*

- That the following Memorial funds be approved:

    - *None at this time*

- That the following Worship Technology funds be approved:

    - *None at this time*

Prayerful Consideration of Session Matters

- Building and Grounds: no recommendations
- Communications: no recommendations
- Mission: no recommendations
- Zelienople Preschool: no recommendations
- Personnel and Finance: no recommendations
- Spiritual Nurture: no recommendations
- Worship and Arts:

    - *That Calvin Presbyterian Church accept Dr. David English's offer to serve as Calvin's choir director on a volunteer basis.*

- Youth Formation: no recommendations
- Nominations: no recommendations
- Clerk and Staff: no recommendations
- Other actions: no recommendations

A Time of Prayer

The Lord's Prayer

Next Session Meeting

Regular Session meeting: Tuesday, [insert date], @ 6:00 p.m.

Note: We will be meeting with confirmands at 7:00 p.m.

To view these materials in their original formatting, please visit http://www.ngrahamstandish.org.

APPENDIX C

Discerning God's Purpose for the Church

The following is a guide to be used by the church board and invited members to discern and articulate what God's purpose and overall calling are for the church. The meeting should be held on a day when there is ample time to discern and discuss. It can also be split up and held over several days in a row or on specific days over the course of several weeks. Things to consider in preparing for the meeting:

- Invite members of the governing board to be a part of the discernment process.
- Invite from outside the church board only those who seem to be respected leaders *and* who have a sense of spiritual maturity.
- Let this process be fluid, allowing for as much time to be spent as needed—some groups are quicker, while others may be slower.

MEETING AGENDA

1. Begin with a time of worship and prayer.
2. Invite the members into a time of Bible study focusing on discerning God's call. Suggested passages are provided below. Depending on the size of the group, three smaller groups can be created, each to discuss a different passage. The group(s) should

be asked to discuss what the passage says about the nature of God's call and our discerning God's call as individuals and as a church.

- I Samuel 16:1–13
- Proverbs 3:5–6
- Ephesians 4:1–16

3. In a large group, have members share what they have heard in their small group discussions. Specifically, have them address the following questions:

- What do these passages say about God's call to us and how we hear it?
- What guidance do they give us as we seek God's calling here in our church?

4. *Small Group Discernment.*

- Divide the group into smaller groups.
- Give each group several newsprint sheets, large enough to draw a large picture on, along with colored markers.

5. Give the following directions: You are responsible for building this church. Each church must have a foundation upon which it is built, as well as pillars that support the ministry of the church. Basing your discussion and final drawing on the earlier Scripture passages we discussed, discussions we have had so far, and what you know of the ministry of this church, draw two elements for this church:

- A foundation that articulates what you sense is God's foundational call and purpose;
- The pillars, which are anchored in this foundational purpose and which support the ministry of the church.

6. *Large Group Discussion.* Have the participants gather in a large group. Invite each group to present its drawing, presenting what its members sensed the foundational purpose of the church is,

along with the pillars that support the ministry grounded in this purpose.

7. *Integration of Discernments.* Engage all participants in a process of integrating the various drawings into a single, cohesive drawing. This may mean jettisoning some aspects while rearticulating and emphasizing others. New insights may also lead to articulating a clearer foundation and pillars.

8. *Formation of a Purpose Statement.* Form a short, one-sentence statement that captures the essence of the one drawing created by the large group.

9. *Refining of the Purpose Statement.* After closing the session with prayer and worship, give the members several weeks to sit with the formulated statement, and invite them back in a few weeks to a month to reflect on the statement and refine it if necessary.

APPENDIX D

Discerning Direction for a Particular Issue

The following is a simple guide to discerning God's voice when seeking God's call in a particular situation. It is most valuable when a church board or committee is stuck on an issue.

1. Identify the issue to be discussed.
2. Offer a Bible study and a time of prayerful reflection as preparation for discussion:

    - Choose a Bible passage or a passage from a book or article that pertains to the issue being discussed.
    - Have the members identify specific aspects of the Scripture that seem to speak to the issue.

3. Spend a short time in prayer seeking God's guidance.
4. Have a time for open discussion and clarification.
5. Before voting on an issue, take time for centering prayer.

    - Invite participants to spend time in quiet prayer, specifically asking them to put aside their egos to gain a sense of what God wants.

6. Reengage in brief discussion, asking people to share what they sense God may want.

7. Vote on the issue. Have the presiding officer call for the vote using these words: "All who sense this may be God's will, say aye. All who don't, say no." These words invite members to seek God's will rather than their own.

8. Afterward, if the members have not come to a sense of agreement over what God is calling them to do, and they remain divided, invite them to lay aside the vote willingly and to postpone the matter. The point of this action is to emphasize seeking unity (a willingness to act as one body even if not all have sensed the same directives from God), even if unanimity is not possible. A lack of unanimity suggests that various members may have sensed conflicting guidance from God. Postponing for prayer allows more time to be devoted to discernment. When members are willing to lay aside a decision to better seek God's will, they create an environment for discernment.

9. When necessary, because a matter has been postponed for prayer, return the following month and prayerfully revisit the issue. If unanimity is not possible, then the board should seek to go forward in unity—meaning that all members, even dissenting members, prayerfully agree that it is God's will that the board move forward together despite disagreements.

Note: This process does not have to become lengthy. For instance, if the division is not great, the Bible study may be unnecessary, and the group can move directly to the short prayer. If the process gets bogged down, then postpone the decision and take time for prayer. On occasion the leadership board must move forward even though it is divided. Moving forward in disunity should be done only when absolutely critical—a rare occurrence.

APPENDIX E

A Prayerful Process for Discerning Committee Budgets

The following is a guide for committees to use in seeking God's will as they prepare their budget for the coming year. A copy of this guide can be handed out to all committee members.

1. Begin by opening the meeting with a short time of prayer, asking God to guide you during your meeting.
2. Read Proverbs 3:5–6:

   > Trust in the Lord with all your heart, and do not rely on your own insight.
   > In all your ways acknowledge him, and he will make straight your paths.

3. Take 15 minutes to discuss the passage and how it relates to the committee's ministry and budgeting for the church.

   - What does this passage say about what our goal should be as a committee?
   - What does this passage say about what our goal should be as a church?
   - What should our focus be as we determine our budget for the coming year?

4. Spend a short time in prayer, asking members to center their hearts in God so that they can hear God. Then gather suggestions from the members about what God may be calling your committee to do for the coming year. Don't worry about the cost yet.

5. Ask people to take a minute in silent prayer to put aside their egos and what they want so that they can ask in prayer what God wants for this committee.

6. Have the members discuss the committee priorities they sense God wants for the coming year. Remember that God speaks through hearts, and it is impossible to know with certainty what God wants. The focus is seeking to do God's will, not necessarily doing it with perfection. Try to avoid setting priorities based on beliefs that:

   - We *should* do this because it is what we've been doing.
   - We *should* do this because it would be good to do it.
   - We *should* do this because we haven't done it before.
   - We *should* do this because we said in years past that we would.

   The focus should be solely on what we sense God is calling us to do in the coming year.

7. After setting the priorities you sense God wants, spend time determining what it may cost to accomplish these priorities.

8. Set a committee budget to be shared at an all-committee budgeting meeting. Invite all your committee members to attend that meeting.

APPENDIX F

All-Committee Budgeting Process

Invite all members of the church board and committees to this meeting. This meeting serves to guide the board and those involved in setting the budget as to what God is calling the church to do. The results should not be binding but should be taken seriously as God's will. As the finance committee and board consider setting the budget for the coming year, they should do so prayerfully, basing their action on the results of this meeting. Hand out this sheet to all present.

Opening Hymn

"Be Thou My Vision"

Prayer

Holy and gracious God, help us to come before you with humble minds and hearts that are ready to listen for your voice and do what you will. Let this be a time of discerning your will so that our leadership and church may be filled with your blessings. Through Jesus Christ our Lord. *Amen.*

Scripture and Short Discussion

Proverbs 3:5–6: "Trust in the Lord with all your heart, and do not rely on your own insight. In all your ways acknowledge him, and he will make straight your paths."

1. What does this passage say about what our goal should be as leaders of this church?
2. What does this passage say about where our focus should be as we discuss the budget for the coming year?

Centering Prayer

- Ask the members to spend a minute in silence, centering their hearts in God's will.

Presentation of Committee Budget Requests

- One at a time, a representative of each committee presents that committee's budget request, explaining the discerned reason for each request.
- After the presentation, offer a time for questions and discussion.
- Afterward, ask someone to offer prayer for each committee.
- During this process, if discussion becomes divisive, stop and ask the group to spend time in prayer, seeking God's unity.

Centering Prayer

General Discussion

Engage members in a general discussion about overall budget priorities. Remind the members that during this discussion, their focus should be on what God is calling them to do for the *whole* church and not just for their committee. Guide members to set priorities for the whole church budget by asking them to reflect on the overall budget, and then sum up what general budget priorities God has revealed through the budgeting process.

Closing Hymn

"Breathe on Me, Breath of God"

APPENDIX G

Guiding Members to Give

The following is a step-by-step yearly stewardship program guide for finance committees and pastors that encourages members to root their giving in prayerful discernment.

1. *Stewardship Sermons.* Encourage pastors and finance committee to talk about prayerful stewardship throughout the year. Instead of speaking of giving only during the yearly stewardship drive, pastors and other preachers should sprinkle into their sermons throughout the year short discussions and stories on the importance of giving. Then people hear an ongoing, cumulative message of the importance of giving and its connection to spiritual maturity.

2. *Scheduling a Stewardship Campaign.* Time the stewardship program so that it begins after the committee and all-committee budgeting processes have concluded, allowing the finance committee to summarize and communicate to the congregation the prayerful processes they have engaged in, along with the priorities that have been discerned by the committees and church board.

3. *Conducting the Stewardship Campaign.* Allow four weeks for the campaign.

- *Week 1*. Send a first stewardship letter along with a one- to two-page stewardship campaign circular. The circular describes changes or additions to the budget in the coming year.

    a. The letter should discuss how important member giving is to God's work in the church. It should also invite people to spend time in prayer, seeking what God is calling them to give, while offering them specific Scripture passages to reflect on. (See appendix H, "Sample Stewardship Letters and Campaign Circulars.")

    b. The campaign circular should explain the discernment process the committees and board have engaged in and tell the congregation what changes they prayerfully sensed God is calling them to make in the budget for the coming year. (See appendix H, "Sample Stewardship Letters and Campaign Circulars.") It should also encourage them to read the Scripture passages cited in the first stewardship letter as well as encouraging them to begin the process of seeking God's will, especially suggesting that they give only what God is calling them to give, even if that means giving less.

- *Week 2*. Offer a brief time in worship and include a sentence in the bulletin to remind people that the church is in the midst of the stewardship campaign, inviting them to use the resources that have been sent to them to ask prayerfully what God is calling them to give in the upcoming year.
- *Week 3*. Send another stewardship letter with a pledge card enclosed. This letter should again summarize what was said in the first letter and document and then offer members a process on the back of the letter for praying about what they are called to give. (See appendix H, "Sample Stewardship Letters and Campaign Circulars.")
- *Week 4*. Have the members bring their filled-out pledge cards to worship and dedicate the pledges during worship.

After this process, the finance committee and church board should match member giving with the discerned priorities and once again engage in a discernment process, asking what budget God wants them to set.

APPENDIX H

Sample Stewardship Letters and Campaign Circulars

FIRST SAMPLE STEWARDSHIP LETTER

[Date]

Dear Calvin Church Members:

How do you know what matters in life? How do you discern between what is important and what isn't? There are a lot of demands in life, all of them shouting for our attention. What makes hearing God difficult is that God generally doesn't shout out for our attention. God whispers. And because God whispers, it is easy for us to miss God's call to pay attention to what really matters.

One place where God has always whispered, and where people have been calm enough to listen, is at Calvin Church. You have heard God gently whisper to you through our worship, education, mission, ministry, drama, small groups, prayers, and so much more. Calming ourselves enough to listen is a critical value at Calvin Church, and it's one we are asking you follow in the next few weeks.

Throughout [month], the committees and session have been listening to that whisper, asking God what the church is called to do in [year] and how to set the budget accordingly. This is never an easy process because it requires putting away "shoulds" and "what ifs" in order to pay attention to what God wills.

Over the next few weeks, please spend time prayerfully listening to God's whisper as God speaks to you about how to support God's work in this church through your [year] pledge. We deeply believe that if the committees and session prayerfully seek God's will in what we are called to do and budget and you seek God's will in what you are called to contribute, God will find a way to bring the two together. To help you, we've attached a flyer detailing what we have sensed God calling us to do in [year] and why. This is a process steeped in prayer, and we invite you now to join us in that process.

In a few weeks, you will receive a pledge card asking for your financial commitment to the ministry and mission of Calvin Church for [year]. We hope that between now and then you will spend time in prayer, seeking an answer to one simple question: "God, what are you calling me to give to Calvin Church in [year]?" We know that if you join with others in prayer, together we all will ensure that Calvin Church remains a place where we hear what matters.

Yours in Christ's Ministry,

The Calvin Presbyterian Church Personnel and Finance Committee

STEWARDSHIP FLYER

How Is God Calling You to Serve in [year]?

The Calvin Presbyterian Church [year] Stewardship Campaign

Calvin Church has gained a reputation, both locally and nationally, as a unique church that creatively leads people to spiritual depth and acts of love. We regularly have people come to our church to study what we do, yet what we do is really simple. We strive to seek what God is calling us to do as a church and as individuals in every part of our lives. You are a BIG part of that because you are a God-seeking person. As we prepare to enter our [____] year as a church that embodies God's presence, please join us in seeking how God is calling you to give in [year].

Youth Formation and Education Committee

The youth formation and education committee supervises and coordinates the church school, the church nursery, and the youth program while cultivating leaders for these programs. At present, more than 120 children and youth, ages 3–18, are growing spiritually through our church school and the youth program. After a number of years of holding its budget steady or decreasing it, the committee has adopted a new curriculum that is getting rave reviews from teachers and students. They anticipate increasing their budget by $300.

Mission Committee

The mission committee reaches out to those in need, both spiritually and financially. After decreasing its budget by $4,500 in [year], it has discerned new opportunities for mission, especially in supporting individual members to do mission. So the mission committee is anticipating a $1,200 increase for [year].

Building and Property Committee

The building and property committee is responsible for the care of the church-owned buildings and surrounding property. The committee does a tremendous job of making sure our buildings are in the finest shape possible, and it is evident, whether you look at the church from the inside or outside. They plan to decrease their budget by $330 in [year].

Personnel and Finance Committee

The personnel and finance committee is responsible for overseeing the staffing, administration, and financial aspects of Calvin Church. We have a tremendous staff in this church, and we are committed to compensating them not only at a rate that is fair and competitive with other churches like ours in the area, but at a rate that will keep them committed to Calvin Church for years to come. After a number of years in which the staff voluntarily held their salaries the same or took only minimal raises, the session is considering returning to the general yearly policy of an across-the-board 3 percent cost-of-living adjustment to all staff members. This adjustment means a general increase of approximately $6,058 in salaries.

Worship and Arts Committee

The worship and arts committee is responsible for overseeing all worship services as well as the drama ministry. It seeks ways to make our worship services meaningful to worshipers of every age, and it works to ensure that the drama program continues to offer an experience that reaches out to others while also instilling Christian teachings in our youth and adults. In the coming year their budget will increase by a modest $100. This increase is to support a new greeter training program, which was a proposal that came out of the future of worship task force.

Spiritual Nurture and Outreach Committee

The spiritual nurture and outreach committee is responsible for creating programs to help members grow spiritually through adult education and small groups. It also supervises the growing prayer and healing ministries of the church. The [year] budget will remain the same as in [year].

Communications Committee

The communications committee has been working diligently to enhance the communications both within and beyond Calvin Church. In [year] it performed a dynamic upgrade of our website that allows our staff members to directly post items rather than having to go through one WebServant. Also, it sponsored the hiring of Toni Schlemmer as our director of communications to facilitate the publicizing of church events. For [year], they are anticipating no increases.

Future of Worship Task Force Matters

The future of worship task force has offered a series of dynamic proposals to enhance our worship after a year spent studying and seeing what is possible in worship. Their focus was to prepare the church for the next 10 or more years so that we can reach out to people of *all* ages for years to come. The session is considering several proposals that will enhance our worship. They are taking their time with this to ensure it's a calling and not just a wish. The most significant proposal is to add a percussionist and a guitar player to our music team. This is *not* so that we can begin to play rock music or offer a more driving contemporary sound. It is to give our music more depth, much in the same way we did when we added the electric keyboards 10 years ago that DeWayne Segafredo plays on Sundays. We are not interested in becoming a rock-driven church. These additions would increase our budget by $10,000. It would also make our soundboard needs more complex and beyond the capacity of our present volunteers. This would necessitate the hiring of a person dedicated to sound, increasing our budget by an extra $3,000.

How are you called to be part of Calvin Church's ministry in [year]?
   In the next few weeks we ask you to prayerfully consider your pledge. Please don't consider what you should give, want to give, or can afford. Please follow the session's lead, which has tried to ask, "God, what are you calling us to do?" Please ask in prayer, "God, what are you calling us to give?"

SECOND SAMPLE STEWARDSHIP LETTER

Trust in the Lord with all your heart,
and do not rely on your own insight.
In all your ways acknowledge God,
and God will make straight your paths.

[Date]

Dear Calvin Church Members:

Thank you for taking the time over the past few weeks to pray and seek what God is calling you to give to Calvin Presbyterian Church in [year]. Whether you have spent time in deep prayer or have just thought about it prayerfully, please trust that God is with you in this. God cares more about intention than perfection when it comes to seeking God's will. This is a time to seek what God wants for and from you, and God is speaking.

Each year our committees and the session budget for the next year by taking time in prayer to ask, *"God, what are you calling us to do in the coming year?"* We are trying to live out the passage quoted above. We genuinely try to put away our own insights so that we can get a sense of what God is calling us to do.

We are asking you to join us in this prayer process as we finalize our budget for [year]. We believe that if we prayerfully seek what God is calling us to do, and you prayerfully seek what God is calling you to give, then God will find a way to bring the two together.

We offered you a prayer guide with Scripture in our previous letter, and we are attaching it here, too. Also, we have included a pledge card for you to use, which helps us to ascertain what the church's income will be in the coming year. Please spend time in prayer over the next week, asking God what you are called to give in [year]. After praying and listening to God, please fill out the pledge card and bring it with you on Sunday, [date], to either worship service, or send it to us in the next two weeks.

Thank you for having been so generous in the past and for taking time to pray for and about the future.

In Christ's service,

The Calvin Presbyterian Church Session

A GUIDE TO PRAYERFULLY SEEKING GOD'S WILL

The following will help you as you seek what God is calling you to give to Calvin Presbyterian Church in [year]:

Please read prayerfully the following Bible passages. After reading each passage, let it guide you to consider what God is calling you to give.

2 Corinthians 9:6–12

Whoever sows sparingly will also reap sparingly, and whoever sows generously will also reap generously. Each man should give what he has decided in his heart to give, not reluctantly or under compulsion, for God loves a cheerful giver. And God is able to make all grace abound to you, so that in all things at all times, having all that you need, you will abound in every good work. . . . You will be made rich in every way so that you can be generous on every occasion, and through us your generosity will result in thanksgiving to God.

1 Timothy 6:13–21

In the sight of God, who gives life to everything, and of Christ Jesus, who while testifying before Pontius Pilate made the good confession, I charge you to keep this command without spot or blame until the appearing of our Lord Jesus Christ. . . . Command those who are rich in this present world not to be arrogant nor to put their hope in wealth, which is so uncertain, but to put their hope in God, who richly provides us with everything for our enjoyment. Command them to do good, to be rich in good deeds, and to be generous and willing to share. In this way they will lay up treasure for themselves as a firm foundation for the coming age, so that they may take hold of the life that is truly life.

- Reflecting on the Scripture, take time in silent prayer to ask what God is calling you to give. God will guide you if you are open.
- Continue to ask God to guide you over the next few weeks on what you should give. Trust that God will speak to you in some way. It probably won't come in a lightning bolt, but more in a sense of peace surrounding a number that seems "right."

- After you've sensed an answer, fill out your pledge card and offer it to God on Sunday, [date], in worship. You also may send your pledge to the church office.

To view these materials in their original formatting, please visit http://www.ngrahamstandish.org.

APPENDIX I

A Guide to Healing Prayer

There is healing power available from God if you are willing to believe and trust. Jesus came not only to preach and teach but also to heal. Almost one-fifth of the stories in the Gospels are about Jesus healing all kinds of illness: physical, mental, and spiritual. After Jesus died, the apostles continued the ministry of healing, as did their followers. Belief in healing has always been at the core of Christianity, whether all churches have practiced it or not.

How can you receive God's healing? It begins with *faith* and *surrender*. Recognize your doubts and put them aside so that you can open yourself to God's healing power. If you have difficulty doing this, tell God that you have trouble giving up your doubts. Ask God to have faith for you. Healing also includes surrender—giving God everything, including the power to choose what kind of healing to give you. To truly let God heal you, you must let God decide what kind of healing is best, even if it is different from what you want. God is not a genie who obeys our commands. God is the loving healer who will do what's best for us. Trust in that.

God wants to heal you, but not necessarily according to the plan you may have for your own healing. Most of us want to be healed on the outside. We want to be healed of physical or mental disease, but God is interested most in healing from the inside out—from the soul outward.

The more open you are to God, the more God can heal you spiritually and then let that spiritual healing turn into mental and physical healing.

The most important things are to try your best to trust in God to heal you and to trust that God is healing you, even if you can't feel anything happening. Like seeds planted in the soil, growth cannot always be seen until it sprouts. You need to be patient and let God work. Healing, like anything lasting, takes time to grow.

The following, then, are suggestions to you as you begin healing prayer for yourself or someone else:

1. *Lay aside your doubts, worries, and cares.* Psalm 46:10 says, "Be still, and know that I am God." As you begin your prayer, be as still and calm as possible. If you can't let go of your concerns, don't worry. God will accept you as you are. Just trust that God will act.

2. *Open yourself to Christ.* Just as we need to plug a lamp into an electrical outlet to receive light, we need to plug into God to receive healing power. Try taking a minute to silently recite to yourself, "Bless the Lord, O my soul." When you feel more open to Christ, ask him to enter you and grow within you.

3. *Pray.* Pray for your healing. Be specific. Imagine what you want Christ to do and ask for it. Ask with confidence. A suggested prayer: "Lord, I know that it is your will for me to be whole and holy. Let your power enter me and heal me. Heal me by . . . [name your specific request]. Thank you for healing me."

4. *Trust and believe that God's power is entering into you.* When the Holy Spirit works, we usually *don't* see, sense, or feel it. Sometimes healing is immediate. More often it is slow and gradual. This is especially true of pervasive physical diseases such as cancer or degenerative diseases and mental illness. Don't spend time analyzing whether you are being healed or not. Just trust and believe.

5. *Thank God for healing you.* When we thank God, we are appreciating God, and the more we appreciate God, the more we allow God into our lives. After you've prayed for healing, thank God for being with you.

6. *Set up a prayer discipline.* Too often people pray once and, when nothing happens, quit praying. God wants us not only to pray but

to pray constantly. It is through our constant prayer that God increases in our lives. Make regular times for healing prayer. Do it two or three times a day. Keep it down to earth and direct. The best prayers are simple: "God, I know you love me and are with me. You know my struggles and pain. In the power of Christ, fill me with your Spirit and heal me."

As you begin to pray for healing, try this simple prayer:

> God, I give you my life to do with as you will. I know that you can heal me, yet my faith is weak. Give me the faith to trust in you. Let your healing Spirit enter me and heal me by [name your specific need]. I thank you, God, for your presence. Let your grace shine in me and through me.

Follow the Guidance of Scripture

One of the best ways to increase the Spirit's power in your life is to follow the guidance of 1 Thessalonians 5:16–18: "Rejoice always, pray without ceasing, give thanks in all circumstances; for this is the will of God in Christ Jesus for you." Rejoicing, praying without ceasing, and giving thanks increases the Spirit's power in your life by opening your mind, heart, and soul to the Holy Spirit's healing power. It creates the confidence we have in God's willingness and power to heal us.

- *Rejoice always.* It is easy to slip into a dark, pessimistic, doubting, and cynical spirit. This is especially true when one is suffering from the depression that so often afflicts us because of either physical or mental illness. Look around and appreciate God's presence. You might notice the love of family, the movements of nature, or anything else that reveals Christ's work in the world. Try to find ways to rejoice, even if it is difficult and you see no joy in life. Rejoicing increases God's presence.
- *Pray without ceasing.* Turn your life into prayer. You don't have to pray in a formal way. Talk to God all throughout the day. Give Christ your burdens. Let the Holy Spirit be a constant companion by constantly speaking and listening to God throughout your day.
- *Give thanks in all circumstances.* The more we thank God, even when we don't sense God's presence, the more we create open-

ings for the Holy Spirit to enter our lives. Think about this. Have you noticed that when you are thankful, others tend to be giving and caring toward you? And the opposite is true: the more ungrateful and grudging we are in life, the less positively people respond. Our attitude can either open or close us to others, and it can open or close us to God. Look for reasons to thank God.

To view these materials in their original formatting, please visit http:// www.ngrahamstandish.org.

APPENDIX J

Nominating Committees

GUIDELINES FOR NOMINATING COMMITTEE MEMBERS

As a member of the nominating committee, you are serving this church in an important ministry. Through your work, you are having a direct impact on the future of the church by nominating future church leaders who will guide our future direction. How you make your decisions will determine the extent to which this church becomes a place that listens to and serves Christ. For that reason, it is important to keep several principles in mind as you go about the process of choosing nominees.

1. *Remember that you are Christ's eyes, hands, and voice.* God is working through you to call new leaders to the ministry of this church. So as a way of being God's eyes, hands, and voice, you are being asked to:

    *   Seek God's will in prayer, asking God the question, "God, who are you calling to be a leader of this church?" Take this process seriously, because it is the foundation of everything you do.
    *   Prayerfully seek people of faith and commitment who you sense will act with faith, hope, and love—not fear, cynicism, and selfishness—in their leadership.

- Avoid choosing people based upon conventional thoughts such as:

  - Let's get someone who will say yes.
  - Let's get someone who has experience.
  - Let's get someone I want, the pastor wants, or the leader of the nominating committee wants.
  - Let's get someone who has been serving on a committee.

2. *Choose leaders who you sense will be spiritual leaders for the church* . Church board leaders are called to be spiritual leaders of the church. The people you nominate should be people who are willing to struggle with the process of listening to God's gentle calling for themselves and the church. They do not have to be perfect (who is?), but they are people who you believe take their faith seriously and will bring their faith into their service to the church.

3. *Give people time to sense whether this is or isn't a calling for them*. When you extend an offer to someone to become a board member:

  - Visit prospective leaders at home or in a private place where questions can be asked and answered in an unhurried environment.
  - Give prospective leaders the sheet explaining the position and expectations.
  - Explain to them why you sense that they may be good candidates for the position.
  - Give them time and encourage them to consider the position prayerfully. This process does take a commitment of time, but remember that the point is to get good people, not to hurriedly get warm bodies to fill the positions. It is better to operate shorthanded with a few excellent people than to operate with a full slate of less-qualified people.

4. *Try your best to avoid these pitfalls:*

- Don't choose only people you know, but seek out also those you don't know. It is easy to keep choosing the same people again and again, but when we do this, we end up weakening the leadership base of the church.
- Don't avoid choosing people who have served in the past. Often, certain people possess wisdom, faith, and skills that have been proved over time. Seek to balance diversity with consistency.
- Don't choose only those people who are successful in the secular realm. Often people who are strong secular leaders have strong egos that inhibit their ability to seek God's will over their own. Faith, humility, and love for others are more important qualities. Still, you do need to assess whether people have the skills necessary to lead a committee.
- Don't make serving on a committee a precondition for serving on the church board. When we impose such a requirement, we end up serving a custom, not God. Sometimes excellent people have not been asked to serve before. At the same time, don't ignore previous service on a committee.
- Be sure that the people you nominate don't have an ax to grind. Sometimes people want to serve on the church board so that they can move the church in a certain direction. It is important for leaders to have a vision, but when elders are more interested in serving their own causes rather than God, their personal drive becomes divisive. Be sure that the people you nominate are willing to ask what God wants first, and what they want second. People who are interested only in their own goals should be disqualified.
- Don't forget to pray, pray, and pray. Prayer is not just a ritual. When we pray, we are asking God to be present among us. So pray constantly that God will help you find the right people to lead this church and pray for it.

A PROCESS FOR NOMINATING COMMITTEE MEETINGS

The focus of the agenda is to help members remain grounded in seek-ing and discerning God's will in calling candidates to the leadership positions of our church.

1. *Centering and prayer.* Begin the meeting with quiet centering for a minute, and then offer an opening prayer asking God to guide the committee.
2. *Grounding in God's Word.* Spend 15 minutes in Bible study to ground what you are doing in Scripture and to open yourself to God's guidance in Scripture. Scripture should be chosen that is relevant to discerning God's will in prayer and faith. Suggested Scripture passages include Proverbs 3:5–8, 1 Corinthians 12:4–31, Ephesians 3:14–21, John 15:1–17, Ephesians 4:1–16, John 13:1–20, 2 Timothy 2:14–19, and James 4:1–10.
3. *Prayer discernment.* Take time in quiet prayer to gain a sense of whom God is calling to be leaders. Have members prayerfully focus for a time and then make a list of names. If the members don't sense much, encourage them simply to spend the time in prayer asking God to lead them.
4. *Compare discernments.* Have members share their lists, and then begin to make a master list from their comments.
5. *Come to consensus.* Be sure that when you discern a candidate as suitable for a position, there is consensus among the members that this person is qualified. This step prevents one person from dominating the process and pushing a particular candidate. If there is division among nominating committee members about a candidate, there is a good chance that this person is not necessar-ily being called by God just now. If disagreement persists, then lead the committee back into prayer to ask God to cleanse mem-bers of their own agendas so that they can be more open to God's will.
6. *Resist discouragement.* If the committee gets bogged down and has trouble getting people to say yes to a position, do not get discouraged or desperate. Such frustration can lead to seeking people just to fill a spot instead of seeking God's will. When a time of confusion occurs, reground the committee in prayer and

Scripture. Devote a whole meeting to prayer and Bible study, and then return to the process in the next meeting.

7. *Close in prayer.* Spend time praying for the work of the church and for God's continuing guidance.

To view these materials in their original formatting, please visit http://www.ngrahamstandish.org.

APPENDIX K

Becoming an Elder at Calvin Presbyterian Church

We are grateful that you are considering the invitation to serve as an elder for Calvin Presbyterian Church. As you take time to make your decision, the following information may help you discern whether this is God's calling for you.

The Calling to Be an Elder

Being an elder is a calling. One of the convictions we take seriously at Calvin Presbyterian Church is that God cares deeply about what goes on in this congregation. The members of the nominating committee may ask you to serve as an elder, but it is really God who calls people to serve. The nominating committee members are merely acting as servants who try to sense God's call for the church. You have been asked to consider becoming an elder because the members of Calvin Church's nominating committee have sensed that God *may* be calling you. They have looked at your leadership abilities and skills, and they sense that you have made God central in your life. As a result, they believe that God may be calling you to serve as a leader of Calvin Presbyterian Church.

What Is an Elder?

Elders have been the church leaders since the earliest church was formed in Jerusalem on the Day of Pentecost. The following points may help you understand what an elder is:

- Elders are called to be spiritual leaders of the church, not political leaders. They are to "lead the congregation continually to discover what God is doing in the world and to plan for change, renewal, and reformation under the Word of God" (*Book of Order*, G-10.0102j).
- Elders' primary concern is trying to discern what God seeks for the church. They act as leaders by listening together for what God is calling all the members to do as a church, and then by creating opportunities to turn what they hear into action.
- Elders are expected to be people of faith, dedication, and good judgment who try to do their best to serve God.
- As the Presbyterian *Book of Order* states, "Together with the pastor, [elders] should encourage the people in the worship and service of God, equip and renew them for their tasks within the church and for their mission in the world, visit and comfort and care for the people, with special attention to the poor, the sick, the lonely, and those who are oppressed. . . . Those duties which all Christians are bound to perform by the law of love are especially incumbent upon elders because of their calling to office and are to be fulfilled by them as official responsibilities" (G-6.0304).

What Will Happen If I Say Yes?

If you agree to serve as an elder, you will become part of an important ministry in this church. You will serve a three-year term and in the process share in the administration of this church. That means serving on and possibly chairing a committee of the church. It means looking toward the future with other elders and helping form a vision for Calvin Presbyterian Church. If you have more questions, please call Dr. Standish at the church office or talk to one of the present elders.

A Guide to Discerning Your Call

As you consider whether you are called by God to be an elder, the following guide may help you:

1. Take time in quiet prayer, away from others, to make your decision.
2. After quiet prayer, ask God whether you should serve as an elder.
3. Try to get a sense in your heart about what the answer may be. If you don't sense anything right away, don't worry. God will still be working to give you an answer.
4. Talk with your family members about their thoughts.
5. Look at your life and get a sense of whether you have the necessary time and personal commitment to the church to accept this important call.
6. Take several days to continue this process of asking in prayer what God's will is, listening to your heart, talking with your family, and assessing your life.

If it is God's will that you be an elder, you will discover three things happening:

1. You will get a sense in your heart that this is the "right" thing to do.
2. The idea of serving as an elder will make rational sense to you.
3. As you assess your life and talk with your family, everything will fall into place and make the way clear for you to serve as an elder.

To view these materials in their original formatting, please visit http://www.ngrahamstandish.org.

APPENDIX L

A Guide to Holding Spiritually Grounded Meetings

A significant problem in making prayerful decisions as members of a church board or committee is that we often are not clear about the foundations of our decisions. For instance, do we decide based on rational judgment? Ease of achievement or efficiency of application? Affordability? Past success? Unfortunately, most church boards ignore the primary spiritual question: *What is God calling us to do?*

Christ tells us that the wise person who listens for God builds a house on rock instead of sand (Matt. 7:24). While many of the concerns stated above are legitimate ones, they are still "sand" because they are not rooted in faith. Still, they look like rock because they are built on what common wisdom says is rock. When we make decisions in the church, we need to make them in the light of spiritual concerns while taking into consideration more functional realities. In short, our decisions need to be based more upon what we sense we are called to do rather than on what we think is practical. The practical is secondary to calling.

A spiritual focus does not ignore questions of practicality, efficiency, and finance, but these concerns are tempered by what we sense God wants us to do. For instance, if we feel genuinely called to some ministry or activity, then we should use our concerns about finances to help us create something that is financially responsible as well as spiritually faithful.

With these principles in mind, then, here is a guide to help your committee make decisions that are spiritually sound as well as pragmatic and realistic.

Spiritual Reflection

Prayerful spiritual reflection means using our hearts and minds *together* to determine whether something is what God wants for us. When we reflect spiritually, we ask whether or not God is guiding us in this or that particular direction. Spiritual reflection is like a thread that runs through all our other kinds of reflection. Here are five steps in reflecting spiritually:

1. *Always begin with prayer.* Begin your discussions and deliberations in prayer, seeking the Spirit's guidance. *Believe* that if you do this, God will lead you. For as Christ says, "Where two or three are gathered in my name, I am there among them" (Matt. 18:20).

2. *Continually check your heart.* During discussions and as you come to conclusions, continually ask whether something feels spiritually "right." Is this possibility something that we sense God does or does not want for us? Some actions may make perfect sense but still be spiritually wrong. Good decisions feel right spiritually.

3. *Continually take time for simplification, clarification, prayer, and silence.* Too often, where there is continued confusion or disagreement, groups get lost in having too many ideas. When there are too many possibilities, confusion reigns. So try to clarify by simplifying what the basic issue is, and then discern between clear, simple possibilities. When the time is right to make a decision and discern, take time to refocus on God through silence and prayer. When the issue is simplified and people are given time to be silent and to pray, decisions become more clear and focused.

4. *Try to reach a prayerful consensus.* While it is silly always to expect to reach unanimous agreement in all decisions, the best decisions are the ones that are so compelling spiritually that they make decisions easy. A seriously divided vote signifies either that the decision is not quite theologically and spiritually sound or that

some in the group are letting their egos get in the way and are not taking spiritual reflection seriously. So I always suggest trying to move forward in *unanimity* (we all sense that this is what God is calling us to do) or *unity* (we don't quite agree, but those in the minority are willing to trust the discernment of others). If we cannot reach either, then *postpone for prayer* (inviting leaders to take more time to discern on their own) for a month or so, and see whether another possibility can be discerned.

5. *Always bless your actions with prayer.* After making a decision, ask God to bless it, and believe that with this blessing, anything is possible.

Reflecting spiritually does not need to be formal. Instead, it should be as natural as possible. Do not be afraid to include spiritual reflection and prayer as part of your meetings. The more you pray, the better you will become at it.

A Suggested Format for Committee Meetings

One of the most important ways to make our meetings more spiritually alive is to structure our meetings around prayer. Like any new activity, grounding the meeting in prayer will be somewhat uncomfortable at first. With time, it will feel more natural. It will also help committee members become more accustomed to bringing prayer and reflection into all parts of their lives.

1. Beginning the Meeting

Begin the meeting with 30 seconds of silence, and ask members to quietly center their hearts upon God. Consider lighting a candle(s) as you begin as a symbol of God's light in the room.

2. Sharing Time

Ask people at the committee meeting whether they have anything that they would like to share with others about recent concerns or joys in their lives. Encourage people to share anything that could be prayed about as a group, such as illnesses, struggles, and difficulties in their or family's and friends' lives. Leaders who share their lives are also more likely to care about one another.

3. Study Time

Invite members of boards and committees to engage in a study of Scripture, a book chapter, or another kind of study so that they can be grounded spiritually. Study resources should be chosen that help leaders become trained in prayer and discernment. One suggestion is the use of "Committee Reflections" that I offer through my website in the "Resources" section (http://www.ngrahamstandish.org). You will find a three-year cycle of free monthly reflections (36 in all) that can be used for boards and committees. These are short, one-page studies devoted to training leaders in prayer and discernment.

4. Business

Discuss the business of the board or committee. As you conduct your business, keep three things in mind.

- Instead of beginning with motions to be debated, have all motions become "recommendations," which allows the ensuing discussion to craft the motion. In other words, emphasize dialogue as leading to a final motion to be voted upon rather than emphasizing debate between options that creates winners and losers over motions. When a leadership board seems to be reaching a discussion through dialogue, articulate the eventual consensus into a final motion to be discerned through prayer.
- When matters become confusing or contentious in the midst of dialogue, it is good to invite members to pause for silent prayer and reflection to reground themselves in God's presence.
- Take time to pray about it in silence and together prior to voting (a few seconds for simple items [approval of minutes] up to two minutes for more weighty issues). When taking a vote, ask the leaders a question designed to seek God's will rather than our own: "All who sense this may be God's will for us, say yes; all who sense it may not be God's will for us, say no," rather than "All in favor, say yes; all opposed, say no."

5. Limitation and Delegation

Most boards struggle to create time for prayer and study because they overload themselves with too many matters that aren't necessary:

- Leaders don't need to give verbal reports. Reports were necessary during a time when many church board and committee members couldn't read and when making and distributing copies of reports weren't possible. It's a remnant of a bygone era (and a major time consumer) in an age when minutes can be easily copied and sent out ahead of time for people to read for themselves. Cutting out reports creates more time for prayer and study.
- If committees are trained in discernment, boards can limit and delegate the number of issues they deal with. They do so by trusting and empowering committees to make decisions on behalf of the board as long as the matter is within their budget and their mandate (what they are authorized to decide). If a committee discerns a call that is within their budget and mandate, boards should be very reluctant to rediscuss and redecide these issues. They should reserve their discernment for issues that go beyond committee budgets and mandates and that deal with more whole-church issues.

6. Prayer

At the meeting's end, clasp hands and form a circle. The chairperson begins a silent prayer, and when she is done, she squeezes the hand of the person to the left. If that person wants to pray, he prays and then squeezes the next person's hand. If he doesn't want to pray, then he squeezes the next person's hand. This continues around the circle. The person who has been monitoring the committee for prayer should pray for the concerns of the committee. Close with the Lord's Prayer.

APPENDIX M

Four Principles of Discernment

Here are four simple principles to keep in mind whenever seeking to discern God's will as an individual or group.

1. Grounding in Scripture

Discernment always starts with Scripture. That doesn't mean that to discern, a person must immediately open the Bible and look for particular guidance. That works at times, but it isn't the best way. For effective and powerful discernment, it is best simply to become a person of Scripture. This means engaging in regular devotional reading of Scripture, becoming part of Bible studies, and listening to Scripture through sermons. Grounding our discernment in Scripture allows us to be formed by Scripture so that the words begin to guide us even when we are not aware of their influence.

2. Listening for Christ's Voice

God's voice is so much richer than ours, and God can speak to us through anything—a song, a poem, a leaf, a graduation ceremony, the lettering on a truck, the stray comment of a stranger—anything. Learn to become attuned to how God is speaking. At the same time, don't assume that everything you hear is from God. Be discriminating and somewhat skeptical. The true voice of God will resonate within. Your heart will leap at its sound.

3. Clarifying

Don't assume because you have heard something that it has to be God's voice. Far too many false preachers, teachers, and prophets have been deceived by their own pride masquerading as God's voice. Have the humility to ask, "Is this really you, God?" Then talk with others, especially those who you believe are spiritually attuned. If God is speaking to you, they will sense it, too. If the voice isn't God's, their doubts will help you go back and listen again. The important part of clarifying God's voice is recognizing that Christ is present and speaks to us throughout life but that our egos, especially when they are immature and afraid of seeking Christ, can speak to us through a false voice that mimics Christ's voice. Discernment requires us to spend time clarifying, to whatever extent we can, whether the voice we hear is Christ's voice. If it is, then it will be affirmed by others who also are seeking to discern God's will.

4. Following in Faith

Following in faith is the thing that separates real ministry and mission from activities that are self-serving. When we follow God in faith, we still have doubts, we still are a bit reluctant, we still have trepidations, but we act anyway. If Christ is really the one calling, something special will happen. The impossible will become possible—and sometimes the possible becomes impossible when our timing isn't God's. Generally, God will find a way to work through us to make what God wants happen. This is how God as Presence works. God as Purpose calls us to ministry and mission, and God as Presence makes it happen through us. To be a blessed church means acting in faith.

APPENDIX N

A Guide to Creating a Prayer Group, with Covenant

A GUIDE TO CREATING A PRAYER GROUP

The purpose of prayer groups is to give members of the church the opportunity to engage in a ministry of prayer for the church, other members, specific concerns, and local and world events. These groups will further the mission of being a church that listens for and serves God in prayer. Prayer groups root the church in the purposes of God the Creator, prepare the church for the presence of God in Jesus Christ, and open the church to the power and work of the Holy Spirit in the church.

How to Invite Others to Join

The best strategy for forming a prayer group is to identify 8 to 10 members of the church who either already take prayer seriously in their lives or seem to have the potential to do so. (The latter may be people who do not have much experience in prayer but have expressed a desire to pray.) The more people initially invited, the larger the eventual group will be. Expect 20 to 40 percent of those invited to drop out of the group at some point. Invite them to a preliminary meeting to introduce them to the idea of a prayer group, explaining the process described below. Then invite them to make a six-week commitment to form a group and meet weekly at a designated time. Explain that you will ask them to assess whether they want to remain in the group at the end of the six-week period. During the assessment, invite those who want to remain to sign the covenant provided below and officially to become part of the prayer group.

Features of the Prayer Group

- Each group ideally consists of six to eight members. Whenever the group grows larger than this, the members should consider dividing it and creating a new group.
- Each group member should have a specific role and duty in the group (although this may mean that some share duties). Having a specific role or duty in the group encourages commitment to the group. The following are suggested roles and duties of the members, along with their responsibilities.

  - The *group coordinator* is responsible for opening the group and for ensuring that the group's agenda is followed.
  - The *assistant coordinator* helps the group coordinator and acts as coordinator whenever the leader is absent. Also, the assistant coordinator is responsible for offering prayers for special concerns that might arise. In addition, she or he would be responsible for dividing up the church directory so that a certain number of members can be prayed for at each meeting.
  - The *church pray-er* would be aware of events in the church and offer prayers for the church, staff, committees, and special events.
  - The *concerns pray-er* would offer prayers for members and nonmembers who have special needs. These concerns would be gathered from Sunday bulletin prayer inserts and from people requesting prayer. The prayer group may need to set up a process for people in the church and community to request prayers, such as placing a prayer box somewhere in the church or providing a contact link on the church's website.
  - The *local and world events pray-er* would keep abreast of events in the world and locally and offer prayers for these concerns.

These roles are all flexible, and each group can create and assign additional roles as seems appropriate. The pray-ers do not have to offer all the prayers for their particular area of concern but can distribute them among the rest of the group. The group is confidential, and no personal matters prayed for in the group are to be discussed outside the group.

Particulars of the Prayer Group

- The group meets for an hour each week.
- The group follows a 10-week cycle (except during the initial six-week cycle).
- Every 10 weeks an invitation to new members is extended, either through the newsletter or through personal invitation, to those deemed by the prayer group as potential members.
- Two weeks after the beginning of a group, a covenant is drawn up. (A sample covenant is provided below.)
- A suggested agenda for the weekly meeting follows:

  - *Opening Prayer.* The coordinator opens with a short prayer, which might be the Lord's Prayer, another written prayer, or a personal, extemporaneous prayer.
  - *Sharing.* Members take time for sharing—10 or fewer minutes.
  - *Centering.* The assistant coordinator leads a one- to two-minute time of quiet centering, a time for members to let go of their concerns and to become more open to God's purpose, presence, and power.
  - *Offering of Prayer Concerns.* When the coordinator believes all are centered, she or he begins by offering a prayer for the group. Each member then offers prayers for his or her assigned area. Those who are not assigned a role, or who share a role and have not prayed, pray for whatever concerns they feel inspired by the Spirit to offer. Members also may offer prayers for any personal concerns brought up during the time of sharing.
  - *Closing.* When personal prayers are finished, members say the Lord's Prayer together.

Covenants

Every 10 weeks, members are encouraged to sign a covenant of commitment to the prayer group. Covenants should address the following issues:

- Who the members of the group are.
- The group's purpose.
- Where and when the group will meet.
- Expectations of the members, such as:

    - Members should be committed to being at the group each week. When a member cannot attend, she or he should covenant to pray for the group and the concerns of the group at some point during the week.
    - All prayer concerns offered each week should be kept confidential.
    - The group should strive to avoid becoming a divisive agent in the church and seek to be a healing one. This aim is accomplished by focusing only on God and God's will in prayer. In other words, the members are not to pray against the ministries of particular staff people or members, against the work of committees or board, or for a certain resolution other than what God wills regarding any issue.

A sample covenant follows.

PRAYER GROUP COVENANT

A covenant is an agreement among people establishing a commitment between them and God. When we make a covenant with God and others, we trust that if we remain faithful to our part, God will be faithful to us and bless what we are doing. As members of this prayer group, we are committed to praying together once a week, trusting that God will listen and bless those for whom we pray.

> As for me, I am establishing my covenant with you and your descendants after you. This is the sign of the covenant that I make between

me and you and every living creature that is with you, for all future generations: I have set my bow in the clouds, and it shall be a sign of the covenant between me and the earth. (Genesis 9:9–13)

Covenant

- We agree to be part of the Prayer Group.
- We agree to meet every _____ (*day*) from _____ to _____ (*times*).
- We agree to make this activity a priority for our lives and to do our best to put aside all other commitments during this time between the dates of _____ and _____. We agree to spend the time praying for: _____.
- We agree to share and pray with one another; to be honest with one another; to keep the names of those for whom we pray and other matters discussed within the group confidential; to affirm one another and the church; and to refrain from criticizing the church, members, or others.
- We agree that the following people will have or share these specific roles:

  - Group Coordinator:
  - Assistant Coordinator:
  - World and Local Events:
  - Church Members:
  - Church Committees and Events:
  - Others:

- We agree to pray for each other throughout the week.

Signed: _____

APPENDIX O

Bibliography of Writers in Spirituality and Spiritual Theology

The following are suggestions for spiritual reading. The focus is not to give you books that present one particular spiritual perspective but to offer a variety of books from great spiritual writers from ancient, traditional, modern times, and contemporary eras. Also, they range in perspectives from Protestant to Catholic and Orthodox as well as progressive, conservative, moderate, charismatic, and evangelical. The point is to offer resources that extend beyond our normal theological and spiritual comfort zones so that we can be exposed to the great depth and breadth of the Christian spiritual tradition.

The order of the resources is a suggested order for using books in small group ministries so that each successive book offers a different level of awareness that can build on the previous books. They include several books by me, which are included because they were written specifically to be used in these kinds of groups. All of these are books that have been used for more than 20 years in spiritual reading groups at Calvin Presbyterian Church:

1. Richard J. Foster, *Celebration of Discipline*, Harper & Row, 1988.
2. N. Graham Standish, *Paradoxes for Living*, Westminster John Knox Press, 2001.

3. Brother Lawrence, *The Practice of the Presence of God*, Paraclete Press, 1985.
4. C. S. Lewis, *The Screwtape Letters*, Touchstone Books, 1996.
5. Henri Nouwen, *Life of the Beloved*, Crossroad, 2002.
6. Ronald Rolheiser, *The Holy Longing*, Doubleday, 1999.
7. Corrie ten Boom, *The Hiding Place*, Chosen Books, 2006.
8. Philip Yancey, *Reaching for the Invisible God*, Zondervan, 2000.
9. Brennan Manning, *Ruthless Trust*, HarperCollins, 2002.
10. David Steindl-Rast, *Gratefulness, the Heart of Prayer*, Paulist Press, 1984.
11. Hannah Hurnard, *Hinds' Feet on High Places*, Living Books, 1986.
12. Richard Foster, *Prayer*, HarperCollins, 1992.
13. Hannah Whitall Smith, *The Christian's Secret of a Happy Life*, Baker Book House, 1952.
14. Agnes Sanford, *The Healing Light*, Ballantine Books, 1983.
15. Thomas R. Kelly, *A Testament of Devotion*, HarperSanFrancisco, 1992.
16. C. S. Lewis, *The Great Divorce*, Macmillan, 1946.
17. Thomas à Kempis, *The Imitation of Christ*, Ave Maria Press, 1990.
18. N. Graham Standish, *Discovering the Narrow Path*, Westminster John Knox Press, 2002.
19. Thomas Merton, *Thoughts in Solitude*, Farrar, Straus and Giroux, 1986.
20. Dorotheos of Gaza, *Discourses and Sayings*, Cistercian Publications, 1977.
21. *Father Arseny, 1893–1973*, translated by Vera Bouteneff, St. Vladamir's Seminary Press, 1998.
22. Richard Rohr, *Immortal Diamond*, Jossey-Bass, 2012.
23. Dallas Willard, *The Divine Conspiracy*, HarperCollins, 1998.
24. Jean-Pierre de Caussade, *The Sacrament of the Present Moment*, HarperSanFrancisco, 1982.
25. Henri Nouwen, *The Way of the Heart*, Ballantine Books, 1981.
26. Philip Yancey, *Soul Survivor*, Waterbrook Press, 2003.
27. Richard J. Foster and James Bryan Smith, *Devotional Classics*, HarperSanFrancisco, 1993.

NOTES

1. WHAT IS A BLESSED CHURCH?

1. Christian Schwarz, *Natural Church Development: A Guide to Eight Essential Qualities of Healthy Churches* (St. Charles, IL: ChurchSmart Resources, 2000), 23.

2. Bill Easum, *Leadership on the Other Side* (Nashville, TN: Abingdon, 2000), 111.

3. Easum, *Leadership on the Other Side*, 113.

4. Stan Ott, *Twelve Dynamic Shifts for Transforming Your Church* (Grand Rapids, MI: Eerdmans, 2002), 14–22.

5. Rick Warren, *The Purpose Driven Church: Every Church Is Big in God's Eyes* (Grand Rapids, MI: Zondervan, 1995), 16.

6. For a clearer understanding of the Trinity as purpose, presence, and power, see N. Graham Standish, *Discovering the Narrow Path: A Guide to Spiritual Balance* (Louisville, KY: Westminster John Knox, 2002), chap. 5.

2. SETTING A SPIRITUAL FOUNDATION

1. For more information on van Kaam's theories, especially as they relate to these four dimensions, see Adrian van Kaam, *Formative Spirituality*, vol. 1, *Fundamental Formation* (New York: Crossroad, 1989); Ellen McCormack and N. Graham Standish, "Formative Spirituality: A Foundational and Integrative Approach to Spiritual Direction, Part I: Understanding the Individual," *Presence: The Journal of Spiritual Directors International* 7, no. 1: 3–19; or N.

Graham Standish, *Discovering the Narrow Path: A Guide to Spiritual Balance* (Louisville, KY: Westminster John Knox, 2002), chap. 3.

2. For a much more detailed exploration of creating a worship based on leading a congregation to an experience and encounter with God in worship, see N. Graham Standish, *In God's Presence: Encountering, Experiencing, and Embracing the Holy in Worship* (Herndon, VA: Alban Institute, 2014).

3. Danny E. Morris and Charles M. Olsen, *Discerning God's Will Together: A Spiritual Practice for the Church* (Bethesda, MD: Alban Institute, 1997); Roy M. Oswald and Robert E. Friedrich Jr., *Discerning Your Congregation's Future: A Strategic and Spiritual Approach* (Bethesda, MD: Alban Institute, 1996).

FORMING A CHURCH OF PURPOSE, PRESENCE, AND POWER

1. See N. Graham Standish, *Paradoxes for Living: Cultivating Faith in Confusing Times* (Louisville, KY: Westminster John Knox, 2000), 4.

2. If you would like to engage in a deeper discussion of God as purpose, presence, and power, see N. Graham Standish, *Discovering the Narrow Path: A Guide to Spiritual Balance* (Louisville, KY: Westminster John Knox, 2002), chap. 4, where I explore the need to become more experiential, relational, and spiritual in our understanding of and approach to God as Trinity—as purpose, presence, and power.

3. GROUNDED IN GOD'S PURPOSE

1. Rick Warren, *The Purpose Driven Church: Every Church Is Big in God's Eyes* (Grand Rapids, MI: Zondervan, 1995), 86.

2. Warren, *Purpose Driven Church*, 62, 63.

3. Bill Easum, *Leadership on the Other Side* (Nashville, TN: Abingdon, 2000), 88.

4. Suzanne G. Farnham, Joseph P. Gill, R. Taylor McLean, and Susan Ward, *Listening Hearts: Discerning Call in Community* (Harrisburg, PA: Morehouse, 1991); and Roy M. Oswald and Robert E. Friedrich Jr., *Discerning Your Congregation's Future : A Strategic and Spiritual Approach* (Bethesda, MD: Alban Institute, 1996).

5. The difference between a context and a situation is that context has to do with particular geographical characteristics of the church, such as whether it

is suburban or urban, high- or low-income, and racially integrated or segment-
ed, whereas situation has to do with more intangible factors such as prevailing
conditions facing the church: Is it in transition or in a stable period? Has it had
conflict or harmony? Has it had growth or decline?

4. ALIVE TO GOD'S PRESENCE

1. Neil Howe and William Strauss, *Millennials Rising: The Next Great
Generation* (New York: Vintage, 2000), 236.

2. Thomas Kelly, *A Testament of Devotion* (San Francisco: HarperCollins,
1992), 54.

3. Kelly, *Testament of Devotion*, 56–57.

4. Kelly, *Testament of Devotion*, 57.

5. Ben Campbell Johnson, *95 Theses for the Church: Finding Direction
Today* (Decatur, GA: CTS Press, 1995), 28.

6. Agnes Sanford, *The Healing Light* (New York: Ballantine, 1983); John
Wilkinson, *The Bible and Healing: A Medical and Theological Commentary*
(Grand Rapids, MI: Eerdmans, 1998).

7. Edwin H. Friedman, *Generation to Generation: Family Process in
Church and Synagogue* (New York: Guilford, 1985); Edwin H. Friedman,
Family Process and Process Theology: Basic New Concepts (Washington, DC:
Alban Institute, 1991), videocassette (VHS).

5. OPEN TO GOD AS POWER

1. For a more detailed account of Müller's life, see N. Graham Standish,
Discovering the Narrow Path: A Guide to Spiritual Balance (Louisville, KY:
Westminster John Knox, 2002).

2. Rick Warren, *The Purpose Driven Church: Every Church Is Big in
God's Eyes* (Grand Rapids, MI: Zondervan, 1995), chap. 1.

3. Eberhard Arnold, *God's Revolution: Justice, Community, and the Coming Kingdom*, ed. Hutterian Society of Brothers and John Howard Yoder (New
York: Paulist Press, 1984), 56–57.

4. Arnold, *God's Revolution*, 57–58.

5. Rufus M. Jones, "Finding the Trail of Life," in *Quaker Spirituality:
Selected Writings*, ed. Douglas Steere (New York: Paulist Press, 1984), 266.

6. Walt Kallestad, *Turn Your Church Inside Out: Building a Community
for Others* (Minneapolis, MN: Augsburg Fortress, 2001), 51–52.

7. Kallestad, *Turn Your Church Inside Out*, 64–65.

LEADING A CHURCH TO BLESSEDNESS

1. Henry T. Blackaby and Richard Blackaby, *Spiritual Leadership: Moving People on to God's Agenda* (Nashville, TN: Broadman and Holman, 2001), 20.

2. Henry T. Blackaby and Claude V. King, *Experiencing God: How to Live the Full Adventure of Knowing and Doing the Will of God* (Nashville, TN: Broadman and Holman, 1994), x–xii.

3. Blackaby and King, *Experiencing God*, xii.

6. LEADING A CHURCH TO LISTEN

1. Many neurological studies done by researchers outside the field of religion are pointing to the fact that our brains seem to not only be wired for spiritual awareness but become healthier when we engage in spiritual practices. See, for example, Andrew Newberg, MD, and Mark Robert Waldman, *How God Changes Your Brain: Breakthrough Findings from a Leading Neuroscientist* (New York: Ballantine, 2010); Mario Beauregard and Denyse O'Leary, *The Spiritual Brain: A Neuroscientist's Case for the Existence of the Soul* (New York: HarperCollins, 2007).

2. Adrian van Kaam and Susan A. Muto, *Formation Guide: Becoming Spiritually Mature* (Pittsburgh, PA: Epiphany Association, 1991), 67–118.

3. Van Kaam actually uses the term "congenial to our *calling*," but considering the previous discussion about how we confuse purpose and call, I believe that it is more accurate to say that we are questioning whether something is congenial to our *purpose*—whether we sense that this is in line with who we really are meant to be and what we are meant to do.

7. LEADING A CHURCH TO DEEPEN

1. "Blessed Are the Meek," *Monty Python's Life of Brian*, directed by Terry Jones (1979; Culver City, CA: Sony Pictures Home Entertainment, 2008), DVD.

2. Richard J. Foster, *Celebration of Discipline: The Path to Spiritual Growth* (San Francisco: Harper & Row, 1988).

8. LEADING A CHURCH THROUGH TRANSFORMATION

1. Gregory W. Lester, *Power with People: How to Handle Just about Anyone to Accomplish Just about Anything* (Houston: Ashcroft, 1995), 8.

2. Lester, *Power with People*, 27.

3. Lester, *Power with People*, 31.

4. "Explore 1001," 1001 Worshiping Communities, accessed September 8, 2015, http://www.onethousandone.org/#!about-1001/c19jr.

5. Chip Heath and Dan Heath, *Switch: How to Change Things When Change Is Hard* (New York: Crown, 2010).

6. Dr. Seuss, *The Sneetches and Other Stories* (New York: Random House, 1961).

7. Chip Heath and Dan Heath, *Made to Stick: Why Some Ideas Survive and Others Die* (New York: Random House, 2007), 20.